W. E. GLADSTONE

W. E. GLADSTONE

By

OSBERT BURDETT

BOSTON · AND · NEW YORK

HOUGHTON MIFFLIN COMPANY

PRINTED IN GREAT BRITAIN BY RICHARD CLAY & SONS, LIMITED,
BUNGAY, SUFFOLK.

NOTE

A PARTIAL portrait of Gladstone is all that has been attempted here. Moving through nearly a century of public affairs, the man is blurred by the events that immersed him, and to read the lives that have been written is to become lost in a chronicle of domestic and foreign politics. Thus the task of Morley with but two thousand pages was, in his *Life of William Ewart Gladstone*, to compile, to edit, to arrange. The technical and detailed explanations necessarily overweight the chronicle, and draw our attention away from the character and personality of Gladstone himself. We receive a mass of information upon a hundred matters besides. Morley was bound to chronicle an unwieldy mass of material, to which Gladstone himself contributed additional memoranda by the score. The result has been to incline a later generation to take Gladstone vaguely for granted, because the approach to him is necessarily very slow. He is encompassed with general facts as with a bulwark, and hedged with historical matters as with stiff robes.

Feeling this condition, however unavoidable in the official record of such a public person, to be unfortunate for our understanding of his human nature, the present writer has ventured to regard Morley as a quarry, and to see if, from Morley's monumental record, with such sidelights as could be gleaned from other memoirs and lives of the period, there could be fashioned a less encumbered but more appreciable portrait. From the

massive setting of events as much as possible has been
omitted, in order to fix upon the more revealing moments
of action, word and growth in Gladstone's life.   Where
illuminating glimpses of him could be gained from other
sources, they have been thankfully appropriated since,
in a sense, the vastness of official materials has hindered
Gladstone from being known.   The public facts which
they recount may leave us as much at a distance as newspaper references to the living.   As Morley himself
remarked, posterity is more interested in what Gladstone
was than in what he did.   All my materials I have taken,
and from this handful of other men's clay a profile in
relief has shaped.   To use an adjective of Gladstonian
ambiguity, it is a partial portrait of a character.

CONTENTS

vii

W. E. GLADSTONE

CHAPTER ONE

HIS ORIGIN AND INNOCENCE

I

At least as far south as Liverpool, and he was born there, Gladstone claimed to be " purely and absolutely Scotch in every drop of blood " in his veins. He was still insisting on this point at the age of seventy when receiving at Hawarden a deputation from his native town. Perhaps a Scotsman so complete as this could have been born safely anywhere; nevertheless a good deal in his development is explained by his origin and upbringing.

The name of the family, originally Gledstanes, was changed to Gladstone by royal licence as late as 1835, during the lifetime of his father. The licence legalised an apparently accomplished anglicism, and its " sad lack of imagination," which his daughter lamented, lies on " his father and grandfather." It happens, moreover, though the pedigree of the Gledstanes family has been traced to the remotest times, that we need not here go more than two generations backward, for its early glories suffered an eclipse till the family re-emerged into prosperity with William Ewart's grandfather, who may be fitly called Gladstone the first. He laid the foundations of the modern family's fortune, marked his undertaking by the change of name, and his successors

B

derived, no doubt, from him the gifts of energy and enterprise in which they too have been conspicuous. This Thomas Gladstone had been a corn-merchant of Leith and Liverpool. To quote his famous grandson's words, " he was a merchant in Scotch phrase; that is to say, a shopkeeper dealing in corn and stores, and my father as a lad served in his shop. But he also sent a ship or ships to the Baltic." His son, John Gladstone, the statesman's father, who was made a baronet in 1845, left Leith for Liverpool, where, beginning as a clerk, he became shortly a partner in the firm of Corrie & Co. When the partnership was dissolved some sixteen years later, John Gladstone with his brother Robert formed a new firm, the principal business of which was in the West Indies. There John Gladstone held large sugar and coffee plantations, worked by slaves, in Demerara. On his death in 1851 he left, according to his son, a fortune of " near £600,000." The previous heads of the family had often been responsible Elders of the kirk, and Gladstone's own mother was a devout Evangelical.

The Gladstones had had issue in abundance: William Ewart's great grandfather begot eleven children : his fourth son was blessed with sixteen; and the grand-father's position enabled him to provide for his seven surviving sons when the turn of each came to be started in business. This vigorous middle-class stock, pushing toward mercantile prosperity, with Presbyterian serious-ness and argute Scotch delight in sermons and disputa-tion, produced the future statesman, whose enormous vitality, shrewd intelligence, debating skill, tireless energy, moral fervour and almost perfect health, were but the prodigy of the fine breed from which he sprang. Such a stock has ever been stock for men of genius, and, in this instance, it came to fruition when either side of the Border was only beginning to be industrialised.

Thus the new opportunity of wealth coincided with natural stamina to produce a combination of vigour, less possible to-day when city life has drained the country of the stock we can least afford to lose, so that our modern commercial magnates are, as a rule, of much poorer physique than the Gladstones of the eighteenth century.

William Ewart Gladstone was born on December 29, 1809, it is said under the sign of Capricorn. The vigour, the impetuosity, the butting head, the agile heels, the sure foothold on slippery places of the symbolic Ram, no one would deny him. In English ram is a better equivalent for capricorn than the astrologer's stricter he-goat. It gives us the fighting qualities, the flashing eye, the head strong in the horns. He arrived appropriately on the crest of the family's fortunes, so that he could be well educated in England for the public career on which his father's hopes were centred for him.

He made his first speech at the age of three. The occasion was political. During Canning's first election in Liverpool Canning stayed at John Gladstone's house. On the day when a great dinner was being given there, the child was taken to the dining-room, placed upon a chair, and directed to say to the company : Ladies and Gentlemen. He was also taken to see Hannah More, who presented him with a copy of her *Sacred Dramas* and wrote his name in it.

Gladstone supposed his parents to have singled him out for these attentions as a child possessing something worth seeing, but his own marvellous memory throws no light on his inner development but this : He recalled no propensity to mortal sin; none even to diligence, earnestness or devotion, but these, doubtless, his mother was soon to arouse. He himself believed his inner life to have been " always dubious, vacillating, and above all complex. During a sermon in St. George's, Liverpool, he remembers, perhaps for the only time in his life, turning quickly to his mother with the question : " When will he have done ? " He remembers praying to be spared the loss of a tooth. Otherwise his religious recollections are a blank, and he supposed his development to have been unusually slow.

His earliest teacher was the clergyman appointed to the neighbouring church built by his father at Seaforth in 1815, where with about a dozen boys he was prepared for Eton. At Seaforth he declared that he showed " a priggish love of argument," possibly encouraged at home, for his father, we are told, discussed every sort of question with his children and would allow them to take nothing for granted. Reasons were expected even when someone said that he thought it would be a fine or wet day. If at Seaforth Vicarage he felt himself to have been under no moral or personal influence, and to have shirked in consequence, yet he taught in the Sunday School at Primrose Bridge. Any lack of moral influence at Seaforth was probably, though he does not say so, more than made good at home. The devoutness of his mother and the Socratic teaching of his father would have seemed sufficient moral influences to most boys. The Seaforth Vicarage may have been a place of instinctive moral relaxation. As we shall see, his home standards survived even the indifference of Eton.

He went there in 1821, when the ferocious Dr. Keate was headmaster, and remained for six years, " the prettiest little boy that ever went to Eton." [1] There were floggings and fights, but two chief impressions remained. The teaching of classics, he said, was " simply splendid " in its accuracy, but the " teaching of Christianity was so dead that it was almost a wonder that its very forms had not been surrendered." His piety none the less survived this strain. Stories were told in after years of his refusal to drink to a coarse toast proposed by some school-

[1] Sir Roderick Murchison, quoted by G. W. E. Russell.

fellow, of his defence of some persecuted pigs, of Bishop Hamilton, then a boy, being " saved from worse things " than idleness by coming to know Gladstone. The few outlets that Eton did provide for his fervour and activity, Gladstone used to the full. He became joint editor of the Eton Miscellany, and spoke regularly at the school debates. As he wrote many of his speeches and kept them, we can see how little his manner changed in after years. It was perfected rather than altered. That curiously impersonal, but fervid, manner of his was his from the start. While most able young men begin with revolutionary notions and become later more sceptical of conventional methods of reform, Gladstone began reverentially content with the existing order. While, again, nearly all able youngsters, whatever their opinions, begin in the exalted style and shed it gradually, Gladstone preserved it to the last. In his style, at least, he was always conservative. The voice of his class was Gladstone's voice, the editorial " we " his instinctive manner, righteous indignation, never personal wrath, the appeal he used, and felt. He believed undoubtedly that everyone held their professions as sincerely as he did himself. He had no conception, at this age, that most people never dream of putting their professions into practice, or that he would make them aghast if he or any other respectable man expected them to do so. So long as actions and assumptions are kept peacefully apart, there is no confusion, but once they start trespassing on one another's ground there is no telling where the trouble will end. To try to turn the world upside down has been, very justly, the accusation against religious enthusiasts in all ages. Later experience, not critical observation, was to teach Gladstone the painful truth of this. The first period of his growth ends with his recognition of it, at the age of thirty-one. Perhaps he never learnt it fully. Using the word in no disparaging sense, he had a credulous rather than a critical mind. In his boyhood and in his youth he believed everything that he was told, literally.

At Eton he made friends with George Selwyn, Milnes Gaskell, and Arthur Hallam, but the personal intimacy that there must have been in the last particularly of these friendships, does not survive in his account of them. His fervour indeed dominated individuals as it was afterwards to dominate the public, but in the same aloof way. It is as if he imported the amenities of public life into private intercourse. He loved boating and was already a great walker and an ardent politician at school.

When he left Eton at Christmas 1827, he read with a clergyman, who afterwards became a bishop, for six months. In 1828 he went to Christ Church, Oxford, where again he appeared to make lofty acquaintanceships rather than friends. After a walk with Anstice to Cuddesdon, there is this significant note in Gladstone's diary : " O for a light from on high ! I have no power, none, to discern the right path for myself." It is a flash of self-criticism. A man does not pray for the insight he already possesses. The unerring choice of the Holy Ghost is felt on the instant it is made. To the recipient, alone of lights this Light is unmistakable. There is more, beyond question, than inherited Evangelical fervour in this revealing confession, perhaps the most searching that its author ever made. He knew the agonising truth, and reacted to it in the way which history shows us by many similar examples to be inevitable.

The eighteenth century Enthusiasts and Ranters, as they were called, invariably began with a sense of their deficiency. Being certain of nothing but their own blindness, they were tormented with the fear of sin. They felt themselves to be sinful, and they prayed, there-fore, to be saved by a power from without. With the divine light withheld, this needs must be the power of human example. The mystics pass through the Dark Night much later, as a rule nearer the middle than the beginning of their lives. The lightless turn obediently to Morality for their guide, since morality is the customary standard of conduct, a rule of convention which the man with an inner light regards with indifference, for it is, at most, a superfluous prop to himself. The good man is freeborn because he is born good. The lightless man, being born blind, knows himself in need of leading-strings : the commandments and conventions of Morality. He worships them as the only light within his reach, and may even go so far as to believe that there is no other light than they. His next step may be to persecute the few freeborn who differ from him. Gladstone never went to that extreme, for he believed that there was a Light beyond his personal apprehension. He was even credulous of those who seemed to claim it, and was ready and anxious to defer almost to anyone. Intellectually he was a humble-minded man, though the fervour of his obedience to adopted ideas often disguised this from other people, especially when they were not in agreement with him. His fervour and dependence on external guidance, outside practical affairs, made him a mystagogue, about as far from a mystic as it is possible for a human being to be. The above entry in his diary gives the first significant clue to his character and after career.

The rest of his Oxford days no more than illustrate the justness of it.

He was said to have known his Bible better than any undergraduate. On Sundays he sometimes heard as many as three sermons. He haunted also Dissenting chapels in his search for light. He consulted a clergyman on the advisability of holding prayer-meetings in his rooms. He recoiled from Archbishop Whately's

" anti-Sabbatical doctrine." Another preacher moved him to expostulate on the " character and doctrines of his sermon " in a letter that Gladstone left at the clergyman's door. He was accused of " ostentatious piety." A writer in 1829 declared : " Gladstone has mixed himself up with the St. Mary Hall and Oriel set, who are really, for the most part, only fit to live with maiden aunts and to keep rabbits." Alas ! the Evangelical nature is always subject to such misunderstandings as these. If Gladstone had known of them, he would not have minded.

His ardour was not exhausted in listening to others. He founded an essay club, called, after him, the WEG, where he contended, among other things, that philosophy was higher than poetry, as a moralist would. He also made one of his rare, right judgments in literature. He said that the poems of Tennyson showed considerable genius.

This eager undergraduate, if not at first, soon became a steady worker, as his ambitions began to stir. He entered twice for the Ireland scholarship. At his second attempt Gladstone was surprised to learn from the examiner that, in a close decision, the prize had gone to one who gave short and concise answers. "Ours," he told his father, " were long-winded." Gladstone's own essay was marked " desultory beyond belief." An unillumined intelligence is apt to be vague. He failed to win the Newdigate with his poem on Richard Cœur de Lion. Whether as a writer or a critic, his literary faculty was small from the beginning.

The copiousness which chilled the examiner in his written papers, however, was far from a disadvantage at the Union, where Gladstone soon began to be both heard and admired. In time he became president. It was his first completed step in public life. He found a larger audience proportionally easier to address, and the

diffuseness of speech more natural to him than the terse
directness of good writing. In debate, especially in the
debating points that quell interrupters, also in reply,
verbal readiness is almost everything. The orator was
finding his feet. The speeches that he made are interesting for the attitude which they reveal. All, I think,
support the positions in which he was reared. His
familiar preceptors were accepted implicitly. He was a
trumpet in their hands : he did not criticise anything
they had told him. One example may suffice us. In a
debate in favour of the prompt emancipation of the West
Indian slaves, he moved and carried an amendment that
" education of a religious kind was the first object of
legislation." Being both lofty and inapt, it circumvented
the issue successfully. It is as if we overheard his
mother's fervour and his father's commercial prudence
merging to a single voice through the young man. As
an echo he was magnificent, but the original murmurs
were theirs. He initiated no ideas, but the ideas of
others impelled him to eager speech and impulsive action.
Since he had not critical intelligence, it is to his honour
that speech and action were never far apart. No one
perhaps has ever combined so much talk with so great
an activity.

Active as he already was, he prays for the habit of
steady application. In his studies, speeches, church-
going, his parties for wine and talk, his long walks, his
letters even, there is an air of suppressed excitement.
Filled with moral enthusiasm and growing conscious of
his latent powers, he was also ambitious to excel in the
public activities of undergraduate life. It was a new
world, a larger world, than Eton or home, and it led to
one more wide than Oxford. His eye became aware of
the political stirrings of the day. His religious ardour
made him welcome Catholic Emancipation; his inherited
conservatism to denounce electoral reform. It was with

a speech against the extension of the franchise that he
made his mark at the Union, a speech that penetrated
beyond its walls. The coming Reform Bill was already
filling the propertied classes with fright, and the young
man, very naturally, had not yet developed his later sixth
sense for rising currents of public opinion. Standing
on the past, he found the fearsome future still impalpable
to him, though his leaping mind was eventually to
inhabit the political day after to-morrow. For the
moment, like his worthy exemplars, he identified reform
with revolution.

The animated debate in the Union at Oxford reflected
the excitement prevailing in the nation at large, and
the youthful Gladstone's speech of three-quarters of an
hour electrified the house. It also pleased his father so
much that he wanted to have it printed. Thereupon,
Gladstone immediately wrote an anti-reform pamphlet,
which even his father thought was too extreme, and then
hurried to London in order to hear a debate, lasting five
nights, in the House of Lords. When the Lords threw
out the Reform Bill by a majority of forty-one, Gladstone's comment was : " The consequences of the vote
may be awful. God avert this ! But it was an honourable and manly decision, and so may God avert them."
This was the first debate that Gladstone attended in
Parliament.

At this time too he conceived a vast work on Morals,
Politics and Education, the materials for which were to
be gathered during the progress of his life. It was
intended to be his bequest to posterity. Morals still
came first in his regard, and he was not content to counsel
us upon them. He wished also for some personal work
to do, and discussed with his friend Hope-Scott a private
plan for the benefit of prostitutes. In the odious
euphemism of the day this was known as rescue work for
" fallen women." The social outcast, leading the most

precarious of lives, exercised an irresistible appeal to
Gladstone's charitable heart. The call, to be up and
doing, on behalf of the forlorn was the form in which
the appeal came to him. A crusader born out of due
time, he responded instantly to romantic causes. At the
moment, the established order seemed politically to be
one of these. It loomed largely, calling for help; but
there was also the unheeded cry of erring sisters to which
one's private ear might well be open. For the present,
however, the ordeal of Final Schools allowed no
trespassing.

At the examination which followed on the heels of
these excitements, an amusing incident occurred. After
questioning Gladstone upon some point of theology, the
examiner said: " We will now leave that part of the
subject." " No, sir," replied Gladstone, " if you please,
we will not leave it yet," and began ardently again. No
wonder that he received a first class. The wonder is that
he also gained a first in mathematics, for the subject was
not then taught at Eton, and Gladstone had had to rely
entirely upon private study and his own brains. This
double first was, then, a feat both of intelligence and
industry. It showed steadfastness of purpose and
pliability of mind : abilities promising and even dangerous, coupled, as they were, to enthusiasm of feeling and
restless activity. His prayers had been answered, and
it was impossible to say where his gifts would carry him
in the end. With this achievement and the presidency
of the Union behind him, Gladstone's Oxford career was
a complete success. Combined activities of this order
at the University are an established preliminary to public
life, and, with his father's wealth to back him, nothing,
unless it were a young man's want of inclination, need
now stand in his way. He had qualified for a political
career at Oxford, and even before he left had made
himself heard beyond the walls of the University.

During the year previous to his Final Schools, Gladstone had become already distracted about his future.
" God direct me !   I am utterly blind," he had confessed.
In this mood he wrote an inordinately long letter to his
father.   In vague and involved sentences he portrayed
his religious yearnings to forsake the callings of this
dusty world and to become a clergyman.   It is characteristic that he proposed to take Holy Orders as much for
public as for private reasons.   His fervour instinctively
aspired to the most exalted form of activity, but his
judicious eye was equally upon the world and pointed
to the need of the world to justify him.   How godless it
was, how vast the opportunity, how precise and sacred the
Christian's trust !   The theme lent itself to expansion,
and then one's own unfitness needed, also, to be made
abundantly clear.   It produced this tremendous letter,
in which the natural, but unconscious, egoism of the
youthful writer is transparent.   Indeed it is disarming,
for he would be indeed a miserable creature who did not
remember to have written or contemplated some such
letter at Gladstone's age.   One does not need to be an
experienced master of novices to realise, however, that
the vocation confessed by this letter is not for Holy
Orders.   In so far as such yearnings can be sifted from
the sands of emotion in which they lurk, they remain
indeterminate.   They show a bias, not a direction.
They indicate no more than an ardent temperament at a
loss for employment, an active mind in search of an aim,
any aim so long as the youthful imagination can recognise
and respond to it.   This, the only positive inference,
is accompanied by one negative disclosure.   A good
master of novices would infer that the young writer is not
destined for the contemplative life : the life where
silence is golden.   The verbal activity is profuse enough
to show that the youth will be a man of action ; perhaps,
if his bias holds, a preacher ; if not, a barrister possibly,

possibly a politician.   Words, whether spoken or penned,
will play a large part in his activity.   To-day, we should
add to the list of his chances, that of a leader-writer and
journalist, but in 1831 journalism was not a calling.
Having no set qualifications, it cannot be a profession
to-day even, for a learned profession without learning is
still unthinkable at present.   We are not arguing backward in having drawn inferences like these.   Gladstone's
letter occupies several closely printed pages of an appen-
dix to Morley's first volume.   It is there to be read, and
is almost a classic document for the psychologist of
adolescence to browse on.

We find in it, then, a vocation to some form of public
life, in which lofty aspirations may be combined with
secular, and probably prominent, activity.   It shows a
crusader who has yet to find his crusade, a recruit
embarrassed by the wealth of moral evils that invite his
attention.

Gladstone's father almost certainly understood William
very well, but his face may have been a study while he
was reading his son's immense letter.   Showing both
tact and judgment in his much shorter reply, he asked the
young man to postpone his decision until he should have
taken his degree, and had returned from a trip to the
Continent.   Obviously so impressionable a nature ought
to receive as many impressions as possible before taking
such a momentous decision as it proposed.   The father's
counsel had been asked, and that was sufficient grace for
the moment.   John Gladstone's tact was justified.   In
reply to this advice, the young man declared that his
excitement had subsided, but that he foresees a crisis in
the history of mankind : upon the new principles
prevailing, the Established Church, and the whole
foundations of society, may vanish.   He must not be
tied to any profession that will not leave him free to
enter the arena ; but, wishing to fall in with his father's

desires, he proposes to study constitutional law " with a view . . . to a subsequent experiment . . . on public life."

This, no doubt, left Gladstone's father much relieved. He had earned the respite, and, doubtless with a lighter heart, continued this second long letter to the end. Substantially it ran as follows : Gladstone wishes to be the humblest of those commissioned to set before the eyes of man " the magnificence and the glory of Christian truth," especially since his temperament is " so excitable " that it might yield to the allurements of other matters. These are indicated in his diary by a note made after he had passed his examinations : " Politics are fascinating to me, perhaps too fascinating." In politics too, become now so serious, the budding orator would be required to vent, as Burke, as Canning had vented, the exalted aspirations of his heart. He can define his ambition only in these solemn words : " To work an energetic work in this world," and by it, under God, " to grow into the image of the Redeemer."

II

Such was Gladstone when the Oxford of his day had done with him. He had been prepared for a career. Had he been prepared for the world in which that career would be passed ? The Union is indeed a House of Commons in miniature. Is the House also the World within four walls ? If it were not, the higher education of Englishmen would have been different, but in these days there is no telling what question will not next be asked. Suffice it to say that, when Gladstone left Oxford, so absurd a question was inconceivable. What other world but the House of Commons could an English university prepare her sons to enter now that the Church had been deprived of political power ? Politics had been a patrician preserve throughout the eighteenth century. The tradition of scholastic leisure for the aristocracy survived in the memory of the Grand Tour, a prelude for the sons of commercial magnates to the politics that would lead them, perhaps, into the aristocracy itself at last.

His four months' trip to France and Italy, where he learned Italian, were notable for two events in Gladstone's life. At Rome and Naples there dawned upon him, for the first time, the Latin conception of the Church as a body and a teacher apart from the Bible. Its ministry of symbols and channels of grace, its historic line of teachers, its body of doctrine, inspired him with his first vision of the Church Corporate, as men had thought of her in the Middle Ages, when the Patrimony of St. Peter was, like the Empire, an international Power. Even now, Evangelical as he was by training, he scarcely seems to have asked whether, if Church and Bible be set side by side, the Church is not the author of the book. His visit to Rome (and without such a visit what European can hope to hold the roots of our past within his mind, for its stones utter more than a library of learning ?) made Gladstone a churchman. His idea of Christianity was transformed, though his language kept its Evangelical tone as instinctively as his voice kept the lingual burr of Scotland. The effect of Rome was great on Gladstone. It made him reflect, and on the one path wherein he found reflection not difficult. What did churchmanship mean ? He remembered Newman, who had become vicar of St. Mary's, Oxford, in 1828, and in this very year, 1832, was to visit the Eternal City. Had not Newman, the impressive preacher, broken with the Evangelical view two years before, while Gladstone was still up ? The kirk compares poorly with the church to a man who has a passion for institutions.

These reflections were interrupted at Milan by a

mundane event more startling, if less pregnant, than themselves. This was no less than an offer of the seat for the
borough of Newark from the Duke of Newcastle, the
former foe of Gladstone's family idol, George Canning.
The offer was the reward of the speech at the Union which
had first made Gladstone known. Though the duke's
son had been one of Gladstone's Oxford friends, it
seemed at first " a stunning and overpowering proposal."
Surprise and doubts, however, soon yielded to his father's
inclinations and his own. It *is* interesting that Gladstone
did not enter political life, but was called to it. In the
person of the Duke of Newcastle, the " light from on
high " had come. The double fitness of Gladstone to
receive it was shown during the election itself.

Newark was a nomination borough, and in his address
to the nominal electors Gladstone professed principles
rather than a programme : to resist change, to remedy
evils by restoring general principles, in particular the
principle that government is a religious duty. In
regard to slavery, then a ticklish question, the young
candidate rested its abstract lawfulness on the regulations
of Scripture, regulations, he explained, which took the
institution for granted. He argued on his own behalf
that moral must precede physical emancipation of the
slaves. He defended the union of Church and State,
especially of the Irish Church ; he favoured the principle
of allotments. His only indiscretion was to startle the
duke by averring that labour should receive adequate
pay, " which, unhappily, among several classes of our
population, is not now the case."

It would be superficial to complain that almost everything else for which he contended now he opposed later.
The consistency of Gladstone is not to be measured by
abstract logic. Just because he had not a logical mind,
it was easy for him to explain away, though not to
explain, his political changes. In this matter he was a

casuist without a case, than which nothing is more delightful to an argumentative mind. His consistency was more real than any logic, because it was temperamental, and therefore much more profound. In the depths of his own unconsciousness he knew that logical necessity is not necessity at all. His genius lay in not knowing consciously just this, for it made him impervious to the intellectual criticism of men far more intelligent than himself. Their intelligence was no match for a vital instinct like Gladstone's, for it is rarely intellect that makes the genius. It is always vitality, to which the intellect even of an intellectual genius is never more than a convenient tool. George Eliot was much more intelligent than Charles Dickens, but, vital as she was, she was not nearly so vital as he. Genius is energy of life, and can survive a considerable infusion of stupidity. The consistency of Gladstone, then, was a consistency of vital energy, which carried him from enthusiasm to enthusiasm, from change to political change.

This made him far more disconcerting to his political rivals than political logic, or even political principle. He hardly understood what political principle means, while he knew, without knowing how he knew, what were the desires of the moment, and, much better than his contemporaries, what were the immediate obstacles in their way. His emotions and enthusiasm were at the beck of every one of them, and thus he was never at a loss like his opponents; on the contrary, he never hesitated to claim almost divine sanction for whatever he proposed. For the most part pygmies in vitality compared with Gladstone, they were tied and bound by the chain of an artificial logic, the merest gossamer to Gladstone, who simply walked through it, like a man. Logic to him, being superior to it, was literally a matter of words. Having a superabundance of words always at his command and increasingly avoiding definite statements, he

c

beat the logicians at their own game, in debate and
controversy. His explanations were an overwhelming
torrent, and as they did overwhelm, the question whether
they were also logically convincing shrank to an irrelevant
trifle. Beside this, he was also extremely shrewd in
practical and immediate matters. As practical in detail
as he was hazy in idea, he relied upon a vital enthuasism
to propel him onward, while he avoided pitfalls with the
canniest of care. His want of inner light was compensated by his enormous susceptibility to outside
influences. Thus he took the lead by identifying himself,
before anyone else, with the changes of opinion around
him. In the strictest meaning of the word, therefore,
he was always morally in the right. His enthusiasm was
his own. His ideas invariably came from other people.
He originated nothing but his own native energy, and
his responsiveness to popular suggestion became ultimately a reflex action, a sixth sense. His emotional
consistency was, with the activity that it invariably
dictated, with the practical sagacity he partly inherited
and partly acquired, the only consistence he had. It was
so complete that he needed none other. Indeed intellectual consistency would have been a handicap. Luckily
there was no alloy in his energetic ore. His energy, in
fact, served him better than inner light serves far more
intellectual men, for, unlike intellect, it does not know
doubt or hesitation. It survives its mistakes. Its only
law is to go forward. Like life itself, it has no end but
to live more abundantly. In political affairs it can
increase mischief or virtue according to the stimulus
that it receives. The virtue of Gladstone was Gladstone's vitality, issuing through his lips first of all, but
the ends which it served are to be measured by our
judgment of the desires of his age. These it reflected
perfectly through all their changes, the changes (that is to
say) which came to the surface of his time. He was

incapable of comprehending the deeper currents. Opinions he understood : ideas never. Darwin and Huxley remained inexplicable to him, but, were he alive to-day, he might be as popular an expounder of evolution, birth-control or eugenics, as he was in his own time of electoral reform, economic *laissez-faire*, or free trade. The proof of this is that, in his own lifetime, when there was no lead on these later matters, the bare mention of such things would have scandalised him. He would have been at home in the ardent atmosphere that heralded the Revolution in France, though whether he would have become its servant or its victim it would be needless to inquire, and is impossible to decide. When strife passed beyond discussion, he tended to become helpless. Whatever the popular movement was, he would have joined it. That is certainty enough. Like the traditional huer at St. Ives, he watched and waited for the tide. Thus he was habitually the first person to detect the incoming shoal, and was then all eagerness to net it. His fervour was not content, for long, to defend the things which are, to dwell among forlorn hopes, or, like Parnell, to let hope itself create a cause out of its ruin. His fervour launched out to meet its kindred, the fervour that was rising to meet him.

Having disposed of the bogey of consistency, which haunted Gladstone from the time when even his speeches as an undergraduate at the Union were examined to provide a repartee at his expense, till his biographers continued to discuss the matter, let us return to Newark. There his second hostages to political logic were un-wittingly given. After what has been said, we need waste no time upon them. The vital matter is this. His strategy at the election was almost all that the Duke of Newcastle and his father had a right to hope. His tactics were shown in his answer to a question. " Are you the Duke of Newcastle's nominee ? " a heckler

inquired. Gladstone was, but the election might have
seemed a farce had he admitted it. He therefore asked
Mr. Gillson what he meant by the term. The heckler
incontinently replied : " A man sent by the duke to be
pushed down the electors' throats whether they will or
no." " In that sense," the candidate answered, " I am
not a nominee. I came to Newark on the invitation
of the Red Club, than whom none is more respectable
and intelligent." If the duke had had a dreadful qualm
about the soundness of his candidate's attitude to the
payment of labourers, the young hand had shown itself
apt to deal with a debating emergency as it arose. Gladstone was, of course, elected at the head of the poll, and
six weeks later, in January 1833, sat as a Member of the
first Reformed Parliament.

III

It requires to-day a slight effort of imagination to
recall the condition of political and social life which
Gladstone was entering, at the early age of twenty-four.
We forget sometimes that the England of the first
Reformed Parliament was still, on the whole, the England
of the eighteenth century. Electors were still wooed
on a system that we call corruption, and the morals of
the reigning aristocracy were still aristocratic, that is to
say, not based on the middle-class assumptions of a later
day. Middle-class morality necessarily seems ridiculous
to aristocrats, as aristocratic manners seem supercilious
or immoral to the middle classes. Ideas of right and
wrong vary, not only from frontier to frontier, but from
class to class. Whichever stratum of society happens
to be at the top imposes its own standards and com-
placently imagines that these are the immutable test of
virtue.

The young Gladstone happened to enter public life

at the turn of the tide, when, that is to say, the aristocracy
was beginning to lose political predominance, and,
consequently, when both its political practices and its
moral code were becoming undermined by the habits
and standards of its successors. Gladstone lived long
enough in his nearly ninety years to see the former
ousted, but he was born early enough to be aware of
the change and to remember in his old age a time when a
different code was taken equally as a matter of course.
We must place ourselves at his point of view, and
become octogenarians of the nineteenth century ourselves, if we are not to feel puzzled by some of his later
dilemmas, the dilemmas of an old gentleman who had a
very much longer memory than almost any of his contemporaries, a memory also wholly beyond the range
of the bulk of his popular audiences. Gladstone himself
had received the mental impress of the rising class of
which he was to become eventually the popular representative. His home seems to have been a pattern of its
virtues. Evangelicalism has never been an aristocratic
product because it is, characteristically, provincial both
in habitat and in ideas. Bunyan himself spoke of the
" village " of Morality and contrasted it with the " city "
of Destruction, in which last, presumably, the men of
Mayfair are to be found. The consequence was that,
hardly had Gladstone taken his seat in the House, when
an elementary discovery scandalised him.

It was this. The cost of the election proved to be
twice as much as he had anticipated, and he was horrified
at the amount which had been spent upon free meals
and free drink. It proved useless to remind him that
many of the voters could not be persuaded to poll
without a breakfast at the expense of their candidate,
a breakfast at which beer was enjoyed in hospitable
draughts. He declared that this " organised drunken-
ness " was not a question of money, but a question of

right and wrong. No doubt the memory helped him
to carry Sir Henry James' Act of 1883 to reduce " corrupt
practices " at elections. Wiser, and a little sad, for this
was his first taste of disillusion, Gladstone turned on his
birthday, December 29, 1833, from this examination of
political morality (the immorality of another means the
difference of his habits from one's own) to glance at the
condition of his own heart. " I wish," he confided to
his diary, " that I could hope my frame of mind had been
in any degree removed from earth and brought nearer
to Heaven, that the habit of my mind had been imbued
with something of that spirit which is not of this world."

He began to view his approaching social duties with
some apprehension. After due consideration, he
resolved not to withdraw " from the practices of my
fellowmen except when they really *involve* an encouragement of sin, in which case I do certainly rank races and
theatres." He limited himself, therefore, for the present
to concerts, safer and, at their best, not far from semi-
sacred ground. Theatres and races Gladstone could
avoid if he chose, and to the end he never crowned any
of his four premierships by leading home a Derby winner
or so much as owning a single racehorse. He could not
avoid meetings and personal intimacy with the men who
rejoiced in such pursuits, who regarded a racing-stable
and a mistress as possessions to boast of, and those who
had them not as scarcely to be called gentlemen. Was
Gladstone to refuse to work with a colleague because he
had, perhaps, been one of the bucks at Carlton House a
few years before ? It would have been manifestly
impossible. Your aristocrat, the typical politician of
that day, who had been brought up under the eye of the
Prince Regent, whose memory of the days of the dandies
was a memory of yesterday, has always been a man who
rejoices in the strength of a horse and delights in the
limbs of beautiful women, who makes a marriage for the

sake of the settlements, and makes love without the consolations of the Church. A very earnest man of Gladstone's type deplores these tastes and the standard that is immensely proud of them, but, if he was not to abandon a political career at the very start, he had, in 1833, to accept them, at any rate for others. This, then, is the place to recall, though by anticipation, the habits that good society took for granted in the Prime Ministers of Gladstone's early political life. Lord Melbourne was twice in the Divorce Court; Lord Palmerston lived for years with the lady whom he eventually married. Disraeli himself, happy and conjugal as his life was, could hardly have taken the theological view of marriage if only because he must have missed it so often in the social life in which he moved. Fifty years later, that is in 1885, we shall find it convenient to have recalled the political and social atmosphere into which Gladstone was introduced when he became, for the first time, a member of Parliament, and thus a welcomed diner-out in Mayfair when William IV was king. The moral relaxation of Seaforth Vicarage was scarcely enough to have initiated Gladstone into this life of pride and pleasure, wherein his fellow-politicians sported as naturally as " troutlets in a pool."

For the moment, to have discovered how the cost of his recent election had mounted was news enough. The time had hardly come to swallow the second pill. Gladstone therefore contented himself with a further experiment in journalism. He let off his moral steam in a series of articles for the *Liverpool Courier*. In one of these he attributed the fall of the Roman Republic to the practice of secret suffrage. In another he welcomed the statement that the condition of the West Indian negro was paradise compared with that of the spinning-mill hands in Lancashire. This was a convenient argument to store against the day when he might have to defend the conduct of the West Indian planters. The comparison hardly led him, however, to become a second Lord Shaftesbury; indeed his critics have been wont to declare that official atrocities in remote lands moved him more quickly than the industrial atrocities in his own country. In the public memory of his numerous crusades on behalf of oppressed persons, Naples, Bulgaria and Ireland come to mind. Shaftesbury complained that Gladstone opposed industrial legislation for his own country. Neither the curious eye, as the old statutes of Henry VIII used to phrase it, of Ruskin the ubiquitous, and Gladstone the Argus-eyed observer, can pounce on everything at once. Sin has the strangest power of escaping even minute search. Already, as this excursion into journalism proves, activity was claiming the most of Gladstone's week. The habit of faithful attendance beneath the pulpit was not, however, abandoned when he arrived in London. On Sundays he continued to attend church services regularly, and to be an assiduous listener to popular preachers, while, in the intervals of his public devotions, he read to himself many of Dr. Arnold's sermons aloud. All this was at once a dear solace and support, and what better preparation could there be for his parliamentary duties in the rapidly approaching session ?

The proposal of the Government for the gradual abolition of slavery gave to the young Member his first chance of making himself heard in the House of Commons. The vigorous opposition of his father to this proposal had made John Gladstone a target for the Abolitionists' attack. Lord Howick called the Gladstone manager a " murderer of slaves," and declared that these were worked to death systematically in the hope of increasing the crop. The young Gladstone was thus called upon to defend his own father, and if his filial piety had been less or his father had not been a slave-owner he might have appeared earlier upon the Aboli-

tionist side.   While admitting in the House that regret-
table cruelties had occurred, and favouring a gradual
emancipation, with full compensation to the slave-
owners, Gladstone forcibly reminded the House that we
had dangerous occupations at home.   He also insisted,
as before, that moral advancement must precede physical
freedom.   He went on to urge that the conditions of
work upon his father's estates were no worse than elsewhere, that, indeed, they were better.   We need not
pursue his persuasive arguments in detail.   The interesting thing is Gladstone's later comment on this speech.
For it is his second flashlight of self-criticism.

The later comment begins by regretting the tone of
this speech.   Having expressed regret, it continues :
" Of course allowance must be made for the enormous
and most blessed change of opinion, since that day, on
the subject."   Gladstone's temperamental test was the
state of opinion around him.   He had already confessed,
as we saw, at Oxford, that he had " no inner light."
What could he do, therefore, but reflect the best opinion
near at hand ? and what better opinion could there be
than the opinions he had learned at home ?   If his
intellect was still imbued with the ideas that it had learned
at his mother's knee, if he naturally wished to follow in
the footsteps of his practical father, who built five
churches, was it not proper and inevitable that he should
still wait for his father's scruples against the abolition of
slavery to subside before venturing to entertain any
opposite scruple himself ?   Those Evangelicals who
have no " inner light " necessarily venerate more fortunate persons, and the habits and opinions of the illumi-
nated, that is to say, the Morality of " their betters,"
become their reflected ray.   Thus we find that the less
inner light a man has, meaning (to be precise) the less
conscience he has, the more scrupulous he is about
Morality.   Morality is the conduct of our neighbours,

and the views of a highly moral person, which Gladstone certainly was, veer, in proportion to his scrupulosity, with the alterations in Morality around him.

To call such a person a man with no conscience is not to condemn him, for a conscience is a divine gift not bestowed on everyone. The majority consists of Moralists, good souls and bad souls, who do what their neighbours do because their neighbours are doing it. To abuse them for this would be as cruel as to abuse a child for having been born colour-blind, or left-handed. The chief difference is that the possession of a conscience, as Bunyan knew, is rare, while left-handers are relatively common, so that a man without a conscience is in the majority. The confusion which occurs over contradictory but seemingly kindred terms, conscience and morality (they are opposites), is a modern one, and happens because modern people do not read their Bibles. If they did, as has often been remarked, they would know that the word Morality does not occur in Holy Scripture, which invites us to consider Right and Wrong, Sin and Righteousness, but never Morality and Immorality. The word of God and the holiness of those whom He has called is the example set before us in both Testaments : not the conduct and habits of whoever, possibly the Philistines, happen to be living over the way. Thus Gladstone, being an honest man, was the first to admit that his guide had to be some external human authority, and how better could he prove his purity of intention than by acting as his father desired ?

Do not too hastily suppose that John Gladstone, therefore, stands in need of a special apology. On the contrary, though the Church may have ever set her face against slavery, it was one of the foundational institutions of the Roman ethics on which she had to build. It was expressly countenanced by Aristotle, who declared that certain men were born slaves, and that a class of such persons was necessary to civilisation. In the course of ages, and latterly in particular since the day when Rousseau asserted that " men are born free," we have grown shy of the word " slavery," but between theoretic servitude and complete practical penuriousness there is not very much to choose, as the unemployed or junior married clerk will tell you, except the hope, one doubtful day, of escaping it. To regard slavery, especially the slavery of negroes, as a natural abomination in John Gladstone's time, seemed to most people as fantastic a notion as the parallel theory of to-day that it is abominable, in the idea of a few, not to pay the same income to everyone, from a private to a Prime Minister. The idea of human equality was the paradox then. The idea of economic equality is the paradox now, and, if one ventured to infer anything from history, the logical inference would be that economic equality might become regarded as obviously the right opinion a century or so hence. What reason has anyone to suppose that John Gladstone should have been specially reflective, or more bound than his commercial rivals to consider the prejudices of the twentieth century ? He took the world as he found it; he made a success of what he found, and that is justification enough for most manufacturers.

The change that John Gladstone made, when he ceased to be a Presbyterian in order to become a churchman, was not made entirely on intellectual grounds. Religious sects inevitably appropriate different social classes, and a man who begins with a small and ends with a large fortune, is naturally more aware of this fact than those with less experience of different classes to guide them. In short, circumstances, which include opinion, were altering. Father and son were both conscious of the change, and the popular maxim, that circumstances alter cases, is not popular only with politicians. If charity does begin at home (and if not where is its origin ?), John Gladstone was bound to consider his own security first of all. His son, having declared for full compensation to the owners, had theoretically taken that security for granted. This said, he was free to yield to the change of view more appropriate to his generation than to his father's. Nor was he in much difficulty over the readjustment that would be necessary in his public speeches. According to one of his friendly biographers,[1] Gladstone had carried down from Oxford " a tendency to distinguish with extreme precaution between statements almost exactly similar."

We have examined these instances of Gladstone's budding controversies, as we did earlier his inconsistency, because they crop up from time to time all through his life, and it is simpler to have done with them on their appearance, so that we need not dwell upon them serially. A cautious start may prove the quickest way of avoiding waste of time on a long journey. The modification of opinion, which the cautious but impulsive mind of Gladstone underwent till the very end, would not have been scrutinised more closely than its parallel in other politicians had not his Evangelical fervour virtually claimed divine assent for whatever he happened to be proposing. He claimed it so often and so regularly because he desired to have it, as other men have claimed a divine parent or else a very remote ancestry because they have thought it would be very nice if it were true. Belief is a prop strong in proportion to its superiority to rational proof; and the faith which shuffles mountains as if they were a pack of cards is, in the last analysis, self-confidence or faith in oneself, the ultimate source and very well of human effort. Almost all men, indeed, are vain of what they do badly, not of what they do well. Shakespeare was even vainer of his middle-class parentage than of his poetry, and no doubt boasted of it more in

[1] G. W. E. Russell.

private talk. A boast, defined as a vain-glory, leads us to suspect that it has little foundation in truth. No one who believed himself to be by birth an armigerous gentleman in Shakespeare's time would have bothered so much as the alderman's son about getting (or reviving) that coat of arms. The same inference applies to vaunts of divine sanction : the more frequently they are made by a man, the likelier it is that he lives in want of this assurance.

IV

In the House of Commons the new Member attached himself to Sir Robert Peel, the then leader of the Tory opposition. Peel was favourably disposed to his new recruit, and indeed both men were similar in type, though not in character. In passing we may note here that, except for the session of 1846, when Gladstone was a Secretary of State without a seat, and for the first session of 1847, Gladstone was continuously in the House of Commons till he retired in 1894. Sixty years in Parliament, breathing the necessarily unrarefied air of any vast assembly, is a prodigious period in a special atmosphere. Whether or not we agree with the abbé Ernest Dimnet,[1] a shrewd observer, that " politics have never been known to be morally improving," or with Parnell, that no party (possibly no Member) can remain unaffected by Westminster for more than ten years at longest, we shall probably agree that an experience so long and peculiar is enough, by itself, to explain some of the streaks in Gladstone's complex character. It is hard enough to maintain spiritual integrity in domestic life, but more insidious and scarcely less searching is the test to character of prominence in Parliament.

During his first session, all that Gladstone advocated

[1] *From a Paris Balcony :* the essay on M. Herriot.

or did reflected faithfully the correct opinions of his
corner in society. He supported the Union with
Ireland, the Coercion Bill, the existing Corn Laws, and a
Bill against work on Sundays. He opposed the admission
of Jews to Parliament, and of Dissenters to the Universities. He opposed the abolition of flogging (of which
he had precious memories at Eton) in the Services.
He opposed the extinction of sinecures (that last hope for
uncommercial ability) in the army and navy; the publication of the division lists; the ballot. He sat on the
fence over Lord Ashley's factory legislation—which may
not have included the principle of a living wage, his
advocacy of which had made the Duke of Newcastle
shiver. For Gladstone, the most real issue during this
session was the question of slavery, in which his piety
and his family's interest were involved. As we have
anticipated this issue, it may be dismissed with the
reminder that, while he defended his father, he wished
devoutly for emancipation in due course. A conservative with qualms rather than a liberal in the making,
it was still uncertain in which direction he would tend.

His diary confirms this hesitation. On the 29th of
December, 1833, his twenty-fourth birthday, he is
writing :

> Where is the *continuous* work which ought to fill up the life
> of a Christian ? . . . I have been growing, that is certain;
> in good or evil ? Much fluctuation; often a supposed progress,
> terminating in finding myself at, or short of, the point which
> I deemed I had left behind me. Business and political excite-
> ment a tremendous trial, not so much alleviating as drag-
> ging down the soul from that temper which is fit to inhale the
> air of heaven.

What delicious egoism is here; though we like to slur
our admission because we know that egoism, at least,
is a youthful failing, and universal; very far from being
a Gladstonian one. His bustling vitality makes him

carry, as it were, the egoism of the world upon his tall
shoulders; and ambitious young men, turning the early
pages of Gladstone's diary, shrink, because it might be a
page of their own. Besides, the man who is not an
egoist does not succeed in getting born, and, far more
than Rousseau, because Rousseau was not the " divinely
average " man, Gladstone has confessed the little sins
of all the world. If we recoil from his admissions, it is
because we have written what we have written too.

Observe, moreover, that this passage implies a prayer
for work. Gladstone, a man of energy, could pray, as
all of us do, only for a chance to exercise his own gifts.
It is true that he longed for " light," but he never prayed
for perspicacity, almost as if intellectual penetration was a
gift beyond his ken, for he aspired to every gift within
the range of his own consciousness. This passage, like
the previously quoted ones, displays the palsy of a soul
hungry for its fit, but still unrecognised, employment.
It confesses a natural fluctuation. Once more we observe
that he was never content or sure, from himself. He
waited in doubt, like his duplicate the spider, to perceive
the handy twig sprouting from the body of some external
opinion before swinging himself toward it to find lodg-
ment for his gossamer. His aspirations confess an inner
emptiness, for you cannot have the strength and want it
too. On the other hand, he was naturally a fountain of
fervour. It was settable in motion, by an external hand.
The wonder is that, intellectual perception apart, he had
received his other gifts in such abundance.

Throughout his first session in Parliament, Gladstone
became obscurely aware of a puzzle hard to define to
himself : the contrast between the pious professions and
the conventional practice of the world. A literal
believer in all that he had been told, he could not conceive that this disparity might be cherished as the Comforter in the hearts of those about him. He could

neither dream that they were lip-servants to their ideals,
nor doubt that their conduct, whatever it might be,
accorded with their ideal standard.   They were too much
respected, too dear, to suffer the disloyalty of criticism.
If they said thus, it was true : if they did thus, it was right ;
for in such as these had not righteousness and truth, on
the admission of good society, kissed each other ?
Parliament was a place, more prominent, but not therefore less exalted, than home.   It was the national centre
whence the influences of religion radiated to the white
walls by the sea of old England.   It would be a moral
experience to participate in the debates, to be intimate
with the idealists who, sifted scrupulously by our
reformed Constitution, congregated there.   One would
grow, one might hope, more earnest, more gentlemanly,
in such an assembly, and feel, as one left its doors, as one
had used to feel when returning from the kirk.

This expectation, to which we cannot be too tender,
did not wholly allow, however, for the social revolution
occurring.

The garish days of the Prince Regent were over; as
George IV he had followed his aged parent into the
tomb; William IV, now in the fourth year of his un-
venerable reign, was hardly a strong prop even for a
corrupt tradition, and the world was indifferent whether
he were its prop or no.   Everything paled before the
political event that had led this first " Reformed Parliament " to be elected.   With the monopoly of the aristocracy gone in 1832, by the arrival in power of the
middle-class industrialist, deriving from Puritans of the
seventeenth century, our present phase of industrial pluto-
cracy began.   In religious terms, a state of commercial
Christianity was being established at a progressive rate.
Gladstone, whose imagination was more responsive than
critical, dimly discerned the process of change but
scarcely accommodated the difference involved in it.

On the one hand, the aristocratic sanctions remained, as persisting examples. On the other, a different theoretic basis of conduct, the middle-class basis, the backwash, as it were, of the Republican wave from France was gradually infesting speech and writing. The former were more traditional, more familiar, so that Gladstone was naturally drawn to these, and they seemed at first to crown his belief that Government was a religious duty. It very nearly had been so in the presbyteries of Scotland, and he was not prepared to find small countenance for the provincial opinion in the capital.

A stranger to London, and inhaling with the clean lungs of a country-bred boy the perceptible breeze of Reform which gave freshness to Westminster, Gladstone found himself confronted with proposals, often admirable but not advocated upon religious grounds. Was it not extraordinary that their strongest argument should be unused? The people whom he was beginning to meet about the House and in society were a little cold, in speech that is. He missed the note of enthusiasm, yet it was far easier to suffer the scoffs of wretches, of whom there were luckily but few, stridently declaring that the naming of principles was the stock vocabulary of political rhetoric. That they spoke from tubs and at street corners proved the wisdom of our Constitution in effectively excluding them from Parliament. These ranters were the cynics after all, and cynics in Parliament would be preposterous intruders. He had better words to listen to than theirs. There was Edward Irving to hear at the new, if heretical, church in Newman Street (since he was now excommunicate by the presbytery). There were more orthodox preachers. There were Dr. Arnold's sermons to read aloud. All these men agreed on the importance of earnestness and principle. His pre-eminence in both had led to Arnold's recent promotion to Rugby School. Irving, who entered no

D

house without giving an apostolic benediction, if mis-
guided, was free from any charge of want of seriousness.
His explicit aim had been to teach " imaginative men,
and political men, and legal men, and scientific men who
bear the world in hand " : a comprehensive audience.
This was enough. One must now study to apply one's
principles; possibly, if it must come to that, with a
higher seriousness because one's colleagues were men
of action rather than of lofty thought. These men, too,
could teach a man much. One must learn their ropes,
if only in order to hitch them to the car of a prophet
ascending.

Gladstone's early years in Parliament show the progress of this apprenticeship. The politician learns the
mode of his calling, while the enthusiast functions usefully overhead. Once he shall have learnt how to avoid
collision between this fire above and this cloud on the
ground, his path will be plainer. In the course of the
following sessions we shall watch how the accommodation proceeds.

V

In 1835 Lord Melbourne was dismissed by King
William, and Sir Robert Peel became Prime Minister.
Gladstone, who was returned for Newark unopposed,
was appointed a Junior Lord of the Treasury. It was
an interesting moment politically. After the passing
of the Reform Bill, conservative reaction became an
acceptable attitude. One accomplished change was
enough, and the process of digesting it should not be
disturbed. Gladstone's address to his constituents had
echoed Peel's, that, while the reform of abuses was a
sacred duty, innovation, as such, could not now be
entertained. It was a time for sober distractions, at the
close of, happily uneventful, Parliamentary days. At

dinner at Lord Lyndhurst's Gladstone met, for the first time, the young author of *Vivian Grey*, but neither Disraeli nor Gladstone seems to have made much impression upon each other that night. Disraeli innocently declared that a tender swan stuffed with truffles was the best company at the table. The evidence of eye-witnesses is notoriously weak.

At the end of January 1835, Peel sent for Gladstone to promote him to the post of Under-secretary for the Colonies. Reporting this gratifying interview to his father, the young man said :

> I expressed . . . my hesitation to form any opinion of my own competency for the office, and at the same time my general desire not to shrink from any responsibility that he might think proper to lay upon me.

Had the occasion been less important, even this "expression of hesitation" (Gladstone might have reflected) was superfluous, since he could not be judge in his own case; but how human it is to presume, on these occasions, egoists as we are, we all know. His new chief was Lord Aberdeen. At the age of twenty-five Gladstone was already in office.

Alas ! by April the new Government resigned, and of one of the adverse divisions preceding its resignation, Gladstone wrote : " No more shameful act, I think, has been done by a British House of Commons." His private feelings may be gleaned from a third of his rare revelations. He wrote on March 31 in reference to a speech :

> I cannot help recording that this matter of speaking is really my strongest religious exercise.

Does the old Adam of Evangelical effusiveness escape in a gush of sincerity here ? Who would have dared to assert such a theory of Gladstone unless he had declared

his belief in its truth himself ?   It is this, ever sought and
sometimes rewarded, self-candour which endears the
great man to us all.   When it comes, it is disarming, and
the unusual brevity of these phrases raises them in our
regard.   Gladstone was more accustomed to beat about
the bush.   If *laborare est orare*, then perhaps the highest
oratory is, in the eighteenth-century sense of the word,
to orate ?   It was a religious exercise to Gladstone.
He tells us so, for religious exercises are congenial to
muscular Christians, who are active believers in good
works, and rarely separate the ideas of religion and
activity.

This release from a brief spell of office gave to Gladstone a momentary leisure.   He continued to read
sermons, political and historical books, and from time
to time he ventured on the secular classics of art.
Roscoe's life of Pope Leo X impressed Gladstone with a
feeling that the book " in some degree subdued the leaven
of its author's Unitarianism," but when he had started
to read Rousseau's *Confessions* he was at a loss whether
to continue or to throw it on one side.

In September 1835, Gladstone lost his mother.   In
what proved to be her last illness he had read the Bible
to her every day.   To his father he continued to read
Spenser's *Faery Queen* and Shakespeare; while, on Sundays,
he would browse upon Anglican theologians and St.
Augustine.   He wrote also, memoranda of his meetings
in society and drafts on " Hypocrisy and Worship,"
adding, " attempted to explain this to the servants at
night."   This seriousness does not exclude susceptibility to fun, or smiles aroused by the foibles of members
of his circle.   Should the unpublished letters of Gladstone appear, they may provide the evidence for Gladstone's playfulness.

If his Sunday evenings were sometimes given to
exposition for the benefit of the servants, how did

Gladstone spend his secular evenings ?   He tells us that
speaking in the House would occasionally interfere with
his night's rest, and notes the experience, saying : " How
useful to make us feel the habitual, and unremembered,
blessing of sound sleep."   Wordsworth, whom Gladstone was shortly to meet, in his sonnets on Insomnia,
spoke of " this tiresome night," and began a third with
the line :

> Fond words have oft been spoken to thee, Sleep !

The philosophic poet wanted Gladstone's piety, and
perhaps suffered more often than Gladstone from
sleeplessness.

To dine out among keen conversationalists is public
speaking in little, should the diner be, like Gladstone,
ready in inquiry, question and retort, for we find this
confession near by : a dinner with Henry Taylor is not
only " a keen intellectual exercise," but " a place of
danger, as it is exercise seen."   What zest and caution
in these words !

In May Wordsworth came to breakfast with Gladstone, for breakfast, at this time, was Gladstone's
favourite form of hospitality at the Albany, where his
father's generosity had installed him.   The party sat till
a quarter to one, talking of Shelley and Tennyson,
travelling and copyright.   The subject of sleeplessness
does not waylay the breakfasters, though a discussion
by the poet and the politician of their common enemy
would have been interesting.   Three weeks later Wordsworth met Gladstone again at dinner, but no details
survive of their talk.   They had several meetings in
Gladstone's rooms, and Gladstone says he found intercourse with Wordsworth, " upon the whole, extremely
pleasing."   Gladstone was sorry to hear Sydney Smith
say that he did not see very much in Wordsworth, and
defended the London sonnet from Smith's charge of

being ridiculous. One of these breakfast scenes is worth transcribing.

> Wordsworth came in to breakfast the other day before his time. I asked him to excuse me while I had my servant to prayers; but he expressed a *hearty* wish to be present, which was delightful. He has laboured long; if for himself, yet more for men, and over all I trust for God. . . . We were agreed that a man's personal character ought to be the basis of his politics.

VI

At this time Gladstone himself wrote several sonnets, read steadily, and occasionally spoke. One of the occasions is still noteworthy. A certain candidate, suspected of unbelief, was asked if the report was true. He replied that the question of a person's religious beliefs was one that no liberal-minded man ought to ask another. The comment of Gladstone was this question :

> Is it not a time for serious reflection among moderate-minded and candid men of all parties, when such a question was actually thought impertinent interference ? Surely they would say with him that men who have no belief in the divine revelation are not the men to govern this nation, be they whigs or radicals.

Two comments must be made on this.

Indifference to the Christian religion has become so common that a remark of the kind may seem very out of date. Just as Englishmen have lost political passion because they have not been invaded within human memory, so they have not now, unless latently among the minorities of different faiths, religious passion. So far as Christian formulæ are concerned, there seems less sign of religious passion than there was one hundred years ago. For the present, no Christian is in danger of being burnt at Smithfield by his brother. The " spread of religious tolerance " is necessarily the " spread of indifference " too. But change belief in the Christian

verity to belief in Communism, and the wooden stan-
chions of the stalls in Smithfield Market are sensibly
nearer firewood than they were. Political passion and
religious passion, for a time, have languished : economic
passion, the fury for or against private property, is the
ember glowing now. If people will not fight for a
metaphysic, they will fight for a bank balance, for way-
leaves and royalties, the minimum wage, or an eight-
hour day. The passion we are feeling on the subject
of property is our equivalent to the feeling upon religion
in Gladstone's youth. He would have been shocked in
this year, 1835, at the thought of admitting atheists to
Parliament. Let the reader ask himself how *he* would
feel if two " Reds " seemed likely to be returned for
the City at the next election. Once we of 1927 have thus
put ourselves in the place of the Gladstone of 1837, his
comment on the man who declined to state his attitude
on " divine revelation " is seen to be natural. Would
not most men in a similar social position to-day
repeat it, did some Parliamentary candidate complain
to some constituents that his opinion on the validity of
private property was one that " no liberal-minded man
ought to ask " ?

The comment of Gladstone reflected the opinion of
the majority of his class when religious profession was
general; as, in turn, his principle of toleration on the
Affirmation Bill of 1883 reflected the opinion of other
men who were ceasing to pretend " to believe." We
need not repeat our examination of Gladstone's consistency. The *Tracts for the Times* had begun to appear
in 1833, and I remember the surprise with which, at
the age of seventeen, I read, and transcribed from the
pages of Newman's *Apologia*, this :

> In one of my first sermons I said, I do not shrink from
> uttering my firm conviction that it would be a gain to this
> country were it vastly more superstitious, more bigoted, more
> gloomy, more fierce, in its religion than at present it shows
> itself to be.

Victoria was still on the throne. One had but a glimmering then of the truth now, by comparison with our present passions on a different order of faith, clear enough. Then, however, one did miss the historical value of Newman's ensuing words :

> I added, of course, that it would be an absurdity to suppose such tempers of mind desirable in themselves. The corrector of the Press bore these strong epithets till he got to " more fierce," and then he put in the margin a *query*.

That " corrector of the Press " was the shadow of a Victorian morrow, with tip more extended along the ground than even Gladstone's, as yet. Fierceness in religion was undergoing a temporary period of eclipse, though the language of Gladstone's peers, in education and fortune and home influences, was closely similar. Let us not forget that both Newman and Gladstone were accused of sophistry. Read Manning, Hurrell Froude even, Dr. Arnold, the contemporary body of successful and earnest persons, not only on their common themes, and you will note an assonance that seems remarkable. Add Newman, Keble, Whately, the wittiest of them, though hardly wittier than Florence Nightingale at her best, the great Pusey also, in sum the names that thread the pages of Newman's *Apologia pro Vita Sua*, and the family accent is unescapable.

In this chorus, therefore, Gladstone's tone was not, at first, distinguishable. It struck the same note, and prolonged it, as the novice at an organ will prolong the stop marked *vox humana*. Whenever we concern ourselves with a single member of the group, we need to remember this if we would not exaggerate his value as a specimen of the style. Yet the dialect is so nearly identical that what seems, on first acquaintance with the idiom, an earnestness peculiar to a single soul is largely a group-character. Religion, at the end of the eighteenth century, had taken refuge with the Evangelicals, consequently the future Tractarians and their sympathisers had usually nourished themselves in youth upon the style of the little Bethel and the Beulah. No doubt the twenty-twenties, a century hence, in any words of our day then remembered, will trace a similar assonance. Let us beware of pluming ourselves on a distinction as unlikely as it is impossible to apprehend, if it exists. It is enough to admit that the authorship of an unidentified sentence, belonging to some contemporary of the young Gladstone, would become a nice question of attribution to a present-day scholiast.

VII

Out of office, and being little active in Parliament though assiduous there, Gladstone began to form his future habit of filling intervals by writing a book. The subject had been long, perhaps always, at the back of his adolescent mind. It was the due relation between Church and State. It had been his inner intention to make politics the application of religion. The House was a pastorate to him. It was, as he has told us, the place where he practised his religious exercises, the congregation that he led, when he addressed it, in a kind of extempore prayer. In his first election address he had declared that the cure for our evils was a return to the sound principles of religion. Was not his own principle, that government was a religious duty, sound? Must not all true Christians so regard it? Did not they profess so to do? Was not he, who had no inner light, peculiarly conscious of the need, and would not a book expounding this theme prove to the world that energies, if untimely deprived of office, were still busy with exalted ends? Teeming with these thoughts, he

attended the funeral of Lady Canning in Westminster
Abbey, and confided to his diary the hope, " May we
live as by the side of a grave, and looking in."

The death of William IV, involving a dissolution of
Parliament, plunged Gladstone into a general election
again. The Tories insisted on nominating him for
Manchester, where he was rejected by the Whigs on two
grounds : of owing his wealth to slavery, and of wishing
to subject the poor negroes on his father's estates to the
tenets of an Established Church. This did not matter,
for he was returned without a contest for Newark once
more, with the added satisfaction that his rising reputation
was undisputed.

He confirmed it further by a speech in defence of
the planters, whom he represented upon a committee
appointed to inquire into the working of apprenticeship.
This system was attacked, especially in Jamaica, for having
proved even harsher than slavery to the slaves. He still
had to trim in debate : to defend the conduct of the
planters while declaring now his belief that slavery was
" evil and demoralising." He discerned that criticism
no longer could be met by conferring benefits upon the
negroes, and he begged his father to let him see the
plantations for himself. This the wary parent, perhaps
knowing his son's excitability, strenuously opposed, by
" a prudent instinct." [1] The father's prudence might
have had an untoward effect upon a less filially trustful
young man. Gladstone still had implicit faith in the
guidance of his elders. How could he be a child of his
father without being also a child of light ?

Moreover, he was being infected by the growing
interest in national education, convinced that, where a
church was established, the State should subsidise the
teachers of the establishment only. Touching Ireland,
he had said in 1835, " the Protestant faith is held good

[1] Morley.

enough for us, and what is good enough for us is also good for the population of Ireland."

It is not the fault of youth that it has so much to unlearn : the phrase indeed is significant for a reason that has nothing to do with statesmanship. Observe : the statement is a syllogism, the first premiss, perhaps preferably the middle term (that " the Protestant faith exists in Ireland), being an ellipsis (as taken for granted). Verbally the logic is perfect, but unfortunately logical conclusions are not vital conclusions. Gladstone was still the dupe of words, obsequious to formulæ. In extenuation of a characteristic Scots failing (for the Scots are contentious over words as we are contentious over bats and balls, and each is but " a serious game " to the respective nation), remember this : Like many of his contemporaries, he had no conceptions at this time that Ireland was more than a name on the map of the United Kingdom. In this it was like Fasque, his family's Scottish home. That the Irish could conceive they were being taxed to support heresy was past a joke. Heresy was not a funny word, and to level it at England was, at best, in doubtful taste.

Gladstone was now fully ripe to transfer his Evangelical fervour to the Churchmanship into which his father had already bloomed. Yet he was prevented from taking any narrow view of orthodox claims by the double-mindedness of one now adding the preservative of Westminster to the milk of doctrine. His views had developed, were still unfolding ; his eye was on the political sky, wary of necessity to the drift of cloud lest it should be massing to a nimbus before morning. How was he to balance experience with idealism ? Obviously by supporting practical proposals, in which he believed, in the language of enthusiasm, in which he believed also. The day was coming when he would be using the language of strict orthodoxy for the contemplation of

measures, even of disestablishment, that then made
many incumbents shudder.

VIII

His book upon *The State in its Relations to the Church*,
published in 1839, was his adolescent attempt to apply
his Evangelical ideal to politics. It proved to be the
parting of the ways. The serpent of practical policy
had not yet insinuated its way into Gladstone's innocent
heart by the gate which is called Westminster.

When Gladstone found no response, even from
friendly quarters, when he discovered that a theocracy
was not a practical political policy, he dropped it at
once. The wavering inner light, fed by precept and
reading, still untrimmed by critical faculty, was about
to be quenched by practical experience. No one can
deny that Gladstone was capable of learning, or that he
learned by sight rather than by intuition; and his consistency lay in using the same language for the new lesson
as for the old.

Gladstone properly took advantage of a prevailing
current of opinion in his first book. The posthumous
Church and State of Coleridge had been published in
1836, and William Palmer, of Worcester College,
Oxford, had issued his *Treatise on the Church of Christ* in
1838, the previous year. In Gladstone's own words :
" the primary idea of my early politics was the Church.
With this was connected the idea of the establishment,
as being everything except essential." He went abroad
while the book, with the aid of James Hope (Scott's)
revisions, was being printed ; met Macaulay in Rome,
received a letter from Dr. Wiseman on the Missal, and
attended innumerable sermons.

Roughly, the effect of Gladstone's book was to please
churchmen and to bore politicians. After dining with

Sir Robert Peel, Gladstone wrote : " Not a word from him, Stanley or Graham yet, even to acknowledge my poor book; but no change of manner, certainly none in Peel or Graham." Gladstone consoled himself with the reflection that Peel was " quite incapable of comprehending the movement in the Church, the strength it would reach, and the exigencies it would entail," points on which Gladstone himself was, perhaps, more clear than on matters of doctrine. This was his instinctive answer to the report that Ministers wondered why anyone, with so fine "a career " opening before him, should go out of his way to write books. Almost immediately he made the discovery that " there was no party, no individual person probably, in the House of Commons, who was prepared to act on it. I found myself the last man on a sinking ship." He simply could not see himself in the part. He was a man of action.

The way out of this dilemma was to dress the opposite and prevailing opinion in language not dissimilar from his previous defence of the establishment : " it was " (he wrote therefore in the retrospect) " really a quickened conscience, in the country, that insisted on enlarging the circle of State support." Beset by doubt on many matters, Gladstone was finely constant to the faith of his time, that, whatever else we might disbelieve, we could not disbelieve in progress.

Meantime, however, against the indifference of Sir Robert Peel the praise of John Keble could not weigh. Perforce he abandoned his desire, sprung from the " sanguine fervour " of a youth who had noted " the many symptoms of revival and reform within " the Church's borders, to create a theocracy in England; of a youth who " dreamed that she was capable of recovering lost ground and of bringing back the nation to unity in her communion." All was not lost yet. Could he not turn entirely to the theorists, the little band which

alone had welcomed him ? Gladstone therefore wrote
Church Principles, which fell flat. His head was, like
Scotland, too misty to handle theology in an interesting
way. It required a debatable borderland between theory
and practice for his arguments to arouse men made
uneasy lest their pockets should be threatened by the
application. Expectation or apprehensiveness concerning the politician ever provided the interest taken in
Gladstone's ideas.

Following the plan of disposing of recurring issues
when they first arise, we may attend to the first of Gladstone's fairly voluminous writings. The influences
displayed by his books form an impressive succession,
but the style, like the man himself, did not change. If
he began as a holy innocent, he ended as a holy elder,
indeed the eldest statesman of his time. It was so also
with his authorship. Between *The State and its Relations
to the Church* and *The Impregnable Rock of Holy Scripture*
there were to be many pamphlets and books, the eight
volumes of *Gleanings from Past Years* being, literally,
no more than gleanings. For the present our purpose
is with the first book, which evoked a yet surviving
criticism.

In his review, published in the *Edinburgh*, of the second
edition of *The State in its Relations with the Church*,
Macaulay wrote :

> His rhetoric, though often good of its kind, darkens and
> perplexes the logic which it should illustrate. Half his acute-
> ness and diligence, with a barren imagination and a scanty
> vocabulary, would have saved him from almost all his mistakes.
> He has one gift most dangerous to a speculator, a vast com-
> mand of a kind of language, grave and majestic, but of a
> vague and uncertain import. . . . The foundations of his
> theory, which ought to be buttresses of adamant, are made out
> of flimsy materials which are fit only for perorations.

This is rather hard on perorations, but it was Macaulay's

way, and his assertiveness has no illusion now for critical posterity. The intellects of Macaulay and of Gladstone were without subtilty, but whereas Macaulay's was as hard as a nail, Gladstone's was as unsubstantial as an eiderdown. To watch Macaulay industriously hammering his tintack into Gladstone's theological patchwork quilt is a spectacle apt to become exhausting. To read the one upon the other is to read the new journalism upon the old. The bright young man turns upon his earnest colleague in this summary way :

> It is not unusual for a person who is eager to prove a particular proposition to assume a *major* of huge extent, which includes that particular proposition, without ever reflecting that it includes a great deal more. The fatal facility with which Mr. Gladstone multiplies expressions stately and sonorous, but of indeterminate meaning, eminently qualifies him to practise this sleight on himself and his readers. He lays down broad general principles about power, when the only power of which he is thinking is the power of Governments, and about conjoint action, when the only conjoint action of which he is thinking is the conjoint action of citizens in a State.
>
> He first resolves on his conclusion. He then makes a *major* of most comprehensive dimensions, and, having satisfied himself that it contains his conclusion, never troubles himself about what else it may contain; and as soon as we examine it, we find that it contains an infinite number of conclusions, every one of which is a monstrous absurdity.

To give the devil his due, which is the duty of a Christian, this would pass for a neat decipherment of Gladstone's mental method, did it not overlook, of course, to some extent the earnest purpose, the cloud of yearning feelings, to which the method was no more than a tool in awkward hands. By the simple process of deleting such abstract nouns as Duty, Justice, Righteousness, of curtailing periphrases, of condensing parenthetical qualifications, the bulk of Gladstone's volumes would shrink to normal size. This, however, could not be

done without sacrificing their quality, which is none the
less a quality because it happens to be a quantitative one.
The play of words is the thing; redundancy the virtue;
fervour the element of the whole.   To bring the Glad-
stonean canon to an intellectual test is to make a cardinal
mistake, very unjust to the author.   Read so, the writings
would become almost a specific for yawning.   Indeed
for Gladstone's publications the term writings is a mis-
nomer.   The author is orating with his pen.   He
opines : he does not think.   He is a fountain of written
speechifying.   He is his own stenographer.

To sound moral, to seem earnest, to indulge in sublime
sentiments, to produce a hortatory effect, in a word, to
edify, was the peculiar gift of Gladstone; but when the
clear baritone voice and the graceful pantomime of the
speaker's gestures were wanting, when the pen detained
the attention that the charm of the voice relaxed, the
substance vanishes and the cloud of words condenses
into a rain of ink that chills the head of the reader.   He
professed so much to rely upon eternal truths that the
ephemeral interest of his books seems their reduction to
" absurdity."

This seeming, however, is not all.   To edify was
Gladstone's gift, and his power in this kind must be
related to the audience that admitted it triumphantly.
His art, whether with voice or pen, was the art of homily,
not strictly of oratory, literature, or delivery of sermons.
The homily is distinct from each of these.   A sermon is
a speech addressed to an audience or congregation however intimate or small : a homily, on the other hand, is an
exhortation or moralising discourse addressed to a
homilos or crowd, a throng, a multitude of hearers.   The
distinction amounts to a specific difference.   Littlemore,
" that small grey church where the worshippers are few,"
was a proper spot for sermons.   The floor of the House
of Commons with men crowding between the benches,

the still vaster arena of Blackheath where an assembly of twenty thousand was to hang on Gladstone's words, was the fit amphitheatre for a homily. Would Newman have been equally moving, had he ever inclined himself, to a large crowd? Would Gladstone have had a fair chance at Littlemore? Such a question is invidious to both men. It is its own answer.

Macaulay makes two other criticisms that are worth remembering. The undergraduate said to have known his Bible better than any of his fellow-pupils is convicted by Macaulay of error in the use of a familiar text. If this was the first public occasion when the impregnable rock of Holy Scripture proved to be pregnable in Gladstone's hands, let us remember how few adults even can distinguish between the two versions of similar sayings in St. Matthew's and St. Luke's Gospels. The criticism, which touches us all in a very tender spot, is interesting for another reason. The learning of Gladstone was, like his scholarship, an alluvial deposit rather than the bed-rock that he and the wider public fancied each to be. This fact may serve to introduce perhaps the best general criticism in Macaulay's essay : " When he says that he is where he was, he means only that he has moved at the same rate with all around him."

The criticism proved to be prophetic, and the movement of Gladstone's opinions, the shifting grounds of which he was aware, encouraged his tendency to parenthesis and qualification. There was more logic than is usually admitted in his claim for verbal consistency. His qualifications allowed room for more interpretations than one, and he was never more delighted than when he was referred to some previous statement. This, once his political nonage was passed, would always bear scrutiny because he always shunned directly to commit himself. The involutions of his parenthetical style made his remarks hard to memorise accurately, and, again and

E

again, when some opponent rose triumphantly in a newspaper or in debate to recall a former statement now apparently being contradicted, he was convicted of having overlooked a saving adjective or exempting clause. The general drift had been remembered, but the grammatical reading of the text often allowed more inferences than one. The meaning, at first and afterwards, might indeed be doubtful : the formula could be defended either way. Bad phraseology, in the theological, literary, legal or technical sense, ceases to be bad if it has been designed to be of doubtful interpretation. Gladstone made a crutch of his intellectual crotchet, and, like all men clever enough so to do, was dangerous to his opponents in proportion as they thought him therefore at their mercy. In self-defence he became an adept at this art, and was eventually acclaimed a master of subtilty because he cultivated indefiniteness. It became impossible for him to make a direct statement at last.

To-day, when politicians are at pains to arrange a dispute between two sides opposed in principle to one another, the newspapers tell us that the officials are busy trying " to find a formula." The object of the formula is to obtain a settlement that shall leave the insoluble issue where it was. To " find a formula " has become the official solution of problems arising from collective bargaining both in trade and diplomacy. Its best disciple was Gladstone, the first of parliamentarians to appeal to the mass of electors between election times.

Finally, Macaulay made a certain diagnosis, also of value when we reconsider the ideas that Gladstone imbibed during his youth, accepted implicitly, and endeavoured to apply, or at least to preach, to the world growing up with him. " Mr. Gladstone's book " (Macaulay wrote) . . . " is the measure of what a man can do to be left behind by the world." Since both men believed in progress, this verdict was severe, but it was certainly the verdict of the politicians. Gladstone, a shrewd judge of such opinion, promptly discarded his thesis. It was part of his humility not to be the last upholder of a losing cause. In the inimitable sincerity of his own words : " Providence directed that my mind should find its food in other pastures than those in which my youthfulness would have loved to seek it." On consideration he sees that between taking Holy Orders and a seat in the House there is little difference, for " reflection shows me that a political position is mainly valuable as instrumental for the good of the Church, and under this rule every question becomes one of detail only."

" I wish you to know," he wrote to his brother-in-law in 1840, " the state of total impotence to which I should be reduced if there were no echo to the accents of my own voice."

CHAPTER II

THE GROWTH OF EXPERIENCE

I

THE winter of 1838 Gladstone spent in Rome, where he joined Manning after having met in Naples the widow and daughters of Sir Stephen Richard Glynne of Hawarden, Flintshire. Gladstone had first visited Hawarden in 1835 and now became engaged to Catherine Glynne, sister and in her issue heiress of Sir Stephen, the ninth and last baronet. Gladstone proposed to her in the Colosseum, the largest amphitheatre in the world, and her acceptance admitted him to membership of the aristocracy.

They were married on July 25, 1839. On the same day, Mary, the younger sister, married Lord Lyttelton. The two marriages were solemnised with great rejoicings at Hawarden. Gladstone's best man was Sir Francis Doyle, Professor of Poetry at Oxford. He commemorated the twofold nuptials in a poem called the *Two Sister Brides*, in the course of which Mrs. Gladstone was told to

> Covet not, then, the rest of those
> Who sleep through life unknown to fame;
> Fate grants not passionless repose
> To her who weds a glorious name.

As Gladstone had not yet reached his thirtieth birthday, and the term was not incongruous, it is evident how welcome the union was to both families.

A portrait of Catherine Gladstone at this time happily exists. It shows a delicate face, at once vivacious and tender, with liquid eyes, a straight nose, a shapely forehead and waving hair. The expression is winning and affectionate, open and intelligent, and the picture is a contrast to the somewhat theatrical portrait of her husband which William Bradley painted about the same time. Like many portraits of its period, this last appears to represent a type or reputation rather than a man. The prominent nose is the chief feature of the face, and there is, again typically, more effect than character in the physiognomy.

II

Having married the heiress of Hawarden, Gladstone was naturally taking a warm interest in the future home, a home which he was to preserve amid many financial difficulties. In 1809 the house was built of brick before being enlarged and cased in stone " in the castellated style," when it became Hawarden Castle. Sir Stephen Glynne further improved it in 1831; the new block containing Gladstone's study was added in 1864. This study contained three windows, two fireplaces, and three desks. One of the desks was reserved for Gladstone's political, another for his literary, papers. The third was Mrs. Gladstone's. Other treasures in the room included busts of Homer, Canning, Cobden and Tennyson, together with an axe from Nottingham remarkable for not being of the American shape that Gladstone preferred. When he brought his wife home to his family, Gladstone learnt that his father intended to hand over his plantations to his sons. The estates were now freed from slaves, for in 1837 a return, opposed by Gladstone, of the sums given in compensation to

the slave-owners recorded that his father had received
£75,000.

Nevertheless Gladstone's marriage was to involve him
indirectly in financial worries.   His brother-in-law, Sir
Stephen Glynne, owned a farm of one hundred acres in
Staffordshire, and the land was found to be rich in coal
and ironstone.   On his marriage Gladstone, through his
wife, was given a tenth share in the enterprise of developing this property.   On the security of Hawarden much
capital was sunk, and, after the company became in-
solvent in 1847, Gladstone purchased the concern.
This arrangement left Sir Stephen in legal occupation,
but with a sum of a quarter of a million hanging over
Hawarden and himself.   To save the estate from being
sold became the anxious desire of the family, and in
the prolonged struggle Gladstone took an arduous
share.   With his father's help Gladstone purchased
nearly half of the portion of the estate that had inevitably to be sold.   This brought in £200,000 and kept
half the land in the family, for Glynne's other brother-
in-law was helped to purchase the part that Gladstone
could not take.   In 1852 the house was partly reopened,
and in 1865 Gladstone purchased the reversion for
£57,000.

First and last Gladstone spent £267,000 on Hawarden,
of which the deaths of Stephen and Henry Glynne left
him the owner in 1874.   He promptly made it over to
his eldest son, who agreed to leave the house to Mrs.
Gladstone for life, so that, with characteristic paradox,
the house most identified with Gladstone was occupied
by another when he controlled it or owned by someone
else for most of the time when he was there.   Gladstone
seems to have managed the whole protracted business
with industry, skill and generosity.   This episode, to
which he devoted five years and then an overseeing eye,
though hardly mentioned outside the exhaustive official

biography, is highly characteristic. As an experience of
business men and business matters, as an apprenticeship
to finance, it was invaluable. Beside this, it brought
out the most authentic of Gladstone's abilities. The
more concrete and immediate his task, the better he was
equipped to perform it. His careful letters to his son,
in which he aired his views on the duties attaching to
property and on the prestige still possessed by territorial
families over commercial fortunes, have a note of conviction clearer than the note struck by abstract, moral
or imaginative themes. The reality, as always, is less
high-flown than the phantasm, and to have saved
Hawarden was a complicated and worthy task on which
any man might warm himself excusably.

III

Macaulay's familiar description of Gladstone as " the
rising hope of stern and unbending Tories," was justified
in so far as his book on Church and State had been
much enjoyed at Oxford, to which " fountain of bless-
ings, spiritual, social and intellectual," it had been
dedicated. Eight years later the University was to elect
him to represent it in Parliament. Meantime the session
of 1840 showed Gladstone in one of his characteristic
dilemmas.

Certain Englishmen were smuggling opium into China
in despite of Chinese law, and when China (whose
engagements were not kept) defended herself, the British
agent found excuse for attacking her. Though orders
had been sent forbidding the protection of the smugglers,
England, once engaged, determined to push the struggle
to victory. The result was that the wretched Chinese
were forced to open four ports, to pay an indemnity,
and to cede Hong-Kong. Having (he records) previously asked whether speaking out would do any harm,

Gladstone denounced our conduct, and then yielded to his colleagues in not bringing forward a motion against the demand for compensation from China. His speech here proved to be his "strongest religious exercise," and, if speech be rightly regarded as political activity, his activity at any rate "could not do any harm." If the speech of denunciation be set against its foreseen nullity of effect, the balance struck is almost perfect. It would be easy, therefore, for a third party to claim the net result of this activity for either side. The point for us to notice is that theoretical considerations prompted the speech, practical considerations the withdrawal of his motion. He was growing.

> In words, as fashions, the same rule will hold,
> Alike fantastic if too new or old :
> Be not the first by whom the new are tried,
> Nor yet the last to lay the old aside.

Gladstone was throwing a bridge between remembered precept and observed example, and his preceptors and exemplars were equally reverenced by him. As Pope remarked a little further on, "fools admire, but men of sense approve." It was "men of sense" with whom Gladstone was now dealing.

There were still moments of relaxation. In 1839 he had been reading *Oliver Twist* and *Nicholas Nickleby*. He said of the latter : "The tone is very human; it is most happy in touches of natural pathos. No church in the book, and the motives are not those of religion." Dickens did not seem much use to an advocate of theocracy. Of *Peter Bell*, which Arnold had read with edification, Gladstone recorded that he had been struck with "the depth of interest which is made to attach to the humblest of quadrupeds." Like all Gladstone's phrases, this is worth pondering, for an "interest . . . made to attach" to a donkey implies that the donkey itself is not interesting. Yet an Evangelical who had written verses might have remembered that this was the creature upon which his Lord rode, and haply had been chosen just because it was " the humblest of quadrupeds." In great men contradictions are the salt of character, and, provided that these are not pressed unduly, bring them closer to ourselves.

Reading apart, Gladstone found " moral relaxation " in a journey to Eton, there to examine for the Newcastle Scholarship. He set a passage from St. Augustine in the paper on divinity, and awarded the Newcastle medal to Henry Fitzmaurice Hallam, the younger brother of his old friend. His brother-in-law, Lord Lyttelton, was his fellow-examiner. In the autumn Gladstone joined James Hope (Scott) in a scheme for founding a seminary in Scotland where the clergy might be trained, and the children of the gentry educated, without recourse to Presbyterians. In 1846, with his father's generous aid the seminary was opened at Glenalmond.

This was one of the many schemes for charitable work on which Gladstone and Hope frequently corresponded. Gladstone's letters and his endeavours to persuade Hope to unite with him in philanthropic activity make interesting reading.

Despite political and domestic cares, Gladstone cherished his Sundays. For example, on March 14, 1841, we read in his diary that he attended the early service at St. James's, the afternoon service at St. Margaret's, and then " wrote on Ephes. v. 1 and read it aloud to the servants." The following Sunday he chose 1 Thess. v. 17, and read it aloud to the servants. During the intervening week he had attended the afternoon service at St. Paul's, and was affected by the contrast between the serene cathedral and the commercial strife without its walls. In his diary he notes also : " no strokes from God, no opportunity of pardoning others, for

none offend me." The diary of Mrs. Gladstone remarks :
" engaged a cook, after a long conversation on religious
matters, chiefly between her and William."

IV

In a discussion on the fiscal system, Gladstone referred
to the slave trade. He called it now " that monster
which, while war, pestilence and famine were slaying
their thousands, slew from year to year with unceasing
operation its tens of thousands." In spite of bringing
up a peer, whom Gladstone reported " to be in a state
of total idiocy," and " evidently in total unconsciousness
of what was proceeding," the Government was defeated,
on Peel's motion of want of confidence, by a majority
of one. A dissolution followed ; Gladstone was returned
for Newark as a Protectionist. The sad thing was that
Sir Stephen Glynne was not returned for Flintshire,
but Cobden, for the first time, took his seat in the
House.

Peel appointed Gladstone to the vice-presidency of the
Board of Trade, an office which he combined with that
of Master of the Mint. He seems to have hoped for
the Irish secretaryship and a seat in the Cabinet, and
was inclined to wonder whether his dual post had not
perhaps been designed to keep him quiet. His ecclesiastical writings and interests had been thought mistakes
by his political chief. Gladstone, therefore, thought it
prudent to deny, in an inordinately long letter to Peel,
the newspaper report that he held Peel's opinions on
Church matters in reprobation.

England was now definitely, though scarcely consciously and officially, committed to industrialism ; and
it fell to Peel's government of 1842 to recognise the
economic revolution. In the following passage Lord
Morley depicts the situation :

If you had to conſtitute new societies, Peel said to Croker, then you might on moral and social grounds prefer corn-fields to cotton faċtories, and you might like an agricultural population better than a manufaċturing; as it was, the national lot was caſt, and ſtatesmen were powerless to turn back the tide. The food of the people, their clothing, the raw material for their induſtry, their education, the conditions under which women and children were ſuffered to toil, markets for these produċts of loom and forge and furnace and mechanic's shop—these were slowly making their way into the central field of political vision, and taking the place of fantaſtic follies about foreign dynaſties and the balance of power as the true business of the British ſtatesman.

Hitherto Peel had been a Proteċtioniſt, and Gladſtone had therefore followed suit, but the accumulated deficits and the prevailing diſtress were causing an outcry, and even thought to demand a remedy. The popular spokesman of this bitterness of spirit was Ebenezer Elliott, the Corn-law Rhymer.

Born in 1781 in Yorkshire, the son of a Calviniſt iron merchant, who was a ſtern radical, the little Ebenezer, a dunce to his schoolmaſters, worked for seven years from the age of sixteen in his father's foundry for the Calviniſtic wage of pocket-money. Already rather a morbid little boy, dazed with ſtifled longings, his ſtarved imagination fed on the sight of the wild-flowers that he met upon his country rambles, on his rare holiday afternoons. Indoors he browsed upon Milton and a few poets of the eighteenth century which fell into his hands through some books that a poor clergyman had chanced to bequeath to Mr. Elliott. Ebenezer began to write verses; his firſt sonnet remains, with other juvenile pieces; and these even, unripe as they are, showed that the eager lad had the root of poetry in him. Once his brief years of popularity were over, Ebenezer Elliott fell into negleċt again, except by our anthologiſts. He is rarely tedious, never unreadable, and there is a glow of suppressed passion in his poetry which redeems the rhetoric to which his Muse was naturally akin. On the loss of his father's money and his wife's, through, he asserted, the Corn Laws, the poet inevitably joined the Chartists, till, that is to say, they gave up the demand for Repeal. He was finally touched to poetry by his political conviction, which came to him now in the guise almost of a religious faith. Indeed Calvinism has often produced admirable agitators.

The *Corn-law Rhymes*, which appeared in 1831, ran into three editions in the year of their publication, and for a time Ebenezer was also meeting with success in the business that, on borrowed capital, he had started in Sheffield after the death of his father. In 1837, however, he was almost ruined again, yet he managed to recover, and retired four years later, to die in comparative peace, at Barnsley, in his native county, in 1849. He imputed the cause of all his family's misfortunes to the Corn Laws, and his assault upon the " bread tax," together with his private sufferings, championship of the poor in our industrial towns, stainless sincerity, and moving rhythm created and, to those with ears, maintains, his niche in English letters. A writer praised by Carlyle and by Walter Savage Landor is secure from the neglect of lesser men, whose disregard is really a quaint compliment. Robert Southey, too, deserves to have recalled the friendly criticism that he sent by letter to Elliott after having read the earliest of *Vernal Walks*, addressed to Night, in 1831. It seems to have been written at the age of seventeen, that is, in 1798, in the manner of James Thomson.

The working men of Sheffield subscribed for a statue to Elliott, by Neville Burhard, on which Walter Savage Landor composed the following, among other eloquent, lines :

> Wisely, O Sheffield, wisely hast thou done
> To place thy ELLIOTT on the plinth of fame.

Three Elliotts have there been, three glorious men,
Each in his generation. . . .
A third came calmly on and askt the rich
To give laborious hunger daily bread. . . .
God heard; but they heard not.   God sent down bread;
They took it, kept it all, and cried for more,
Hollowing both hands to catch and clutch the crumbs.
   I may not live to hear another voice,
Elliott, of power to penetrate as thine,
Dense multitudes; another none may see,
Leading the muses from unthrifty shades,
To fields where corn gladdens the heart of man. . . .

But louder than the anvil rings the lyre;
   .   .   .   .

Genius is tired in search of gratitude;
Here they have met; may neither say farewell.

With the insight of his genius, Landor in one fine
line conveys the ringing heart of Elliott's poetry at its
best.   The rhythm does seem to be that of a hammer
upon an anvil, and the finer lines to have been written
in the foundry where the boy found warmth, and the
honour of his metals, to set an example to the slum,
called a town, of greed and poverty in which his generation was bred.   His quality, of which his popular
appeal was the recognition, may still be felt in lines like
these, from " The Emigrant's Farewell " :

England, farewell ! we quit thee—never more
To drink thy dewy light, or hear the thrush
Sing to thy fountain'd vales. . . .
                              In our prayers,
If we forget our wrongers, may we be
Vile as their virtues, hopeless as their heirs,
And sires of sons whom scorn shall nickname theirs !—
And to such wolves leave we our country ?   Oh,
The heart that quits thee, e'en in hope, despairs !

Another Corn-law rhyme is a virtual sonnet entitled " A
Poet's Prayer " :

Almighty Father! let thy lowly child,
Strong in his love of truth, be wisely bold—
A patriot bard, by sycophants reviled,
Let him live usefully, and not die old!
Let poor men's children, pleased to read his lays,
Love, for his sake, the scenes where he has been;
And, when he ends his pilgrimage of days,
Let him be buried where the grass is green;
Where daisies, blooming earliest, linger late
To hear the bee his noisy note prolong—
There let him slumber, and in peace await
The dawning morn, far from the sensual throng,
Who scorn the windflower's blush, the redbreast's lonely
song.

The line about the bee, and the charming final alexandrine, recall the eighteenth century. There is a short and eloquent poem, like a so-called ode, upon " The Press," the rich rhythm of which has a certain added flavour from the sincere but unintended note of its concluding apostrophe. How ironical it sounds to-day:

O pallid Want! O Labour stark!
Behold, we bring the second ark!
The Press! the Press! the Press!

Hopes were high then, because the chances for our millionaires lay still hid in the distant future. No one then foresaw that the popular Press of a century later, in the firm grasp of a few colossally rich men, would live up to its name very largely by suppressing information. Devised by human cormorants for human gulls, popular papers of England and America are exactly what we should expect from the conditions which they reflect and their proprietors thrive upon. We cannot blame Ebenezer Elliott for not having divined that if the newspapers were freed from the Paper Tax, the Second Ark, to which he compared the Press, would be, as the Epistle to the Hebrews puts it, the " mediator of a new covenant " very different from " my covenant of peace,

and he shall have it, and his seed after him . . . because
he was zealous for his God," as the Lord phrased it to
Moses, with the original Ark in His mind.

Another poem of Elliott's, called the " Triumph of
Reform," is mainly political in its challenge. A better
example of the same class is the short lyric on the Revolution of 1832. It is perhaps in " Reform " that we come
near the heart of Elliott's Corn-law rhyming :

> Too long endured, a power and will,
> That would be nought, or first in ill,
> Had wasted wealth, and palsied skill,
>   And fed on toil-worn poverty.
>
> They call'd the poor a rope of sand;
> And, lo ! no rich man's voice or hand
> Was raised, throughout the suffering land,
>   Against their long iniquity.
>
>   .   .   .   .
>
> They murder'd Hope, they fetter'd trade;
> The clouds to blood, the sun to shade,
> And every good that God had made
>   They turned to bane and mockery.
>
>   .   .   .   .
>
> A murmur from a trampled worm,
> A whisper in the cloudless storm—
> Yet these, even these, announced Reform;
>   And Famine's scowl was prophecy !
>
>   .   .   .   .
>
> O years of crime !   The great and true—
> The nobly wise—are still the few,
> Who bid Truth grow where Falsehood grew,
>   And plant it for eternity !

If the voice of that which we now call Labour can be
heard in the sentiment that stars this poem with exclama-
tion marks, there is a ring in it, due not only to the
measure, which reminds one of the cadence that Rossetti
was to use with fine effect too. A single quotation more
must here suffice; it is taken from one of the Rhymes
called " The Recording Angel " :

> King of Dear Corn ! Time hears with ceaseless groan,
>   Time ever hears, sad names of hate and dread :
> But thou, thou only, of all monarchs known,
>   Didst legislate *against* thy People's bread !

This argument, however, burgeoned into two lyrics
which are irresistible in their own kind and degree :

> No toil in despair,
>   No tyrant, no slave,
> No bread-tax is there,
>   With a maw like the grave. . . .

> And their mother, who sank
>   Broken-hearted to rest;
> And the baby, that drank
>   Till it froze on her breast;
> With tears, and with smiles,
>   Are waiting for thee,
> In the beautiful isles
>   Where the wrong'd are the free.

> Child, is thy father dead ?
>   Father is gone !
> Why did they tax his bread ?
>   God's will be done !
> Mother has sold her bed;
> Better to die than wed !
> Where shall she lay her head ?
>   Home we have none !

Hood, at his best, was a more ingenious master of rhyme,
but, in his poems of parallel appeal, was he more moving ?

   With the bitterness and distress of the recent Coal
Stoppage in mind, we can well understand the feelings
of Sir Robert Peel when poetry of this sincerity, written
too by a poor man, was eagerly sung, to the familiar
tunes for which Elliott composed his songs, by thousands
of his wretched fellow-countrymen.

   The distress was undeniable, and Peel was in the most
wretched of the plights that can befall a politician, the
occasion when something must be done.   In order that

he might be free to reduce duties on food and on raw materials, Peel proposed therefore to raise revenue by an Income Tax. At the Board of Trade the alert eyes of Gladstone were beginning to be opened, in his own sphere, to the necessities of the moment. Unlike Peel, moreover, Gladstone was not forced to keep his eye on the agricultural interest and the House of Lords. Trade necessarily dominated his horizon, and perhaps his susceptible mind dimly responded to the political consequences of the coming change. His queer sense of the morrow was roused from its lair. We now see what may have dawned on him, that free trade could not become a workable policy in industrialised England unless and until the extenson of the franchise to holders of urban property accompanied it. Obviously, if agriculture and the landed interest were to be sacrificed to manufacture and industry, the agricultural voter must be securely outvoted henceforth. In political language this meant that the old talk about liberty must be revived, even though, politically speaking, this meant to the engineers of the new policy no more than a dressing to disguise the shifting of political with economic power.

The threefold policy of Peel—the Corn Bill, the imposition of an Income Tax, and the Reform of the tariff—left to Gladstone the third and most laborious task. The field was entirely new to him; there was nothing in his education, save over the Hawarden affair, to fit him for it; and it presents us with another of his engaging contradictions. He came reluctantly to finance, for (having no inner light) he was inclined to speculation and moral fervour. Yet events and the judgment of posterity, where that has happened to be impartial, show that he had next to none of intellect, whereas he was lucid and clear-headed over business and figures, and astute, in his odd way, when dealing with men whom he did not understand. That he was self-deceived is not odd,

F

nor that he succeeded in deceiving others.   His immense
energy, the most vital of his qualities, finely expressed
in his vigorous physique, found congenial scope in the
flood of detail that the reform of the tariff entailed.   He
was copious in effort, inquisitive of detail, ceaseless in
pains, and his minute study of the import duties, with
his consequential recommendations for their reduction,
was a more solid and useful performance than either of
his books.   He could opine, but he could not speculate.
All his thoughts came to him at second hand.   He
never originated an idea in his life, or understood what
an idea was, but his vitality, and the restlessness that
came from having no centre, nourished by the school-
mastering that he had received, led him to pour out in
speech and writing the effect of whatever mental stimulus
happened to have excited him at the moment.   Thus
the more concrete his task was, the better suited it was
to Gladstone's ability.

He never complained of want of inner light when
confronted with business or financial details.   The man
of activity was as precise as the man of reflection was
hazy, and he was at his best with dead things, such as
tariffs and figures.   He needed his antithesis to find a
form for his fluidity, as water does to display its resistance.   With men, curiously enough, he was rarely at
home or at ease.   He could not bring himself into touch
with other human beings.   The more he groped anxiously in their direction the more they eluded him, as
we can conceive a river to grope disappointedly for some
final form in the sea.   The men whom he could not
manage he could manœuvre, and a large part of this
manœuvring took the form of copious speech.   The
more at sea we are the longer are our explanations.
Lucidity is difficult because it needs to be brief, and
Gladstone, very wisely, was terrified of brevity.   So
well, however, did he acquit himself over the prepara-

tion of the new tariff that Sir Robert Peel wrote a letter
of congratulation to Gladstone's father. In a reply,
embarrassed by paternal joy, the father remarked that
he had already given two sons to Parliament, and was
waiting a favourable opportunity for his third, a piece
of family news that may have caused a smile to flicker
across the impassive face of the Prime Minister.

In 1843, and in reward for his services, Gladstone was
promoted to succeed his departmental chief as President
of the Board of Trade, and thus entered the Cabinet at
the age of thirty-three, after less than eleven years in
Parliament.

V

Though now committed with Peel to Free Trade,
Gladstone had to speak warily, for a policy need not
arouse the fears that the statement of a far-reaching
new principle awakens. Morley quotes the anonymous
remark of someone that " Gladstone's arguments were
in favour of Free Trade and his parentheses of Protection." He had been growing fast. He was qualifying for popular statesmanship.

The first Cabinet attended by Gladstone was held on
May 15, 1843. It was concerned with Irish Repeal
meetings, and it was part of Peel's policy to conciliate
O'Connell. With this object he proposed to establish
non-sectarian colleges in Ireland to placate Protestants,
and permanently to increase the grant to Maynooth,
the training college for Catholic priests, from £9,000 to
£30,000 a year. To understand what followed it is
necessary to recall the state of public opinion at the
time. The Catholic Emancipation Act was fifteen years
old, but notwithstanding this, Peel himself feared that
his proposal would be fatal to his Government. Gladstone also was perturbed : not because he resented the

policy himself, but because it contradicted the chief contention of his book, published six years before. He
thought that if he went back, or, strictly, if he confessed
to having gone back, on his earlier opinion, he would
seem unreliable to others : a fear that shows fundamental
weakness of mind, for only the dead, of whom many
are walking, do not modify opinion by experience.
Apparent consistency was highly valued by Gladstone
because, as he had not interior guidance, the sustained
support of other people was essential to his self-esteem.
We can change our opinions as St. Paul did without
turning on those from whom we have come to differ.
It is true that Gladstone had no inclination to persecute;
he was essentially a pacifist, hoping beyond all things to
find men in agreement with him. Nevertheless his
bogey remained, and how was he to exorcise it ?

Was he to admit that he had abandoned the principle
on which he had expended so much eloquence, and thus
to risk offending those who fancied such eloquence to
be the sign of an exalted mind ? The dreadful alternative was not so much to support a measure to which
he privately assented, or even to oppose a Government
to which he was happy to belong, dreadful as was this
prospect for a young Cabinet Minister. Lesser beings
hardly realise how sacred to its holder is the portfolio
of office. What would his father say ? What his wife ?
What his friends ? What his colleagues ? What would
become of his " career " ? It is impossible to sympathise too deeply with Gladstone at this trying moment.
Like the natural politician that he was, he sought to
" find a formula." If a middle way existed, it must lie
clearly here. The formula should be verbally or apparently consistent with his previous utterances and yet
should leave him free to support the policy which they
had condemned. He had been credited with a subtle
mind, and he perceived that the formula could not be

verbal.   The trouble was that action, some action, with
all its dreadful obviousness, was required.   A speech
would not meet the case.   Perhaps he recalled how he
had met a smaller difficulty over the affair in China.
Then an action, foreseen to be of no effect, had saved
him.   Could not he devise some kindred action now?
The present difficulty was immensely greater.   To seem
consistent in principle, and yet to act against his eloquent
thesis, required more than sleight of hand.   To preserve
his reputation he needed some obvious sacrifice.   The
martyr's is always a sympathetic rôle.   It is the eloquence
of action.   Once discovering that the latter was unavoidable, Gladstone hesitated no longer.   He resigned his
post, the political form of suicide, but, having resigned,
he supported the Government's proposal.

The grounds that he found for this shall be given in
a moment.   The interesting thing is that he could find
no ground for the simple admission that he had changed
his mind.   Supposing that he had admitted this, there
would have been no reason, save the misconception to
which all candid minds are liable, for his resignation,
and one cannot become a politician and at the same time
avoid all imputation of self-seeking.   It is the price
that a man pays for adopting politics as a " career."
In an ethical sense, therefore, to have acted as he did and
to have retained office would have been a greater sacrifice
than to have resigned, for to the vulgar eye Gladstone
thus would have sacrificed nothing.   A sincere man is
not swayed by considerations of popularity.   He does
not make the opinion of the rabble the test of right and
wrong in his own decisions.   The popular value of a
sacrifice that will seem much to them is irrelevant to
himself.   The ideas of expiation and of sacrifice are
superstitions to him.   He does not believe that suffering
is well pleasing to God, or that happiness and advantage
must be " paid for," and are paid for most effectively

when we deliberately inflict blows upon ourselves. The issue came to this : Should Gladstone admit his previous thesis to have been mistaken and proceed openly in that belief, whatever people thought of him; or should he put himself right in *their* eyes by inflicting on *himself* a loss that would seem to them, quite irrelevantly, to purchase him the right to forgo his earlier opinions ? If he indulged their sentiments in this way, the act would have an eloquence to them equivalent to the eloquence that they had admired in the thesis that he was abandoning. The rhetorical consistency would be maintained, and that was what he most wanted. The sacrifice of office was as spectacular to the crowd of onlookers as his glowing periods had been to readers of his book. It provided the continuity of emotion that Gladstone wanted *them* to feel; it was their sentimental equivalent for consistency. As his own daughter, Mrs. Drew, has put it :

> It would be rare nowadays to find a tenderness of conscience so acute as to cause a man to resign office on a measure with which he was really in sympathy.

The gesture, as the modern phrase goes, was perfect because it was painful. A man who voluntarily resigns office is the martyr of politics : no cross nor crown (in the eyes of the crowd).

As Gladstone put it himself : " It is not profane if I now say, ' with a great price obtained I this freedom.' " After listening to Gladstone's explanation in the debate on the Address the House of Commons became restive. To resign one's post for the sake of a reputation for disinterestedness produced a disagreeable sensation in some of his hearers. To a few it seemed a kind of simony, to others disingenuous or absurd. Mr. Greville remarked : " Gladstone's explanation was ludicrous. Everybody said that he had only succeeded in showing

that his resignation was quite uncalled for." Most
people thought that to have resigned without opposing
the measure was more equivocal than to have supported
the plan without resigning would have been; but then
they were forgetting the " gesture " of it. What he
had actually done was to have discarded one principle
because the opposite principle had prevailed. What
could have been more politic ? The practical argument
was as simple as the moral proceeding was obscure. If,
he pointed out, the State was to give a more indis-
criminating support than previously to various forms of
religious education, it would be improper and unjust to
exclude the Church of Rome in Ireland from its benefits.

VI

Before he had decided to resign, however, a characteristic incident had occurred. Possibly because of
the Maynooth proposal, Peel was considering whether
to renew official relations with the Vatican. The overtures would be made by indirect communication through
the British envoy at Naples or Florence. When Gladstone learnt of the idea, his imagination ran away with
him. He seized his pen and wrote to the Prime Minister :
" If you and Lord Aberdeen should think fit to appoint
me to Florence or Naples, and to employ me in any
such communications as those to which I have referred,
I am at your disposal." Nothing came of the project,
and the world was deprived of seeing Gladstone in
diplomatic dalliance with the Vatican, the still young
theocrat conducting negotiations with the oldest political
organisation in the world. It would have been a centre
of activity more congenial to his enthusiastic Evangelicalism than the laborious Board of Trade; but
nowhere else than at the Board could he have been
equally useful.

It was apparently his presumption in putting himself forward that weighed later on his mind. In 1894 he wrote :

> I have difficulty in conceiving by what obliquity of view I could have come to imagine that this was a rational or in any way excusable proposal; and this, although I vaguely think my friend James Hope had some hand in it, seems to show me now that there existed in my mind a strong element of fanaticism. I believe that I left it to Sir Robert Peel to make me any answer or none as he might think fit; and he with great propriety chose the latter alternative.

Perhaps the tension under which he was labouring made him a hasty judge of some chance word that Hope may easily have dropped in talk. A new post, particularly a post with an ecclesiastical tinge, would have been very convenient at this moment. No one can blame him for indulging the hope of it, even if the chance led him to put himself forward provisionally. The step that was rebuffed is precisely the step which makes us sympathise with him. How agitated he was, not to speak of his family, is abundantly on record. " Nerves a little unruly between (official) life and death." He told Manning that parting with colleagues feels " much like dying, more like it than if I were turning my back altogether upon public life." To confess such feelings to an unsympathetic House must have been an ordeal. The explanation for which he was asked occupied an hour, and at the end of it all Cobden exclaimed : " What a marvellous talent is this : here have I been sitting listening with pleasure for an hour to his explanation, and yet I know no more why he left the Government than before he began." Perhaps this made the eloquence more impressive. It is distracting to learn that the general verdict was " a piece of political prudery." Political prudery was not popular in the House of 1845, and scruples ill understood are open to impatient expressions. On the second reading of the Maynooth Bill, Gladstone voted for it. He supported his vote with these curious words :

> I am prepared, in opposition to what I believe to be the prevailing opinion, and in opposition to my own deeply cherished opinions, to give a deliberate, and even anxious, support to the measure.

The prevailing opinion to which he referred must have been apparent, since Peel himself was dubious of the effect which the measure might have on the administration of the day. Yet wider considerations showed some such step to be necessary. It was desirable to placate O'Connell, and this could not be accomplished without meeting the opposition of O'Connell half-way. Political necessity, as judged by a man with the long experience of his chief, was the deciding fact to Gladstone. Theoretical principles lay behind him : practical considerations lay ahead. He had crossed his Rubicon. He was politically grown. It necessarily seemed an enormous step to him, yet he had the exaggerated love of writing that marks the amateur of letters. He could not abandon his cloudy towers of theory without a heavy sigh. On them as on an altar he laid the sacrifice of his portfolio.

With the Maynooth affair the shadow of Ireland first rose upon Gladstone's political horizon, and it happened that Gladstone proposed that James Hope should accompany him on a walking tour in Ireland itself. Unfortunately the plan fell through. How interesting it would have been to see how far his quick susceptibility to political oppression would have been aroused in that then remote corner of the United Kingdom. As it was, in the following December, " with a clear conscience but a heavy heart," Gladstone accepted the post of Colonial Secretary. His seat at Newark therefore became vacant. In spite of having represented that constituency for thirteen years, Gladstone prudently refused to stand again. A converted Free Trader could hardly offer himself to an agricultural constituency, the member for which, in truth if not in name, was the Duke of Newcastle's nominee. Thus the new Colonial Minister remained without a seat till the General Election of 1847.

In the meantime Gladstone's father had become a baronet. With a son in the Cabinet and an hereditary title in the family, the Gladstone family had arrived within a century of the re-foundation of its fortunes at the fullness of success. In wealth and dignity the Gladstones need now fear no comparison that their ancestors, the Gledstanes, might make.

CHAPTER III

THE MIDDLE YEARS

I

WITH his retirement from the constituency of Newark, Gladstone entered the middle period of his life. His career on the prominence of the Front Benches was assured, but there was still a doubt in his mind on which side of the House he would permanently settle. His sympathies were " conservative " but his opinions were becoming " liberal." He was a Peelite, and beyond the shadow of the elderly Peel, which could not shelter him for ever, it was becoming difficult to see and necessary to prepare. We have now to watch the oscillation before he himself became the centre towards which others turned for leadership. These distracted years, full of experiment and episodes, have chiefly his triumph as a financier to confirm his ability to lead. For the rest his adventurous energies reach out in many directions. He himself was uncertain what his future direction would be, but began to learn also the value of excursions beyond Westminster.

In 1845 the Anti-Corn Law League, gaining adherents through the eloquence of Mr. Charles Villiers, although the recent good harvests had been making Protection less unpalatable, was nearing the victory of its hopes. On the other hand, the failure of the Irish potato crop proved too severe a test for English statesmanship. To relieve the famine one duke recommended the poor to rely on curry-powder as a nutritious and satisfying food. Another peer implored the Government to promote the supply of salt fish and to appoint a day of public prayer. The council of the R.A.S., composed of the nobility and squires, drew the attention of labourers to the sustenance of thrice-boiled bones. When Peel himself urged that all restrictions upon imported food should be suspended, only three Cabinet Ministers supported him. In November Lord John Russell announced his conversion to Free Trade. Gladstone published a pamphlet on "Recent Commercial Legislation," and, in 1846, the Corn Laws were finally repealed.

In the public mind these important events were some-what blurred by the news in 1845 that John Henry Newman had been received into the Church of Rome, to which, we may note in passing, Gladstone's own sister had retired three years before. To the repeal of the Corn Laws Gladstone had been converted by the pressure of immediate facts and by the detailed study of our trade in relation to our revenue. He could boast that he had prepared the way, by having removed duties from four hundred and thirty articles. In the intellectual ferment that had risen round the Tractarian controversy, and now culminated in the explosion over the defection of Newman, he was naturally less definite. A *via media*, the foundation of which might elude logical analysis but whose practical working accorded with national senti-ment, was indeed the reflection of his own mind. Nationalism has always been the foundation of the religion of the English. Even before the Reformation we had been restive and rebellious sons, jealous of external interference and unwilling to submit to appointments made from Rome. Henry VIII, on his death-bed, believed himself a good Catholic and supposed himself to be asserting no more independence than that which Francis I had secured to the Gallican Church in 1516 by

the Concordat of Bologna. This intense national sentiment was an instinct in Gladstone as in most of his
fellow-countrymen. Like the majority, he welcomed the
increasing sway of Catholic principles, as they were
called, in the Church of England, and, again like them,
he could no more imagine himself deserting the fabric
of the Establishment by passing over to Rome than he
could imagine himself reverting to Wesleyanism because
the awakening in the Church of England had spread
undoubtedly from there. English instinct, always
aristocratic, demanded independence at home, but liked
that local independence to be, in religious as in secular
affairs, an ordered hierarchy. While he lamented Newman's departure, Gladstone tried to preserve the middle
way himself. In this spirit he voted against the condemnation of W. G. Ward and of Pusey at Oxford. He
declared the alleged "choice," between an avowedly
Protestant church and obedience to Rome, "miserable."
It is delightful to see him for once choosing a middle
course precisely where the mass of his countrymen was
choosing it. He clung to this course by the tendency also
of his mind, as the majority did by instinct. Indifferent,
since his time, as most Englishmen have come to be to
the Christian beliefs, there are still few, among sceptics
even, who would not be sorry if the Church of England
dissolved into parties and passed, as an entity, away.
The revision of the Prayer Book in our own day and
kindred controversies are deplored by average laymen
because they feel that the integrity of the English Church
depends upon not dragging deeply disputatious matters
into light. Any change that is not formal or precise
is tolerated; any deliberate alteration or revision is deplored. Nor is this attitude, characteristic of Englishmen
though it may be, peculiar to us. The Latin Church
herself, while regarding her formulas sacrosanct, allows
latitude of interpretation; but among the Seven Candle-

sticks the Church of England burns with a Laodicean
flame, and it remains to be seen whether " the faithful
and true witness, the Amen," will spue her out of his
mouth because she too is lukewarm.   Laodicea, like
England, was a large commercial and manufacturing
centre, and have we not echoed her boast, " I am rich,
and increased in goods, and have need of nothing " ?
In the confidence of these things, at any rate, the
Victorian Englishman was reared, and a few years later
it was to be publicly declared that " it is the cheapness
and abundance of our coal that has made us what we are."
The departure of Newman was an affront to English
nationalism, and to that sentiment Gladstone responded.

In intellectual matters Gladstone was a weathercock,
instinctively answering to the way of the wind, and as
such readily mistaken for the wind's dictator by the crowd
gazing upward from below.   He felt the nation behind
him when he wrote to Manning in 1850 : " the faults and
virtues of England are alike against " the Church of
Rome.   According to his own idea he was still in public
life for the service of the Church.   He foresaw the day
when the State would cease to be Christian, and regarded
every step in that direction as a necessary, but disquieting,
recognition of the process.

In the General Election of 1847 Gladstone was
returned as a Member for Oxford University.   While his
relations with the Oxford Movement were debated freely,
Liberals, churchmen, and moderates combined to give
a fair majority to him.   Both opponents and supporters
had no difficulty in finding that his political record failed
to uphold, and triumphantly upheld, the principles of
the Church of England.   Gladstone was a more ardent
churchman than many of his supporters, but part of the
truth was that, as an active politician, he had to deal with
facts and forces which constituents in the seclusion of a
cathedral city can ignore.   Since, however, clerical

Oxford was mainly and naturally bigoted, it did not seem
unlikely that the constituency would repent, eventually,
of its choice. The Oxford voters wished events to stand
still, while the career of their Member depended on keeping even step with them. Oxford, of course, was the
constituency nearest to Gladstone's own heart. He had
dedicated his own first book to it. With the calm of the
cloister it combined the prestige of the world. It was
a place which abounded in abstract discussion, the home
of the lecture, the school of debate, the nursery of
politicians. Oxford in his day was not unlike a cure of
souls. Before such an audience the line between the
speech and the sermon need not be arbitrarily drawn, and
religious matters were political matters in the University.

In the electoral controversy one amusing comment
was made. Gladstone was charged with having argued
that none need leave the Church of England because it
offered to its loyal members everything that might be
" enjoyed " in the Church of Rome. The cream of the
quip was not its plausibility, but the contrast of its terse
word with the verbal festoons in which Gladstone draped
a not dissimilar view. If, for classification, we must
define religious bodies, the Church of England would be
described to a stranger rather as a reformed Catholic
Church than as a Protestant body, and it is hard to see
why any Anglican need object to such description. The
flavour of the joke was best appreciated, of course, in a
collegiate atmosphere, and on the combination to be
found there of Oxford die-hards and less elderly Liberals
Gladstone was carried to success. He had the power of
attracting both sides, and it was not until each found
that he was identified with neither that both repudiated
him. His political hold on Oxford was precarious, as
was his intellectual hold on life. For the moment,
however, he was happy and contented.

The revealing sentences in his address to the University

electors are those in which he stated that he had abandoned
his earlier advocacy of the exclusive support of the
Establishment by the State because it had proved in
vain; that he had yielded to the force of circumstances;
that he had surrendered his position because his principle
was out of date. In other words, the arrow of his ardour
was yet at the mercy of the wind, and because he hardly
dared to admit his inner want of conviction, it was
natural for him to proclaim divine the only call he heard.
The *vox populi* was indeed the divine voice to him.

II

With the fall of Peel in 1846 Gladstone had entered a
period of transition, and the dividing lines between the
two political teams became increasingly personal. He
was a Conservative free-trader with Liberal leanings,
and threatened to become no less an embarrassment to
others than to himself. Under Lord John Russell the
Whigs were in power, and those Peelites who were asked
to coalesce with them did not do so. Indeed since
Free Trade, carried by Peel, was not a Conservative party
measure, the old labels were losing their meaning, and
the country was confronted with a family party of Front
Benchers uncertain on what questions they should differ.
The party system is most systematic in the arrangements
by which differences are mutually agreed, and when the
necessary division cannot be determined the real covert
coalition has to be confessed. Then it becomes incon-
veniently clear that Party is no more normal to politics
than to municipal life. In this interval Gladstone was
largely occupied with the problem of saving Hawarden
from being sold, and in the spring of 1848 he was enrolled
a special constable during the Chartist riots.

The following year the wife of one of Gladstone's
friends, who had been travelling abroad, was thought to

be compromising her reputation. There was a family
council over what had best be done, and, after due debate
and many heart-searchings, Gladstone and Manning were
appointed ambassadors to persuade the lady to protect
herself. Manning could not go, and we are left to
imagine how Gladstone approached the lady and how
she received his overtures of help. He left our shores
" not unhopeful," but discovered that he was too late.
The facts that he had to report on his return led to a bill
for divorce, introduced a little later into the House of
Lords. Gladstone's evidence was invoked to show that
the friends of the lady had spared no pains to avoid the
rupture now demanded. It is to be feared that Gladstone returned from his long journey a sadder man, and
at this time of day, when there are no feelings to be hurt,
it is difficult not to see in this one of his Quixotically
chivalrous enterprises. With the vain boasting of a
Pelagian or the gloomy error of a supralapsarian Gladstone might have been a persuasive reasoner. He sunned
himself in women's eyes and found refreshment in their
society, but with a woman whose feelings were in
opposition to the prevailing notions of duty Mr. Gladstone perhaps might not have been the aptest of pleaders.
A woman whose feelings were involved seems the one
person who might be deaf to Mr. Gladstone, charmed
he never so wisely. If the day comes when his character
attracts the playwright, one indispensable scene will be
the rescue by Gladstone of some unwilling Andromeda,
a scene in which his sense of propriety and her feelings
are opposed. If the shade of Meredith could be induced to look obliquely on the twain, the rich matter of
such an interview would not be missed. In the historic
episode that suggests this scene Gladstone arrived too
late, but if this fact were withheld by the lady till the
curtain were falling it certainly would not spoil the play.

With the death of Sir Robert Peel in 1850, a more

G

engaging if less stolid statesman emerged in the person
of Lord Palmerston. Peel and Gladstone, by birth and
by temperament, were both typical members of the
commercial middle classes. Palmerston was as typical
an English aristocrat, to whom public business was one
of a patrician's pleasures. He had the secret of that
genuine popularity which Gladstone only seemed to
win. The one responded to a generous impulse in the
spirited half of the nation; the other knew how to in-
toxicate crowds. Palmerston, a schoolboy to the last,
had a sense of comedy and high spirits. He brought a
spirit of slightly reckless sportsmanship into the conduct
even of foreign affairs. Gladstone had the ardour of a
romantic hero uttering sublime platitudes on a quarter-
deck at Drury Lane. If Palmerston was something of a
holy terror, Gladstone was the enthusiast at large. The
touch of superbity which led Palmerston nearly to pro-
voke a European war on behalf of a Jew who happened
to be a British subject, evoked a public response that
Gladstone's moral criticism could not quell. When
Palmerston declared that a British subject, like a Roman
citizen of old, could always feel, wherever he might be,
that the watchful eye and the strong arm of England
would protect him, Gladstone's reply that the test of
foreign policy was not success but righteousness seemed
trite. It sounded well on his baritone, but the nation
felt that something more definite was needed for the
conduct of foreign affairs. In the matter of Don Pacifico's
expensive bed Palmerston had a poor case and a high
hand, but a spirited fellow is more moving to national
pride than a homilist however eloquent. This speech of
Gladstone's was the first in which he touched foreign
affairs, but the excitement that the incident aroused
quickly taught him that they were a political distraction
not to be neglected. You could gain attention by their
means that was invaluable when home politics were

Stagnant, and employ the public interest which they excited to embarrass, and possibly to defeat, your political opponents. This was a lesson that Gladstone never forgot afterwards.

The death of Peel was expected by many to give to Gladstone the leadership of the Conservative party. It was plain to him, however, that the elements of the party were coalesced rather than united, beside which the prominent figure of Disraeli stood in the way. Whatever group Disraeli chose would find Gladstone eventually in the opposite camp. He knew that he would not follow, and could not permanently lead, that dazzling adventurer. If the obstacle of Disraeli were to be removed from Gladstone's path, Gladstone knew that it must be by the foil of party opposition. In Gladstone's moral nest Disraeli would be a cuckoo, and, when he offered to combine, Gladstone instinctively felt such help to be embarrassing. Disraeli, for a time, could probably have understudied and flattered anyone, as he flattered later Queen Victoria. Gladstone, equally histrionic, mistook his attitudes for eternal truths, and was the first to be convinced by them. The actor lost, for the moment, in his part, and the artful dodger, fully conscious of his audience, would dissolve any duet. Already Peel is reported to have muttered : if Gladstone ever becomes Prime Minister, nothing nearer than India will give Disraeli sufficient elbow-room. The Oriental and the Scotsman met, therefore, across the floor of the House.

In this period of political transition, during the late 'forties, Gladstone opposed marriage with a deceased wife's sister as being " contrary to the law of God for three thousand years and upwards." He deprecated the appointment of a Commission to inquire into the Universities on the ground that it would deter benefactors, and declared, in the troubled year of 1848, that Free Trade was the best guarantee for national stability.

To the dismay of his Oxford following, Gladstone, the memory of whose book on *Church and State* survived his recent recantation, voted in 1847 for the removal of political disabilities from the Jews. He repeated the argument that emancipation could not stop half-way, and that the grant of the franchise and the magistracy must logically be followed by admission to the House of Commons.

Gladstone's father was annoyed, and the piqued parent, whose son, he once said, had never given a moment's pain to him, despatched the following rebuke :

> There is a natural closeness in your disposition, with a reserve towards those who think they may have some claim to your confidence, probably increased by official habits, which it may perhaps in some cases be worth your inquiring into.

Sir John had thought that he should have received some notice of his son's change of opinion before the indication given by his vote. The University at all events seemed to forgive its peccant Member, for he received the degree of D.C.L. the following year, despite some obstinate hissing from the gallery.

Dr. Hampden, who had been regarded as a heretic eleven years before, was now revenged on being made a bishop by the Whig Government. The excitement aroused by his appointment was quickly followed by the Gorham judgment, which is said to have occasioned almost as many secessions from the Church of England as Newman's withdrawal. Gladstone, of course, was deeply exercised. The case was this. A bishop had refused to institute a clergyman on the ground that he professed unsound doctrine on baptismal regeneration. The clergyman appealed against this refusal to the ecclesiastical Court of Arches. He lost his case. When he carried it, however, to the judicial committee of the Privy Council, a majority, with the two Archbishops

sitting as assessors, reversed the decision of the Court
of Arches.   Undismayed at this defeat, the bishop in his
turn determined to fight to a finish.   He resorted to
Westminster Hall, tried every device in the Courts of
Queen's Bench, Exchequer and Common Pleas, and even
denounced the Archbishop himself, denying communion
with him.   The issue was this : should the High Church
party have the power to expel Evangelicals, and, if not,
were matters of doctrine to be determined by a secular
court ?

Like other churchmen, Gladstone was greatly perturbed.   He is said to have declared that the Church
must recover its lost prestige by some overt act, and,
then, to have refused to sign a declaration of protest in
the fear that such a signature might conflict with his
Privy Councillor's oath.   This he denied, and his admitted plea for delay may have taken some other ground
for hesitancy.   To the Rev. W. Maskell he wrote : " I
do not consider that the time for any enunciation of a
character pointing to ultimate issues will have arrived
until after the Gorham judgment shall have taken effect."
In other words, if the judgment were swallowed, the
nature of the court need not be scrutinised too curiously.
The Church of England, like other cherished English
institutions, is a monument to evaded logical issues.
While it exists and endures, what Englishman cares
whether it has a logical right to do so or not ?   This,
the effect of the judgment, was the real point, though the
logical point also required just so much attention as it
might need.   Gladstone therefore indited a letter to the
Bishop of London on the Ecclesiastical Supremacy.   The
fact and the effect were distinctions which he delighted to
mark in all such controversies.

He looked within, and distinguished two characters
in himself, " that of a lay member of the Church, and that
of a member of a sort of wreck of a political party."

He must not sacrifice his party, he goes on, until justice
evidently cannot, *i.e.* will not, be done by the State to
the Church. Her apparent defeat was, he added, a noble
opportunity for doing battle for the faith : to rise
mysteriously through the struggle into " something
better than historical Anglicanism." It was a time to
establish truth. It was a time to display fervour. It was
an opportunity for men of good-will, that phrase so dear
to the well-meaning and the puzzled ! His mind was
like a saturated solution that refuses to condense until
some speck of solid matter is dropped into it from
without. Only the immediate and the concrete could
give form to the cloudy vapours in that vacant and
impressive skull. It was apparently Ireland that made
religious matters real, because immediate, to him. He
had already apostrophised her in one of his letters written
in 1845 :

> Ireland, Ireland ! that cloud in the West, that coming
> storm, the minister of God's retribution, upon cruel and
> inveterate and but half-atoned injustice ! Ireland forces upon
> us those great social and religious questions—God grant that
> we may have courage to look them in the face, and to work
> through them. Were they over (he adds in one of his
> perennial suggestions of retirement), were the path of the
> Church clear before her . . . joyfully would I retire from the
> barren, exhausting strife of merely political contention.

Mrs. Gladstone was the recipient of this outburst.
A characteristic passage follows, which gives another self-
revelation of an extraordinay man.

> As to ambition in its ordinary sense, we are spared the
> chief part of its temptations. If it has a valuable reward upon
> earth over and above a good name, it is when a man is enabled
> to bequeath to his children a high place in the social system
> of his country. That cannot be our case. The days are gone
> by when such a thing might have been possible. To leave
> Willy a title . . . without wealth . . . would not, I think,
> be acting for him in a wise and loving spirit—assuming, which
> may be a vain assumption, that the alternative could ever be
> before us.

The qualified conclusion does not dim the value
upon social esteem, the emblem of the middle class ;
of the moralist, who need the support of others to
sustain their self-respect. The commercial magnate has
a regard for social pretension because this has come but
now within his reach. He is still a little breathless at
the end of his long journey.

The confessedly secular State, which every non-
sectarian concession was manifesting, was robbing Gladstone of the theocratic ideal with which his combination
of Evangelical fervour and political ambition had furnished him on his entry into public life. The fading ideal
and the prevailing tendency were contradictory. Since
he could part neither with fervour nor with the future,
he began to idealise the tendency under the names of
religious freedom and progressive views. In idealising
the new morality he was perfectly sincere, for morality
(the habits and standard of our neighbours) *is* the religion
of the middle class. He had its ambition to make the
best of both worlds, and there was no doubt about his
success in this. To assimilate it to other-worldliness, the
ideal of Duty is invented, and Duty is the recognised
excuse for whatever happens to be respectable. Yet
humanity has a sound instinct that our actions should not
need excuses, and that the more exalted the excuse the
more distasteful is it. Thus unction has an apologetic
air which sometimes recoils on the head of those who
indulge in it. It seems to be dragged in gratuitously,
and, like all apologies, infuses suspicions. Gladstone's
speeches were all high-sounding, all explanatory, all
hortative. His life was one long public apology, and
this is why he gathered suspicion throughout his long
career. He was simple-minded without being simple,
for simplicity is direct, and his changes are interesting
because they were the reflection of the changes in public
opinion in his time. As this veered, he veered with it,
and he is important because he was a curiously complete

embodiment of middle-class prejudices throughout his century.

In his development we trace the phases through which the now dominant middle-class mind of his countrymen was passing. We find it advocating at one moment slavery, at another freedom, at one time Church and the landed interest, at another toleration and commercial expansion, and all are advocated at the call of Duty, the ideal given to whatever public opinion happens to desire. It is this which has made some aver that Gladstone was a hypocrite, but a hypocrite is not one who is self-deceived. He was sincere in all his beliefs, if belief is the proper word for ideas that have no inner prompting. Our suspicion of that character is not of its quality but of its kind. A great man, we feel, should be more than a mirror : not merely a school slate on which others have scribbled with no authentic superscription of his own. Moreover, indulge as we may in the vocabulary of unction, it is not, really, popular in England. The virus of Puritanism has gone far enough to make us suppose that we ought to be uncomfortable, but we do not like being uncomfortable and cannot stifle our recoil from those who preach self-denial and wear long faces. Earnestness and striving are distasteful precisely because they have not the manner of ease. The hero and the saint are known, like the athlete, by their apparently effortless mastery. To uphold the strainings of apprenticeship is to forfeit the confidence of an alert audience. The vital quality of Gladstone, in his moral aspect, is the ready fervour, the joyous physical energy, which he threw into all he said and did.

The secession of Manning and Hope-Scott on the same day in 1851 were " terrible blows " to him. " Their going," he wrote, " may be to me a sign that my work is one with them," but he adds, " one blessing I have :

total freedom from doubts. These dismal events have smitten, but not shaken." In December of the same year Gladstone's father died, a few days before his eighty-seventh birthday.

III

The revolutions of 1848 on the Continent had left Gladstone unaffected, for he was not primarily interested in foreign affairs, and stability at home was not seriously threatened by them. In the autumn of 1850 he went with his family to Naples, then the capital of the Kingdom of the two Sicilies which formed part of the Austrian domination of Italy since the Peace of 1815. Reaction and absolutism had quelled the rising of 1848, though Mazzini and Cavour were still occupied with their respective schemes for a united Italy and the young revolutionary movement. Panizzi, when a refugee in this country, had told Gladstone something of the latter, but the future Liberal statesman had little natural bias to criticise the established order in any country. He was temperamentally conservative, and inclined to take an insular view of foreign affairs. His lively interest and natural impulsiveness, however, were open to suggestion from immediate facts of any kind. When, therefore, he met in Naples certain Italians interested in political movements, and discovered that the sense of grievance was as active and positive as the desire to maintain the existing dynasty, he attended the State trials of Poerio, and was horrified to find the counsel for the Crown giving perjured evidence unchallenged by the officials of the court.

Poerio was sentenced to twenty-four years in irons, a punishment hardly worse than the imprisonment inflicted for the unproved political offences of other men. With admirable promptitude Gladstone visited the prisons to discover their condition for himself. He threw himself into the investigation with characteristic ardour, as if, for the time, there were no other interest in his life. The gaols in which these unfortunates were confined were filthy and diseased. Some were so loathsome that the doctors refused to visit their recesses. The physical condition of the prisons was the counterpart of the moral corruption of the courts. The constitution that King Ferdinand had sworn to defend was everywhere violated. The inhumanity that he was witnessing left Gladstone deeply moved, but he did not make it the excuse for his zeal for its amendment. The moralist in the politician comes out in his words :

> Even on the severity of the sentences I would not endeavour to fix attention so much as to draw it off from the great fact of illegality, which seems to me the foundation of the Neapolitan system; illegality, the fountain-head of cruelty and baseness and every other vice; illegality, which gives a bad conscience, creates fears.

It was the wary traveller and the practised hand which seized on the technical flaw in procedure, a matter not easily open to denial; and, no doubt, this was the point to urge upon the diplomatic world that Gladstone was addressing through his, shortly to be published, letters to Lord Aberdeen. This may perhaps be regarded as the first of Gladstone's spectacular crusades, the first at least on behalf of oppressed nationalities. It was also a display of his infectious personal enthusiasm.

He began by suggesting friendly remonstrance through the other Cabinets of Europe, but Palmerston, the terror of diplomacy and now in power, was not the safest instrument though he might prove a very effective one. The alternative was a public exposure; and, if the Conservative party in England could be identified with it, the absolutists at Naples, according to Poerio, would tremble in their shoes, for they relied upon Conservative support in England to shield them, as it were, in a common cause.

Full of his proposed crusade Gladstone returned to London, to secure either the intervention of Lord Aberdeen or immediate publicity. By April 1851 Gladstone had prepared a full statement of his case. Aberdeen, whose youth had involved him in responsibility for the settlement of 1815, a settlement which seemed to the diplomatists the only bulwark against the anarchy that had raised its threatening head in 1848, moved cautiously. After all, conservatism was a common cause in all countries now, and for a Conservative Government to probe evils in a friendly State was to invite inconvenient prying into grievances in the United Kingdom. At length he wrote to Vienna, and was told, after due delay, that Gladstone's statement would be brought to the notice of King Ferdinand. The reply appealed to England to remember that her own treatment of the Irish, the Ceylonese and the Ionians should warn her to be careful not to countenance abroad bad men posing as the martyrs of sacred Liberty. It is one of the delicacies of the situation that this letter from Prince Schwarzenberg, so long, so carefully phrased, so judicious in tone, so mindful of the proprieties, and respectful of abstract right, is not unworthy of Gladstone when upon the defensive.

The difference to be observed is this. Gladstone had the same ardour in attack that the ordinary Minister has in defence, and when the impulse descended upon him he would launch upon highly unofficial activities that seemed almost scandalous in an established man of affairs. His impulsive nature transformed the expert official, explaining inconvenient criticisms away, into a dangerous enthusiast, who, sword in hand, used his official prestige to assault men in the same position in other countries. It was a ghastly and incredible spectacle to his colleagues in foreign governments, comparable to a distinguished doctor who should harry the General Medical Council, an Archbishop of York who should rend the province of Canterbury, a Field-Marshal who should assault the Army Council, a Viceroy of Ireland who should have espoused the Swarajists at the close of a Delhi Durbar. On the defensive Gladstone had the histrionic power to seem guarding the last ditch. In the attack, like Shakespeare's king, he summoned his supporters to the breach with the ardour of a romantic actor. In both rôles he had the sincerity of a great player, wholly identified for the time being with his part.

Gladstone did not enjoy evasiveness or delays for which he was not himself responsible. He talked widely of the subject that suffused his mind, and, four months after his return from Naples, he published his letter to Lord Aberdeen and enlarged his indictment in a second document a fortnight later. Consent had been assumed, and there was no room for protest in the sensation that followed. Translations were multiplied, and Gladstone was overwhelmed with letters of thanks and invited to become a member of the Society of the Friends of Italy. Italian women composed odes in his honour. The journalists echoed the excitement, and the respected " Conservative " became the hero of the " Liberal " newspapers. Such gratuitous activity was astonishing in any Front Bencher, and, as such, was more congenial to those outside official circles than to the stately figureheads within. Because his party was the recognised supporter of established governments in Europe, Conservatives everywhere were horrified, but their reproaches lent force to exposures made by a man in general sympathy with them.

Lord Palmerston, who rather enjoyed an uproar, sent copies of Gladstone's letter to our representatives at all the Courts of Europe with instructions to present them to the Governments. He further told the Neapolitan envoy

that his " flimsy " reply was beneath contempt, and that
the exposure could be disregarded only at the peril of
King Ferdinand. This, as Morley justly noted, was the
sort of attitude that conferred on Palmerston his
authority in England and his dreaded reputation abroad.
The immediate effect of the outcry at Naples was to
increase the rigour in the prisons, until fear of the indignation that would be aroused if Poerio died, or should
lose his reason while in fetters, led King Ferdinand to
commute the sentence on him to exile. Thereupon
Poerio and sixty-six other prisoners were despatched to
America. If, then, the reforms produced by the intervention of Gladstone were limited, it is hard to see what
more he could have done. When indeed the crash came,
Ferdinand had no defenders, but till it came his oppression continued with little check. At all events, no other
politician upon holiday was capable of similar enthusiasm
or activity, and the effect that Gladstone's ardour produced was enormous. It made him, for the first time, a
public figure in European affairs. It added to his stature
and repute at home. It made the public no less curious
than the political heads concerning his future. It taught
him, indeed he could not miss, the political value in
London of activities that seemed as remote from the
narrow world of Westminster and Mayfair as the utter-
most parts of the earth. The political dark horse was
proved capable of bursting, without warning, from his
stall, and kicking his heels on the wide pastures of
Europe.

The Russian war was to make it inconvenient to annoy
Austria on Italy's behalf, and at this time Gladstone, like
most Englishmen, had little idea beyond that of local
grievances, and no vision of Italian unity, though the
expulsion of Austria was the political axiom of all shades
of Italian liberalism. Morley reminds us, with devastat-
ing aptness, that Gladstone's favourite author, Dante,

makes the moral plain. It was characteristic of Gladstone to overlook the practical inference from the poetry,
but he did not miss another inference from the existing
state of affairs. " I have learned," he wrote to Manning,
" that the temporal power of the Pope is . . . gone. . . .
God grant it may be for good. I desire it because I see
plainly that justice requires it." Was this the Gladstonian way of prophesying that the event would happen ?
He did not discuss the question whether an international
hierarchy ought to have some territorial sovereignty, or
apparently infer that, in modern times and with modern
armaments, such territory, with its embarrassing political
responsibilities, was as dust in the balance compared to
the guarantee of world-wide reverence for religious
Primacy. Rome can never be an insulated centre. It
is more than the see of St. Peter. The capital of a united
Italy must be centred there.

The position of the Papal States was too interesting
to Gladstone for him to remain at rest, and, in the absence
of other activity, he translated Farini's book on the Roman
government from 1815–50, in order to acquaint his
countrymen with the latest phase of the Temporal Power.
His old bias towards theocracy here found an inviting
field for study. Here was a church and state in one, and
what was his opinion of it ?

> The covetous, domineering, implacable policy represented
> by the term Ultramontism . . . an unceasing, covert, smoul-
> dering war against human freedom, even in its most
> modest and retiring forms of private life and individual
> conscience.

The bitterness of his denunciation is in the very vein of
his recent indictment of Neapolitan tyranny.

Both governments were supported by foreign bayonets.
Both systems were antiquated and abused. The Temporal Power, moreover, was still a bogey to England, as
became clear from the panic aroused in the autumn of

1850 when the Vatican, encouraged by the recent trickle of prominent converts, restored the Catholic hierarchy to England. The news that Rome was dividing England into dioceses and giving territorial titles to her bishops, that Cardinal Wiseman had been appointed Archbishop of Westminster, created an outburst. The cry No Popery! spread even to pot-lids, and those who collect these lids, for the sake of the coloured designs originally devised to ornament receptacles for bear's grease, will recall that one of the best shows Lord John Russell playing chess with his Holiness. The Pope is exclaiming, " Check to your Queen ! " " Pooh-pooh," John Bull retorts, " your bishop is out of his place, man."

This repartee is a polite version of what the Premier, Lord John, actually said in an excited letter to the Bishop of Durham. A Bill against ecclesiastical titles was hurriedly passed, to remain a dead letter until Gladstone repealed it twenty years later. Gladstone, need one add, lamented the Papal proceeding, but opposed the Bill. The other opponents of the measure argued more logically that the Bill was inconsistent with the toleration of the Roman Catholic religion. They also attributed the popular outcry to public impatience with the Puseyites, though the great Pusey himself remained loyal to Canterbury to the last. English nationalism raised its sleepy head. To tread on the lion's tail is not permitted to the Pope in England.

If the whole question was good copy, or convenient humbug, to the journalists, it gave to Gladstone an occasion for one of the historical speeches in which he delighted. He discoursed on Boniface VIII and Honorius IX; he reminded the House that Catholic laymen preferred diocesan bishops to Vicars Apostolic, and thus prepared the way for his final criticism :

> Here, once for all, I enter my most solemn, earnest, and deliberate protest against all attempts to meet the spiritual

dangers of our Church by temporal legislation of a penal
character.

The speech is a favourable specimen of Gladstone's
oratory, and more readable now than most of his utterances, which are more often mentioned than quoted or
read.   One of its passages runs as follows :

> Show, I beseech you—have the courage to show the
> Pope of Rome, and his cardinals, and his Church, that England
> too, as well as Rome, has her *semper eadem* ; and that when she
> has adopted one principle of legislation (religious tolerance)
> which is destined to influence the national character, to draw
> the dividing lines of her policy for ages to come, and to affect
> the whole nature of her influence and her standing among the
> nations of the world—show that when she has done this
> slowly, and done it deliberately, she has done it once for all ;
> and that she will then no more retrace her steps than the river
> that bathes this giant city can flow back upon its source.

Exuberant Gladstone's utterances were bound to be.
His eloquence was Burke and water, but the use of
semper eadem has its note, if only the diminishing note of
an echo.   In Gladstone's style we observe what Parliamentary oratory was becoming; the decadence of the
grand manner, the resonance of words becoming drained
of the intellect that had once given reality to them.   If
we contrast it, in the permanent form that is the abiding
proof of great oratory, as distinguished from the passing
effect of its sound, with the varied rhetoric of Disraeli,
the biting directness of Parnell, the incisive play of Lord
Randolph Churchill, with the subdued loftiness of Lord
Rosebery, even with the sprightly sarcasm of Mr. Lloyd
George, we see that it was becoming a monotonous
anachronism.   Between the old majesty of the earlier
organ music and the new terseness of strict prose, Gladstone's prolixity does not survive the mellow baritone
voice that died with him.   Oratory was necessarily
tardier than prose to mark the departure that the pam-
phleteers of the late seventeenth century had led, and that

the great Swift had brought to perfection. Johnson and Gibbon, stately as they were, began the declension, which only the genius of Burke, in his magnificent reaction from the democratic faith of France, was able to revive. None of Gladstone's similes can compare with the metaphor in which Burke likened the estates of the realm to Windsor, " girt with its double belt of kindred and coeval towers." The old oratory was addressed primarily, if not exclusively, to the assembled House, in days when the report of speeches seemed at first a breach of privilege. The reporters' gallery extended the audience, and it was natural that the first of modern statesmen to seek the following of the populace should be pre-eminent in the qualities that are palpable to the crowd : a fine voice, an oracular presence, a glowing eye, a copious rhetoric that lulled criticism to sleep. Gladstone was becoming a great parliamentarian, and already in his day the machine of the assembly was producing a form of oratory mainly directed to those beyond its walls, because it was not expected or allowed to have effect on the voting that it heralded. The parliamentary orator is encouraged to be unreal, and parliamentary language, as it is called, is in fact a legislative patois.

IV

The first Derby administration was formed in 1852, and Gladstone has described his situation in the retrospect : " The key to my position was that my opinions went one way, my lingering sympathies another." Conservative by leaning, Liberal in tendency, he was at home in neither party, and as a surviving Peelite was not used to be left in the cold. If Disraeli had not been a Conservative, the position of Gladstone might have been even more unsettled than it was. The minute and

H

copious memoranda that he compiled and preserved
throughout his long life give little clue to the intricacies
of his character. His private diaries seem designed for
publication. The personal note is rare. He resembles
an outside that has no inside, as if his coat, to be always
presentable, had no lining or reverse. For the moment
he nursed a political aloofness, till it could be seen
whether conservative liberalism or liberal conservatism
was the likelier road. As a Peelite or third-party man,
he felt that there was now no prospect for him. The
only third party at this time was the Irish, who were
held in derision at Westminster. The initiative possessed
by Gladstone was for political escapades within, and
not beyond, the existing playground of practical politics.

In 1852, when there was no dividing issue, hesitation
hovered round the foregone question whether the Free
Trade policy should be maintained. Both sections were
slightly ullaged, and needed to be fortified into opposing
teams by a spirited issue, which unfortunately did not
exist. At the election Gladstone was once more returned
for Oxford, despite the antagonism of those who objected
to his attitude to the Jewish question and to the Ecclesiastical Titles Bill. Eclipsed by this fog at Westminster,
Gladstone was compared by Lord Malmesbury to a
dark horse. He declared himself that the Liberal side
of the Conservative party rather than the Conservative
side of the Liberal party appealed to him. All beyond
was obscure.

Other politicians agreed that " Disraeli's leadership
was the great cause of Gladstone's reluctance to have
anything to do with the Government." Disraeli's
Budget evoked the criticism : " I am convinced " (wrote
Gladstone to his wife) " that Disraeli's is the least
Conservative Budget I have ever known." He said too :
" I have a long speech fermenting in me, and I feel as a
loaf might in the oven." The froth was gathering in

his head, and, set down to reply to Disraeli, he found
it "weary work sitting with a speech fermenting," until
he was carried away by listening to Disraeli's speech
himself. He declared it afterwards to have been "as a
whole grand, the most powerful I ever heard from
him," though "disgraced by shameless personalities."
Gladstone began his reply by attacking them, and, being
satisfied with his speech, was "mortified" to find the
following morning only an abbreviated report in the
newspaper. "Such," he confided to his wife, "is
human nature, at least mine." Consolation was provided by an article describing the climax of the debate.
In this "the redoubtable antagonists gathered up all
their forces for the final struggle, and encountered each
other in mid-career." Disraeli's speech, said this descrip-
tive reporter, was "pointed, bitter, telling, keen in
sarcasm, often cogent, in all ingenious and in some
convincing." Gladstone's "was pitched in a high tone
of moral feeling, now rising to indignation, now sinking
to remonstrance—which was sustained throughout without flagging or effort." The Ministry was beaten by a
score of votes; Lord Derby resigned, and party petulance
found its way into Gladstone's club. The room in
which he was sitting was invaded by a knot of Tories who
declared that he ought to be pitched out of the window
of the Carlton on to the steps of the Reform. Their
own gathering was a dinner-party at the Carlton to one
of their friends who had been accused of bribery at
Derby.

The new coalition under Lord Aberdeen included
thirty Peelites, who received between them six Cabinet
posts. Gladstone became Chancellor of the Exchequer.
The jealous comments aroused by this allotment led
Gladstone to retort : "If the Whigs had less than their
due share, they were an used-up, and so far discredited
party . . . whereas we, the Peelites, had been for six

and a half years out of office, and had upon us the glow
of freshness."

Thus the critic of the late Budget was chosen to
design its successor. Palmerston was safely stalled in
the quiet of the Home Office. Gladstone's new appointment involved him in another election at Oxford, where
he was returned by the small majority of 124. He was
losing some supporters because they disliked the politicians with whom he was now associating. His immediate pin-pricks, however, did not begin at Oxford, to
which he paid an enjoyable visit, but in Downing
Street itself, where he was taking over the Chancellor's
official residence from Disraeli. The quaintly contrasted
pair corresponded over the official valuation of the
furniture, over the transfer of the official robe. In the
hope of calming his agitation, Gladstone drafted one of
his later letters on Sunday itself, while Disraeli begged
him to consult a third party " who is, at least, a man
of the world." Could either correspondent have implied
a more unjust reproach to the other ?

Finance was to be the test of the new, as it had been
the failure of the former, administration. By exchanging
Protection for Free Trade, precedents were out of date,
and it seemed hazardous to alter or impose new taxes
upon industry. The simple expedient of the Income
Tax was not yet normal. Indeed a commission appointed
in 1851 to examine the impost had failed to produce so
much as a report. Many incomes are not permanent,
especially if they happen to be earned. Are the professional and the speculator to be treated as a pair ?
Is the winner of a State lottery or of the Calcutta sweep-
stake, the rigger of the share-market, or the monopolist
of a lucky hour, to be regarded by the Exchequer on a
parity with the playwright whose one success may be
the fortune of his working life, and, if not, how shall
we discriminate between them ? This is still a debated

issue, and the question lay at the root of the Income Tax proposals. Gladstone's principle was that national expenditure must be estimated over a period of years, and that we must assume this expenditure to be uniform during the period. He began where he had left off when at the Board of Trade. He reduced and further simplified the tariff. Then he renewed boldly the Income Tax for seven years, on a sliding downward scale, with the inducement that, at the end of that term, it might be repealed altogether. To balance this the legacy duty was extended from personal to real estate. Landed property thus seemed to lose the last of its inherited privileges. With wonderful energy Gladstone worked at his novel and complicated task. Early and late he was occupied with calculations, forecasts, and figures. He found time also to give a Latin lesson every day to one of his boys.

Rumours of the complexities that he was proposing were whispered abroad, and the Prince Consort requested and received an hour's explanation of the proposals. Then Gladstone hurried to the Cabinet and spent three hours explaining it to them. Lord Aberdeen was pleased. " It is," he said, " as ingenious, as clear, and for the most part as convincing, as anything I have ever heard." On a later occasion he remarked that Gladstone, unrivalled at proving a seeming argument to be specious, was less happy at weighing one good argument against another. Perhaps this was an element in his persuasiveness, the persuasiveness and the clarity that made the speech with which he introduced his first Budget memorable. It was an exposition which made figures charming and calculations clear. The combination of lucidity and detail captivated his listeners. Probably it was Gladstone at his best, but it cannot be quoted because it is impossible to revive interest in obsolete Exchequer figures. Even a professional accountant, who looks forward to the preparation of his annual balance sheet as lesser men to their summer holiday, might approach the Budget of 1853 with languid feelings. Between minute detail that is lost in time, and exalted rhetoric not of the finest, the speeches of Gladstone have become more threadbare than seemed possible to his entranced hearers. His first Budget speech was not only a personal success; it was balm to his colleagues. The Cabinet had had qualms. They feared that the Budget proposals would antagonise the Irish, alienate indeed, at some point, every section of a House in which their majority was precarious. Their apprehensions were forgotten on the morrow. The House in all its corners was impressed: much by the eloquence of the speaker, perhaps more by the comprehensiveness of his proposals. The boldness of these gave a welcome lustre to the Cabinet; congratulations descended like manna from the skies. The Prince Consort was moved to hope that Gladstone's "Christian humility will not allow you to be dangerously elated."

Gladstone's first Budget was the making of his political reputation. Cabinet status was his already, but now the leadership was plainly but a matter of time, on whichever Front Bench he chose to seat himself. Nothing he had said or done hitherto made an impression equal to his first Budget. Facts were his concern, and facts, for once, his argument.

At this moment too a generally unsuspected side of his character was now publicly revealed. One night as the Chancellor of the Exchequer was returning home from a late sitting in the House of Commons, a prostitute accosted him. He let her walk by his side and listened to her talk. Hardly had she departed when a man, who turned out to be a clerk in the General Post Office, appeared, and recognising Gladstone attempted to blackmail him. Gladstone allowed him too to follow

until a policeman came in sight, whereupon Gladstone
gave the man in charge. In the police court on the
following day Gladstone gave evidence against the man,
who was sent to gaol, and eventually wrote a letter
begging Gladstone to forgive him. The proceedings
revealed that for years Gladstone had been in the habit
of assisting such people, a work abetted by his wife, to
whose care he would sometimes entrust them. The
incident, which was recalled in the *Daily Chronicle* of
May 20, 1898, and has been given in Mr. E. A. Pratt's
little book on Mrs. Gladstone, is an example of that
personal charity which he and Hope-Scott had discussed
at Oxford, and to which Gladstone persuasively returned
in later letters to his friend. Mrs. Gladstone and her
husband founded several institutions for prostitutes, and
her homes were, I believe, the first that allowed unmarried mothers to keep their babies with them. Those
whose personal memories of London are longer than
my own declare that the number of these women was
much more conspicuous fifty years ago than now, and
explain the matter by saying that, before women were
generally employed in business, the streets were the
only refuge for women thrown suddenly by misfortune
upon their own resources, while the wages which
female workers received in the occupations open to
poor women were so wretched that they had to supplement them, in the idiom of the time, by work upon
their backs. Gladstone was naturally a compassionate
man; charity, to him, should involve some more personal act than a gift of money, and the outcasts appealed
to a romantic strain in him which demanded some
immediate personal service. Indeed they are said to
have called him Daddy-Do-Nothing among themselves.
Mrs. Gladstone also was a fountain of private activities,
and in the midst of her husband's affairs was always
reminding him of little commissions and private pur-

chases for others that it is a marvel he had both patience
and time to fulfil. His enormous correspondence and
the number of his famous poſtcards show that no one
was turned away without an answer, and the ſtrain of
simplicity, which was as much a part of the man as his
myſtifications, would lead him to be no less indulgent
to petitions in the ſtreet. Mrs. Gladſtone was motherly
to a very large number of friends and acquaintances,
and there can be no doubt that this work was common
ground to both.

V

He was now forty-four, and had spent twenty-one
years in politics. The firſt of his thirteen Budgets raised
him from one among Miniſters to a possible leader.
Already known to be a capable adminiſtrator and a
fountain of rhetoric, he was now claiming recognition
as a ſtatesman capable of initiating policy, even in a vital
and thorny branch of home affairs. He had helped to
introduce Free Trade under other leaders. He now
proved himself the firſt to apply the principles of the
new finance to the needs alike of trade and of the Exchequer. At a public speech made soon after his introduction of the Budget, he unbosomed his heart on the
moral value of Free Trade, and prophesied that it would
bring the Powers into closer amity. As we now know,
the fight for new markets and raw materials was to
prove a potent cause of war and imperial rivalries. As
if to remind the world that the millennium was ſtill
tarrying, the Crimean War was about to begin. Not
only did this war upset the hope of repealing the Income
Tax by increasing the national expenditure; it also
proved how useful the tax and the Budget were to
provide the new revenue required. The war, in fact,
juſtified the Budget's policy.

Turkey in Europe, that is to say, a Mahommedan Power governing Christian peoples, was an inconvenience that might produce an explosion at any time, for Constantinople under the Turks divided the European Powers. They neither liked Turkey to possess the city, nor would stomach Russia in her stead. Orthodox Russia and Catholic France were at issue, in particular, over the custody of the Holy Places in Jerusalem. This arranged, another dispute rose over the Tsar's claim to be the recognised Protector of all the Christian subjects of the Porte. The Sultan, encouraged by our ambassador, repudiated this, whereupon the Tsar invaded the Danubian principalities. He said that he would hold them as a pledge, pending the fulfilment of his claim. When the British fleet arrived to protect Turkish territory from Russian attack, Turkey declared war on Russia, relying on England and France to see her through. The two Powers finally sent an ultimatum to the Tsar which demanded his withdrawal from the Principalities. On its expiry, at the end of March 1854, the Crimean War began.

In this Gladstone played a minor part. He said that we were defending " the moral law of Europe " because the Tsar had invaded countries not his own, inflicted wrong on Turkey, and, " what I feel much more, cruel wrong on the wretched inhabitants of the Principalities." As a Cabinet Minister he shared a joint responsibility, but no more; and he did what he could to divert from his political colleagues the charges of mismanagement that this like every other war brought in its train. If he had not been a member of the Government, he might have opposed the war, but public opinion, as usual, was bellicose, and easier to inflame than to chill.

Gladstone, moreover, had been preoccupied with other matters. The controversy that the Tractarians had excited in Oxford had sharpened party feeling in the

University. One of the consequences was to inspire a minority to move for a Royal Commission. Thus in 1850, under Lord John Russell, a body had been appointed to inquire into the discipline and revenues of the University, and to report what action, if any, Parliament should take to encourage religion and learning in their sacred stronghold. Gladstone, as Member for the University, was at once involved, and, as yet, Oxford must have felt little qualm over her representative. After learning the state of opinion in both parties at Oxford on the project, Gladstone rose in the House to denounce the Royal Commission. A Commission, he declared, was probably illegal; it would dismay benefactors; self-government, even if abused, was preferable to reform from without by Parliamentary interference. The delegate had the stock objections at his fingers' ends; he faithfully reflected his sources of opinion. By a happy allusion, he instanced Sir Robert Peel as answer enough to any doubter of the sufficiency of Oxford teaching and Oxford example! This plea was in vain. When Gladstone, like the University, was forced to yield, he surrendered his political conservatism also. At the moment he was only determined to make any changes that could not be shunned as little unpalatable as might be.

By the spring of 1852, and despite a petition to the Crown, the Commission, conducted in every circumstance of difficulty, made its report, and the report won Gladstone's admiration. The illegal had become the actual; the impossible the inevitable; the assumed well-being of the University a body of fact from which no impressionable reader could run away. Probably the report was no less an eye-opener to Gladstone than to others, but his eye devoured new facts with the speed and sensitiveness of a negative in a camera. He embraced the evidence as ardently as he had originally denounced

the Commission of Inquiry. Moreover, though he
represented the University, as a working politician he
knew better than the Oxford men that the way to meet
the report was less to oppose than to make the best of
it. He urged his constituents to begin to reform themselves before more drastic changes were pressed upon
them.

The University was allowed a year to digest the recommendations, after which the new Government under
Lord Aberdeen would draft a Bill. The task fell to
Gladstone himself, and he attacked it with characteristic
energy in the autumn of 1853. While the minds of his
colleagues were filled with the spectres of Russia and
Turkey, Gladstone's was pullulating with academic proposals. He corresponded at length with everyone
concerned, as who was not in Oxford, and preserved
over five hundred letters and documents touching his
measure. He saw that a Liberal bias was the bend for
the Conservatives to take, and in a scriptural sentence he
passed the hint to them :

> As one of your burgesses, I stand upon the line that divides
> Oxford from the outer world, and, as a sentinel, I cry out to
> tell what I see from that position.

Was it necessary to add that the defeat of this measure
would mean another more drastic than itself ?

The principles of " reform " were little to the palate
of many. A no less thorny problem was, who should
carry them through ? When objectors said that Oxford
could enforce them better than any outsider, since
Parliament could not cope with the throng of societies
and bodies whereof Oxford is knit, Gladstone urged the
appointment of an Executive Commission with statutory
powers. It seems a sore rod for him to seek, but none
had had a better chance to learn the difficulties to be
met, and his immediate task always absorbed his energies.

The Member for Oxford had had to express the original indignation of his supporters. The member of a Government, in charge of a Bill, had to make its effectiveness his first care. The real objection to a Statutory Commission was that it would be effective. Thus Gladstone passed insensibly from chief obstructor to chief reformer. One of his admirers, after listening to the " superb speech " that Gladstone made on the second reading, said : " he vainly endeavoured to reconcile his present with his former position." As susceptible as a mirror to external impressions, our doubt is not of his sincerity, but of himself. A mirror is at the mercy of its latest impression. If Gladstone gave some people the creeps, it was because he inspired them with the nightmare that were, say, cannibalism showing signs of revival, they could not be certain that he had any instinct in himself against the practice. Man might appear a sacred dish to him. A pamphlet entitled " The Argument from Theophagy " can be imagined.

The details of his measure have faded into the series of more recent reforms. Its main objects were to abolish sinecures, by which pensions used to be dignified ; to encourage competitive tests, to the impatience of such survivors from the eighteenth century as the venerable Thomas Love Peacock ; to attach active duties to office-holders, and to increase representation on the governing body. The University was sharply divided by the Bill. To some it was the " greatest boon that the University had ever received " ; to others it was a deplorable tyranny. A petition against it, by passing Convocation with a majority of two, defeated itself. The tide of Gladstone's activity bore him to the conclusion that " Oxford is far behind her duties or capabilities, not because her working men work so little, but because so large a proportion of her resources remains practically dormant, and her present constitution is so ill-adapted

to developing her real but latent powers." Touching
the Church and the clamour of Dissenters to be admitted
to the University, Gladstone laid down this principle :

> The whole teaching and governing function in the Uni-
> versity and in the colleges, halls, and private halls should be
> retained, as now, in the Church of England, but everything
> outside the governing and teaching functions, whether in the
> way of degrees, honours or emoluments, should be left
> open.

It was not till seventeen years later that the Church
test for college fellowships was removed, though Gladstone's Bill removed it from matriculation and the
bachelor's degree. This was already thought a far-
reaching step in Oxford, and left the disquieting question,
how much longer Gladstone could be allowed to represent the University in Parliament.

At this date, too, the Civil Service, if hardly the
Treasury and the Foreign Office, was thrown open to
competition, a parallel proceeding that Gladstone necessarily approved. The landed aristocracy, formally dis-
placed by the repeal of the Corn Laws, was now destined
to lose the patronage which it had acquired at the
expense of the Crown. The middle classes, which were
thriving in the turmoil of unrestricted competition in
industry, were now strong enough to replace patronage
by competition at the portals of Whitehall. This change
received a fillip from the cry for administrative reform
produced by the blunders attending the Crimean War.
The immediate effect of the war at home was to raise
the Income Tax from seven pence in the pound to fourteen. Its second effect was to overthrow the Coalition,
and the lesson was to prove the soundness of Gladstone's financial imposts.

VI

In January 1855, on the first night of the assembled Parliament, Mr. Roebuck gave notice of a motion to appoint a Committee of Inquiry into the management of the war. The same evening Lord Aberdeen, the Prime Minister, was startled to receive Lord John Russell's resignation. Next day, when the Cabinet met for anxious discussion, in spite of some dissent wherein Gladstone joined, Aberdeen offered the resignations of the entire Cabinet to the Queen. She refused to accept them, as well she might, considering the stampede, at a critical moment, that a motion for inquiry had created. The Cabinet therefore remained, and Gladstone was put up to oppose the motion of Mr. Roebuck. The reader must not infer, however, that this was Gladstone's preliminary to acceptance of the chairmanship of the proposed committee. Beaten, in spite of his eloquence, by more than two to one, the Government immediately resigned. After many discussions, Lord Palmerston formed a Ministry which Gladstone joined, to retire almost immediately on learning that the Committee of Inquiry was not to be resisted. At the time Gladstone was criticised severely for this resignation, but in the retrospect his acceptance of office seems the obvious equivocation. That those who had resigned rather than accept the investigation should join the new Government committed to inquire into their conduct seems odd; that Gladstone should have supposed that the new team could resist the motion for inquiry that had placed them in office would seem hard to credit. But the political shiftings of Front Benchers are so much a family arrangement that those in the thick of them are apt to forget that their divisions may be taken seriously in the nation, especially at the close of a mismanaged campaign. With his customary minuteness of detail, Gladstone recorded

in his diary the hesitations and decisions in the course
of which his brief association with this Government of
Palmerston occurred.

The popularity of Gladstone was somewhat blown
upon by these events, and he suffered a further rebuff
when he joined the peace party before Sebastopol was
taken.   It was easy to exclaim that he had not left the
Government upon any issue of the war itself, and was
turning ungratefully on his recent associates.   Gladstone received this execration with good-humour.   " It
is hardly possible," he wrote to Lord Aberdeen, " to
believe one is not the greatest scoundrel on earth when
one is assured of it on all sides with such excellent
authority."

He consoled his energy with a holiday in Wales, and
spent much of his time " with Homer and Homeric
literature," in which, he added, " I am immersed with
great delight up to my ears; perhaps I should say out
of my depth."   The result, two years later, was his
fantastic book.   He was in Wales when Sebastopol was
taken, and the Peace of Paris, 1856, neutralised the Black
Sea.   In politics, with a few Peelites, he remained
unattached; party divisions were not clear, and it was
still a question with whom he would ally himself.   At
this interval of political repose he turns his eye within :

> I have never known what tedium was, have always found
> time full of calls and duties, life charged with every kind of
> interest.   But now, when I look calmly around me, I see
> that these interests are for ever growing and grown too
> many and powerful, and that, were it to please God to call
> me, I might answer with reluctance.

The thought of his political ties, his Church interests,
of " the new and powerful hold " which literature had
taken on his mind, of his wife's family affairs, of his
seven children, was disquieting.   It made him realise

how many inducements he had to remain alive. Their
number was depressing to an Evangelical.

After Disraeli and Gladstone had spoken in succession
against the Budget of 1857, and a General Election had
confirmed Palmerston in power and left Gladstone in his
seat at Oxford, it seemed that he might really join Derby
and the Conservatives at last. He still resolved, however, to stand apart, though aware that the undefined
position of himself and his friends was irksome to the
House and to the country.

When the Divorce Bill of 1857 was brought forward,
he emerged into the limelight once more. In 1853 a
Royal Commission had recommended important changes
in the means whereby marriages could be dissolved. A
year later the Cabinet, to which Gladstone then belonged,
had introduced a Bill, on the lines of this report, which
did not proceed much further. Moral questions were
Gladstone's favourite hunting-ground, and he opposed
the destined change as he had opposed the Deceased
Wife's Sister's Bill in 1849. We may recall that when
the Divorce Bill of 1857 was introduced into the House
of Lords, the Archbishop of Canterbury and nine bishops
helped to pass it. In the Commons Gladstone was
taunted with his previous silence. As a man, he thought
divorce an evil : as a politician, he was ready, if the
principle were accepted, to consider how and on what
grounds it might be obtainable. In point of fact, the
principle was not at stake. There had always been some
means of dissolution, however costly, tedious, and
restricted to the rich these means might be. It was this
underlying fact, no doubt, that defeated Gladstone and
his fellow-objectors.

Early in 1858 Lord Palmerston was defeated on a
measure arising out of a plot, hatched in London, to
kill the French Emperor, and Lord Derby became
Prime Minister. When he asked Gladstone to join his
Cabinet, Gladstone declined :

In your party, reduced as it is at the present moment in numbers, there is a small but active section who avowedly regard me as the representative of the most dangerous ideas.

Bringing Derby no friends and upsetting some of his following, Gladstone felt that he would aid neither the Premier nor himself.   On the very day when he penned this opinion, he received the following letter from John Bright :

A Derby Government can only exist upon forbearance, and will only last till it is convenient for us and for the Whigs to overthrow it. . . . If you join Lord Derby, you link your fortunes with a constant minority, and with a party in the country which is every day lessening in numbers and in power. If you remain on our side of the House, you are with the majority, and no Government can be formed without you. . . . I think I am not mistaken in the opinion I have formed of the direction in which your views have for some years been tending. You know well enough the direction in which the opinions of the country are tending.

This letter was admirable in shrewdness, tact, and tone.   It disclosed an astute perception of Gladstone's personal position without intrusive interference.   The reply of Gladstone is characteristically vague.   Its single direct statement, " before I received your letter yesterday afternoon I had made my choice," can hardly be said to blurt out his decision.

Perhaps the coaxing of John Bright was less decisive than a mysterious allurement, which Gladstone declined, from the other side.   Moreover, only by perching somewhere could he end the annoyance of lonely dartings to and fro.   It was now 1858, and Lord Aberdeen's description of him, two years previously, was still plausible :

With an admitted superiority of character and intellectual power above every other Member, I fear you do not really possess the sympathy of the House at large, while you have incurred the strong dislike of a considerable portion of Lord Derby's followers.

Gladstone was publicly labelled a speculative creature,

I

unpractical in party politics, the best orator but the weakest Member in the House, " a Bedouin of Parliament," and so on. The anglers were showing irritation, and the most dexterous determined, or was bidden, to show that there was no menace in *his* cast.

Thus it was that a curious letter was one day delivered at Gladstone's door. " Mr. Disraeli to Mr. Gladstone : confidential "; thus, abruptly and without preface, it began.

> I think it of such paramount importance to the public interests that you should assume at this time a commanding position in the administration of public affairs, that I feel it a solemn duty to lay before you some facts, that you may not decide under a misapprehension.
>
> Our mutual relations have formed the great difficulty in accomplishing a result which I have always anxiously desired. . . . Thus you see, for more than eight years, instead of thrusting myself into the foremost place, I have been, at all times, actively prepared to make every sacrifice of self for the public good, which I have ever thought identical with your accepting office under a Conservative Government. Don't you think the time has come when you might deign to be magnanimous ? . . .
>
> To be inactive now is, on your part, a great responsibility. If you join Lord Derby's Cabinet, you will meet there some warm personal friends; all its members are your admirers. You may place me in neither category, but in that, I assure you, you have ever been sadly mistaken. The vacant post is, at this season, the most commanding in the Commonwealth; if it were not, whatever office you filled, your shining qualities would always render you supreme; and if party necessities retain me formally in the chief post, the sincere and delicate respect which I should always offer you . . . would prevent your feeling my position as anything but a form. . . .

Party necessities and the chief post : were not these the barely conspicuous barbs on the bait that was cast so sympathetically ? but could even so great a fish really master his angler, in the end ? Mr. Gladstone's discreet reply therefore ran as follows :

My dear sir, the letter you have been so kind as to address to me will enable me, I trust, to remove from your mind some impressions with which you will not be sorry to part. You have given me a narrative of your conduct since 1850 with reference to your position as leader of your party. But I have never thought your retention of that office a matter of reproach to you. . . . You consider that the relations between yourself and me have proved the main barrier in the way of certain political arrangements. Will you allow me to assure you that I have never in my life taken a decision which turned on those relations ?

You assure me that I have ever been mistaken in failing to place you among my friends or admirers. Again I pray you let me say that I have never known you penurious in admiration towards anyone who had the slightest claim to it, and that at no period of my life, not even during the limited one when we were in sharp political conflict, have I either felt any enmity towards you, or believed that you felt any towards me. . . . Were I at this time to join any Government, I could not do it in virtue of party connections. I must consider, therefore, what are the conditions which make harmonious and effective action in Cabinet possible—how largely old habits. . . .

And so on till the end.

The Scotch salmon was not to be netted by the Jewish angler. Gladstone remained aloof, except to support the construction of the Suez Canal. He met the argument, that it would place the new route to India at the mercy of other nations, by observing that the canal must be under the control of the strongest sea-power, which was England, and reminded his hearers in the nation at large that it promised also wide opportunities for traders.

VII

If he would not move from the middle of the political road, he was a nuisance to be moved out of it by both teams. The opportunity occurred in 1858, and he was

suddenly invited to leave England as special commissioner to the Ionian Islands in order to inquire into our
Protectorate there. His political friends were dubious.
Some advised him not to go. His adventurous instincts
urged him to accept, and his recent studies reminded
him that he would be following the footsteps of Ulysses,
footsteps, moreover, which would also lead him into the
dominion of the Greek or Orthodox Church. He was
to be away from November 1858 till March 1859. Would
Ionia, like Naples, provide him with a second foreign
crusade ?

By the treaty of Paris in 1815, the islands had been
entrusted to us, to keep them out of mischief. They had
received a nominal constitution which placed them at the
mercy of a resident High Commissioner, until the rever-
berations of unrest in 1849 introduced certain more
popular changes. The Italians formed the upper class.
Below, a swarm of officials competed for the posts now
determined by popular election. As the bureaucracy
grew in number, the public works established by the
British Government fell into decay; laws were ignored,
taxes uncollected; the revenue was in arrear, and the
debt increased. Discontent abounded, and there was an
undisguised desire for union with Greece. The agrarian
risings a few years before had been repressed with
cruelty. The time was ripe for an inquiry, and the man
to send so far was conveniently obvious.

Gladstone had hardly started on his way when the
newspapers printed a recent dispatch which had been
stolen from the Colonial Office. This advised the
Government to hand over the seven islands to Greece :
if not seven, then five, and to convert the remaining pair,
Corfu and Paxo, into a British colony. Thereupon
Gladstone was popularly supposed to have been appointed
to carry out this policy. The islanders were naturally
elated, and Gladstone, hearing of this publication in

Vienna, had to reassure the Austrian Minister that annexation was no part of his mission.

On arrival at Corfu, Gladstone was received with a salute of seventeen guns and all ceremony by the resident Commissioner. Deputations hastened to present him with petitions for the Queen protesting against annexation, and praying to be united with Greece. After holding levees and making speeches, Gladstone observed that our severities had done our reputation much harm. Had not, by the way, Prince Schwarzenberg reminded us of them in reply to Gladstone's denunciation of misrule at Naples? He observed also that the conduct of Englishmen toward the inhabitants and their religion was often contemptuous. Forty years of muddled administration had produced their inevitable fruits. Another shock had been the aspect of Corfu and Ithaca, which did not strengthen his pious trust in Homer's knowledge of geography. Disappointed but undismayed, he danced at a ball given at Ithaca in his honour. In Cephalonia, where the disturbances had been ruthlessly crushed, his carriage was crammed with protests against the Protectorate into which he had come to inquire. At Zante the islanders greeted him with shouts of Philhellene. At Athens he was found to be without credentials or instructions, and learned that opinion was divided on the wisdom of uniting the islands to Greece.

In these distractions we gain a glimpse of the man himself attending a *Te Deum* at Athens in honour of Victoria's birthday; visiting a mosque at Sayada, which he was allowed to enter shod; listening to the call to prayer, proclaimed two hours before the ordinary time; kissing the hand of a bishop, to the ire of the anti-Puseyites at home; and occasioning the rumour that he had attended the very Mass, somewhere or other. In other respects he created little stir, and corresponded freely with the Colonial Secretary, Bulwer Lytton.

From his coign in Whitehall, Lytton dubiously remarked
that demagogy would continue to be the most fascinating
of trades because it is animated by personal vanity, and
its venality is disguised, even from the demagogue
himself, by the love of country that often accompanies
it. With what relief the Colonial Secretary must have
turned, from the dismal prospect around him, to Gladstone's copious letters from abroad! Despite the
publicity of his official progress, the importance of his
task, the beauty of the scenery, the opportunity of visiting
Homeric sites, the chance to enter other than Anglican
temples of worship, Gladstone confided to his diary a
melancholy emotion : " the whole impression is sadden-
ing; it is all indolence, decay, stagnation; the image of
God seems as if it were nowhere. But there is much of
wild and picturesque."

He reported that the present Protectorate was bad for
the Ionians and for ourselves, yet he considered union
with Greece undesirable for the islanders. He proposed
to reform, and not to suppress, the constitution : in
other words, to convert a sham into a reality. Since,
however, the Ionian Islanders were supposed to be free
already, the proposed concession of reforms was taken
in bad part, and an inconvenient definition of the meaning of the term Protector was demanded. Gladstone
offered, if he seemed the right person, and if the resident
Commissioner would be in any case recalled, to introduce
the reforms himself, and to remain Commissioner for the
limited time that this work required. The Government
welcomed a plan that promised to rid them of an irksome
task, that kept him also abroad while connecting him
with them more closely. It was Gladstone's first attempt
to govern men : to preside, instead of participating in
an assembly; to manage persons rather than figures.
He accepted the task. It was then found that acceptance
of office vacated his seat at Oxford, and that he would be

occupied at Corfu, and thus ineligible to stand for re-election. Various solutions were tried for this unwelcome complication, which invited caricature and heartless jests. He was accused of supplanting his predecessor, and twitted with accepting a fifth-rate post from Disraeli, who was said to wish to crown him king at the remoteness of Corfu. His very friends declared that he would return shorn of his laurels.

Meanwhile a new Commissioner was appointed with an order to delegate to Gladstone all his powers until his own arrival, so that Gladstone might be deemed to hold, or not to hold, the office as convenience was best served. At the moment he was deemed to have vacated the post which had cost him his seat, but was re-elected without opposition. From the pin-pricks of home politics Gladstone then turned to the local Assembly, which was convoked in extraordinary session.

He invited the members to consider his proposals for reform, whereupon they passed a resolution affirming their single and unanimous desire to be united to Greece. The resolution, of course, had been phrased in Greek, and Gladstone, after scrutinising the formula with loving care, pronounced that " will " must be interpreted " wish " because it ($\theta\acute{\epsilon}\lambda\eta\sigma\iota\varsigma$) was not the word for will ($\theta\acute{\epsilon}\lambda\eta\mu\alpha$) used in the Lord's Prayer. Unfortunately the meaning of the Assembly was beyond so nice a doubt; and, when they persisted, instead of accusing them of violating the Constitution, dissolving them, and stopping their salaries, Gladstone told them that they must express their wishes in a petition to the Queen. They did so with noise and alacrity, with illuminations and *Te Deums*, activities wasted upon the Cabinet, for, in Morley's words, " neither the English public nor the English Parliament likes any policy that gives anything up."

After duly conveying the refusal of his country to these demands, Gladstone adjured the Assembly to pronounce on his proposals. Once more they declined : some, because reform would make separation more difficult : the rest, because it would place their perquisites in jeopardy. On this adverse vote the new Commissioner arrived, and Gladstone accepted the defeat of his brief rule in the archipelago. With characteristic philosophy, he said, without bitterness :

> The only real importance was to get the [proposals] out, in order to redeem the character, that is, to save the face, of England.

The publication of the stolen dispatch, he went on, had aroused hopes and implied intentions that he could not now circumvent. Within a few years, in 1862, the " undesirable " wishes of the Ionians were realised.

VIII

With his mind full of liberal constitution-making, Gladstone returned to England. He found the Conservative Cabinet tinkering with parliamentary reform, but did not take much part in the discussions beyond defending nomination boroughs as nurseries for statesmen, and speaking against a Whig amendment, which was carried. Lord Derby resigned, and after two years the ill-distributed parties probably welcomed a dissolution. The Government, however, improved its position by thirty votes, to be once more shortly defeated. Gladstone did not speak on the motion of no confidence, but he followed Disraeli into the lobby. Thus the Derby Government fell, and Palmerston returned, with Gladstone once again Chancellor of the Exchequer, after an interval of four and a half years.

His acceptance of office was much criticised. The supporter of Lord Derby had entered the Cabinet of his successor, Lord Palmerston, a statesman whom Gladstone had frequently condemned. To wonder at this is to misunderstand party politics at moments when parties are transparently names. Most of the time party politics are a family pact arranged by the Front Benches, enlivened, of course, with the attachments and aversions that are the staple of family life. Party governments are personal coalitions in fact if not in name, except when, at intervals, some genuine issue actively divides opinion. There were but two great issues in Gladstone's long life : the Corn Law quarrel that was over, and the Irish quarrel still to come. At the present stage of his career the family party could find nothing to differ about. Consequently politicians grouped themselves round men rather than policies; and, since politicians become interesting when they stand for something, and dwindle in interest when they do not, the groups were almost fortuitous and invariably shifting. To relieve the monotony, Ministries came and went, and the proposals for reform by the Conservative party, which seemed to encroach on the Liberal programme, were hardly more than a device to divide the Front Benches into confronting teams once more. All this was useless to Gladstone, whose gift was to place his ardour and enthusiasm at the service of someone else's ideas. If there was nobody with any ideas, what could he do but hesitate round the men who might be expected, politically, to have them. The Last Trump itself remains ineffective till it is seized and blown.

He was inevitably weary of being a politician without a pitch :

> For thirteen years (he wrote to his fellow-member for Oxford), the middle space of life, I have been cast out of party connection, severed from my old party, and loath irrecoverably to join a new one. So long have I adhered to the vague hope of a reconstruction that I have been left alone by every political friend with whom I have grown up.

After taking office and seeking re-election at Oxford, Gladstone was opposed, but returned with a majority of under two hundred. He had not become a Liberal yet. He had chosen between two leaders, and might have joined either, but he could only take office under the one who was in power. Both men had wanted him. Which would endure? It was very difficult. In a sense, too, the entire portmanteau of beliefs with which he had left the university and entered political life, Time had overturned and emptied on the ground. In Morley's opinion, " it was the fates that befell his book, it was the Maynooth grant, and the Gorham case, that swept away the foundations on which he had first built." It seemed sad, yet he needed not the intellect to tell him that his energies were unimpaired. These were, as they had always been, his real resources, enabling him to accept and shed beliefs like skins because his vitality lay in the very power to don and doff them. He was crying for something to do, that is, for some office to hold, since, though he would spend holidays on a foreign crusade, on writing a book, or governing a distant community, his home was the rostrum at Westminster, and he had been below that rostrum for five weary years.

Was he drawing the moral from his chastening isolation when, in 1859, as the first Lord Rector of Edinburgh University, he told his youthful audience :

> He who does his acts in order that the echo of them may come back as a soft music in his ears plays false to his noble destiny as a Christian man . . . ?

IX

By having voted with the previous Government Gladstone had done what his Oxford constituents expected, and by taking office in the new he told them that he was entitled not to be blamed, if only because another

General Election was in prospect. Nonetheless, and
whatever reasons he might give, his action identified him
with the Liberals, and he now had a seat in a Cabinet
wherein Disraeli had no inconvenient share. He found
a new recreation in negro melodies, which Lord Malmesbury heard him sing "with the greatest spirit and enjoyment." Though he was understood to be fond of music,
he came away from a performance of Bach on a Good
Friday feeling that, though it was very beautiful, it was
not what he would have chosen for that day. His main
thought must have been directed to the coming Budget,
always to prove the event of the parliamentary year to
him, and meantime he was concerned over the growth
of expenditure, not upon fortifications alone. To this
last, Palmerston told the Queen, Gladstone gave
" ineffective opposition and ultimate acquiescence."

The Budget of 1859 had increased the Income Tax
from fivepence to ninepence in the pound, its highest
figure in time of peace. When Disraeli made a motion
to " trip me up," Gladstone remarked : " it was not so
that I used him. I am afraid that the truce between us is
over, and that we shall have to pitch in as before."
Bright had been meditating a commercial treaty with
France, and in September 1859 Cobden came to Hawarden to talk it over. On his return he wrote : " Gladstone is really almost the only Cabinet Minister of five
years' standing who is not afraid to let his heart guide his
head a little at times." Having overcome resistance in
the Cabinet, Gladstone reported to Cobden in January,

> Criticism is busy : but the only thing really formidable is the
> unavowed but strong conflict with that passionate expectation
> of war, which no more bears disappointment than if it were
> hope or love.

The treaty involved further changes in the tariff;
it also promised expansion of trade and soothed excite-

ment on both sides of the Channel—excitement aroused by our attitude to the French annexation of Nice. Out of all this the Budget of 1860 grew. A fortunate lapse of fixed charges released two millions which allowed the reductions of duty required by the French treaty. The most interesting of these reductions, which benefited all countries besides France, were those on wine and brandy. Gladstone gave his name to a collar, a bag, a four-wheeled carriage for two persons with a driver's seat and a dickey, and to the cheaper claret that his reductions made possible. Of these, who will deny that Gladstone claret was the most honourable to him? He also abolished the excise duty upon manufactured paper, those " taxes upon knowledge " that the Corn-law Rhymer had deplored. But if this, as he said, marked the zenith of Free Trade, it was also the high-water mark of expenditure. The new ironclads were more costly, so was artillery, to mention only the most palpable items. Gladstone foresaw a period of high charges, and the whole question began to loom in the popular conciousness. He had always a way of attracting interest to his doings, an overflow of their immense interest to himself, and by February 1860 excitement over approaching Parliamentary reform was swallowed by eager concern in the coming Budget and the commercial treaty.

At the beginning of the month Gladstone had slight congestion of the lungs. The introduction of the Budget had to be postponed for a week. Excitement became suspense as the tensity of anticipation quickened. The promised speech was one of his great performances and it lasted for four hours. A brief jotting in his diary records the tension :

> Spoke 5—9 without great exhaustion, aided by a great stock of egg and wine. Thank God! Home at 11. This was the most arduous operation I have ever had in Parliament.

The allusion to egg and sherry refers to a famous mixture with which Gladstone used to sustain himself. " It was an odd thing," H. W. Lucy has recorded, " to see Gladstone just now taking advantage of the pause occasioned by the ringing cheers his eloquence drew forth to seize a short, thick-set pomatum-pot, remove the cork, and proceed to refresh himself. . . [It was] oval in shape, four inches in height, and supplied with an ill-fitting cork that baffled the frenzied efforts of the orator to replace it." The mixture was of Mrs. Gladstone's brewing, and was more than once referred to by her husband in public letters and remarks. One is so characteristic that, though uttered in 1878, it should be given here.

> When I have had very lengthened statements to make, I have used what is called egg-flip—a glass of sherry beaten up with an egg. I think it excellent, but I have much more faith in the egg than in the alcohol.

Who else would have sought to draw moral discrimination between the ingredients of an egg-flip ? It was just this habit that made some people distrustful of Gladstone, who often dragged in morality without cause. As the habit is Pecksniffian, people can hardly be blamed for saying that Gladstone was a Pecksniff himself. In small things as in great he often missed the language of sincerity, though he was a simple-minded man. He never outgrew his Evangelical upbringing, and the sentiments that he thought he ought to feel he expressed ; he never apparently questioned whether it was not a superfluous pretence to feel them. The result was a language of unction disagreeable to those who have more respect for human nature. It is time to admit that his character was far more vital and personal than his terms.

The effect of this speech can be judged from a remark of the Prince Consort to Baron Stockmar : " Gladstone is now the real leader of the House, and works with an

energy and vigour almost incredible." He was forced
to do so because reaction soon made itself felt. The
great man of the day became the popular suspect of the
morrow as his opponents recovered the presence of mind
of which his oratory had temporarily deprived them. He
resigned his membership of the Carlton Club, another
step towards Liberalism. The success of his speech had
not placed his proposals out of danger, and Lord John
Russell played into hostile hands by introducing his
Reform Bill on March 1, when neither the treaty nor the
Budget was secure. The Paper Duty Bill only passed
the Commons by a narrow majority, and it was thrown
out by the Lords, an act that Gladstone declared to be an
interference with the Commons' control of finance.
This was another goad in the direction of Liberalism. It
brought him support from the Radicals, and his share in
opening the way to cheap newspapers was one of the
causes of his rapid rise in popularity. To the fury of
his opponents and the delight of his new friends he
circumvented the Lords in the following year by
including all his taxes in a single Finance Bill, which the
Upper House therefore had to accept or reject at a
stroke. A contemporary mentioned the "glow of
pride" with which Gladstone was now regarded, and
described him without irony as "a transcendent mouth-
piece of a nation of shopkeepers." He had an uphill
fight for economy, and remained unmoved by the scare
of a war with France, yet when he left the Exchequer in
1866, expenditure on the Services was less by two
millions than it had been on his arrival in 1859. While
he preached economy on public platforms, his opponents
denied that he was economical himself. His calculations
were said to be delusive, and Disraeli in 1862 called him
the most profuse peace Minister we had had. He himself admitted that the ease with which revenue could be
raised by the Income Tax encouraged expenditure, but

two matters to his credit are not in dispute. In 1861 he established the Post Office Savings Bank, and three years later a means for obtaining small annuities that should be safe to the purchaser and financially sound. Both were of great service to the masses, who could neither plan nor acquire such benefits for themselves. The House of Commons was indifferent to these changes; they were also distasteful to the banks and insurance companies, which might have been expected to have provided them themselves. The Savings Bank, moreover, was a source of revenue to the Exchequer, and thus helped to free it from dependence on the City, which began to watch Gladstone with a jealous eye. In finance he came nearest to initiative, and we see him already " warming the climate in which his projects throve." In the spring of each year, he afterwards confessed, " I begin to feel an itch to have the handling of the Budget."

A characteristic fragment of his oratory occurs in his speech on the Budget of 1866 :

> We propose to reduce the duty on pepper. The fate of pepper might well excite the commiseration of any humane man. . . . The present appears to be a good occasion when, without exciting feelings of jealousy in the agricultural or any other class of the community, we can afford to do justice to pepper. The case is a hard one, and for this reason : all the spices and condiments in which the wealthier classes have an exclusive interest have been long ago set free from duty. But pepper is a condiment common to all classes of the community; and, though I cannot say whether this is true or not, I am told that it is largely consumed in Ireland.

The characteristic caution displayed in this last sentence was carried to its extreme limit in a speech that he made at Hawarden in 1884. " It is in everybody's power to rear poultry, and, if I may say so, from eggs."

It is odd that the humane side of social legislation appealed to him little unless it had some bearing on

finance. Lord Shaftesbury, the father of the Factory
Acts, said :

> Gladstone ever voted in resistance to my efforts. He gave
> no support to the Ten Hours Bill; he voted with Sir R. Peel
> to rescind the famous decision in favour of it. He was the
> only Member who endeavoured to delay the Bill which
> delivered women and children from the mines and pits; and
> he never did say a word on behalf of the factory children until,
> when defending slavery in the West Indies, he taunted Buxton
> with indifference to slavery in England.

In regard to slavery he had pleaded the " blessed
change of opinion " which had helped to bring his conversion about. There was no such blessed change in
regard to sweating at home. Shaftesbury was almost
alone in his repudiation of it. The contrast between the
sensitive and insensitive spot in Gladstone's sympathies
needs no better illustration, and such contradictions are
the salt of human character. He was hardly alive to
issues that were not astir in many minds.

X

Perhaps it was a lingering trace of his early sympathy
for the planters that led him into an indiscreet remark
in favour of the South during the American Civil War of
1861. By the autumn of the following year the war had
lasted eighteen months, and the blockade of the Southern
ports had stopped the export of cotton. There was
consequently grievous distress in Lancashire, and Gladstone employed factory workers from the cotton towns
on improvements at Hawarden in order to give relief to
some of them.

In September 1862 he had one of the earliest of his
triumphal progresses. The northern Liberals invited
him to visit the Tyne and to address them at a public
dinner. He received a regal reception. Bells were rung,

cannon fired, steamers followed him in procession to
the river mouth. The workmen of the shipyards and
factories, who had shared in the abounding exports that
followed the commerical treaty with France, thronged
the banks. Gladstone was now a recognised popular
spokesman, with a following outside of Parliament
that was amazing his fellow-politicians. One of these
triumphal processions lasted for six hours. He says :
" I made as many speeches as hours," and this was but
a single day's experience. Nothing seemed to tire him,
and no wonder he had written in his diary on his fifty-
first birthday :

> I cannot believe it. I feel within me the rebellious un-
> spoken word, I will not be old.

Two months before, he had fallen under the spell of
Wilkie Collins :

> I did not get to the play last night from finding *The Woman
> in White* so very interesting. It has no dull parts, and is far
> better sustained than *Adam Bede*, though I don't know if it
> rises quite as high. The character drawing is excellent.

His other recreations included enormous walks, of over
twenty miles, and in 1863 we have glimpses of him at
Balmoral.

> So far as I can see, the form and mode of life here does not
> differ for visitors from Windsor. All meals and rooms are
> separate, but sometimes, it appears, some are invited to dine
> with the Queen. The household circle is smaller here than
> at Windsor, and so less formal and dull. . . .
> I do not think that Sunday is the best of days here. I in
> vain inquired with care about Episcopal services; there did
> not seem to be one within fifteen miles, if indeed so near.
> We had something between family prayer and a service in the
> dining-room at ten; it lasted about forty minutes. . . . You
> are better off at Penmaenmawr.
> The service at Ballater has made a great difference in favour
> of this Sunday. It was celebrated in the Free Kirk schoolroom
> for girls !

K

> Lady Churchill . . . was very submissive at dinner in her
> manner to the Queen, and I told her it made me feel I had been
> so impudent.   Only think of this : both through her and
> through General Grey it has come round to me that the
> Queen thinks she was too cheerful on the night I last dined.
> This she feels a kind of sin.

He took long walks, climbed Lochnagar, and, if he
" could not do all that the others did in looking down the
precipices," on one occasion he walked a measured mile
in twelve minutes, by the side of the Dee.

XI

Gladstone was now settled in office and evidently a
predestined leader in the Commons, but much as Dickens
had crossed the seas to receive in person the homage
of American citizens, so Gladstone was carrying political
prestige beyond the accustomed circuit of Westminster;
on platforms throughout the country he was creating
the same amazement and sense of change.   If the
audiences which danced delightedly to his piping were to
be admitted to the franchise, it seemed to many that a new
epoch was at hand.   The ideal of quantity on a new and
vast scale was being felt in many departments of life.
The prospect or possibility that Parliament might cease
to be the privileged arena of political activity was
exciting to many and disquieting to some.   The
enormous welcome given to Garibaldi and the public
joy over the unification of Italy roused a desire for
liberalism at home, which took the form of asking how
much longer the vote should be limited to the reforms
of 1832.   The rising tide was in want of a leader who
should combine personal fervour with practical capacity.
The name of Whig, once applied to a group of aristocratic houses, was now giving way to the term Liberal,
which implied a less exclusive choice.   The line " genius

better is than birth " had occurred in one of the songs
sung in his honour when Gladstone had received his
popular welcome on the Tyne. His own appeal to
popular liking was varied and confused. His pleas for
peace and retrenchment were popular at Manchester,
however much the straitened city might deplore his
neutrality over the American Civil War. His support
of a united Italy pleased the Whigs, Nonconformists
and Churchmen were both drawn to him, workmen felt
that they had in him a friend. The old fear of ideas
connected with the French Revolution was over, the
Chartist agitation was giving way to a desire for the
vote. The quiet in which the Lancashire men had
endured the recent distress was held or claimed to show
capacity for constitutional privileges. In May 1864
Gladstone told the House of Commons :

> Every man who is not presumably incapacitated by some
> consideration of personal unfitness or of political danger is
> morally entitled to come within the pale of the constitution.

This was altogether too much for Lord Palmerston and
for many others as well. There was an outcry. Gladstone was said to " minister aliments to popular turbu-
lence and vanity, to preach the divine right of multitudes,
to encourage, Minister of the Crown though he was,
a sweeping and levelling democracy." Palmerston
expressly objected. " I entirely deny that every sane
and not disqualified man has a moral right to the vote.
. . . What every man and woman has a right to is to be
well governed and under just laws." To his brother
Gladstone wrote :

> I have been astounded to find it (my speech) the cause or
> occasion of such a row. It would have been quite as intelligible
> to me had people said, " under the exceptions of personal
> unfitness and political danger you exclude or may exclude
> almost everybody."

Palmerston had the better argument because he had the clearer head, but it is amusing to see Gladstone criticising himself as others often criticised him, for ambiguity. Feeling had inspired his speech, and feeling had interpreted it, but, as usual, his words and his qualifications admitted equal emphasis and, not for the last time, he rode the more convenient horse away.

This did not discourage his activity, however. A month later the same speech induced the voteless workmen of York to present him with an address of congratulation. They mentioned, among less definite matters, his Post Office Savings Bank and his Government Annuities Bill. These excellent deeds gave a foundation to the set of speeches that he delivered in Lancashire during the autumn of 1864. He was feeling the rising of the tide, and advanced himself, before others, to meet it. He spoke of working-class progress during the previous thirty years. Opening a park he enlarged on that " communion with nature " which was now part of the life of the poorest citizen. At Liverpool, with the touch of a musician, he warned his eager audience against " political lethargy." He reminded them of the moral responsibility of Imperial politics and referred openly, and for the first time, to Ireland, where " the state of feeling was not for the honour and the advantage of the United Kingdom." " So ended " (in his own words) " in peace an exhausting, flattering, I hope not intoxicating circuit. . . . Somewhat haunted by dreams of halls, and lines of people, and great assemblies." He had become the first popular hero of workaday politics, and the success of his proceedings filled other politicians with alarm. When his brother-in-law reported their criticisms to him, Gladstone replied : " Please to recollect that we have got to govern millions of hard hands ; that it must be done by force, fraud, or good-will ; that the latter has been tried, and is answering." As Bishop

Wilberforce put it, " Gladstone is certainly gaining power. You hear now almost everyone say he must be the future Premier, and such sayings tend greatly to accomplish themselves."

His friendly attitude to an old grievance about the burial of Dissenters brought him into touch with the Nonconformists, and on one occasion they sounded him on the question of laying the foundation-stone of one of their chapels.   While he continued to oppose Palmerston on the estimates, he was beginning to raise the question of the disestablishment of the Irish Church.   In politics, however, one cannot make new friends without risking the confidence of original supporters, and after the dissolution of Parliament in the summer of 1865 he was defeated at Oxford.   This occurred partly through the postal vote, which was largely that of elderly clergy to whom the very word disestablishment was abhorrent. He found consolation in a verse from one of the lessons : " they shall fight against thee, but they shall not prevail against thee, for I am with thee, saith the Lord."   The last official tie with his early influences was now severed. Politically he had outgrown the control of Oxford and of Westminster and was looking to the people at large.   No longer a Tory or a Churchman, he was revealed as a Gladstonian at last, and in the welcome that awaited him lay the elements of a party that should seek its inspiration from the man himself

XII

Though he wrote in his diary that " a dear dream is dispelled," the weight of Oxford opinion, which he was ceasing to represent, must have already become an oppression to him.   He had been invited already to stand for South Lancashire, and hurried off to Manchester and Liverpool.   " At last, my friends," he began, " I am

come among you, and I am come among you un-
muzzled." There is more relief than regret in these
words, apt as they also were to rouse enthusiasm. When
Manning wrote in a letter : " you say truly that Oxford
has failed to enlarge itself to the progress of the country,"
and warned him not to entangle himself in extremes,
Gladstone replied : " in a cold or lukewarm period
everything which lives and moves is called extreme."
To another old friend, the Bishop of Oxford, Gladstone
wrote :

> There have been two great deaths or transmigrations of
> spirit in my political existence. One very slow, the breaking
> of ties with my original party. The other very short and
> sharp, the breaking of the tie with Oxford.

In October 1865 Lord Palmerston died, and Lord
Russell became Prime Minister with Gladstone once more
at the Exchequer, and leader of the House of Commons.
The obvious man for this position, Gladstone managed
to excite suspicions of exactly opposite kinds. A
politician declared that Gladstone " would not perceive
the difference between leading and driving," while his
brother-in-law reported grumbles from another quarter :
" There is an impression that you are absorbed in questions
about Homer and Greek words, about *Ecce Homo* [which
he had been reviewing], that you are not reading the
newspapers, or feeling the pulse of followers. The
people don't understand it; they consider you their own,
as a husband claims a wife's devotion." Church, the
future Dean of St. Paul's, noted that " they love him
much less in the House than they do out of doors ";
and Jowett, the Master of Balliol, said : " It is the first
time that anyone of such great simplicity has been in so
exalted a station." Gladstone himself bore out this
description in the sentence, " I have not refused to
acknowledge and accept the signs of the times."

These signs can be summarised in the word unrest, which was evident in Gladstone's favourite spheres, the religious and the political. In 1859 Darwin had published his *Origin of Species*. Its effect was enormous, and, though we are still living under its shadow, we hardly realise the importance of the change. In the ferment of opinion the appearance of *Essays and Reviews* during 1860 created grave disquiet, and two of the clerical contributors to that book, who had questioned the inspiration of the Bible and the doctrine of eternal punishment, were haled into court. The hostile verdict was reversed on appeal to the Queen in Council, and thus confirmed the principle of the Gorham judgment of ten years before. Gladstone was moved to declare that the spirit of this judgment " established, as far as a court can establish it, a complete indifference between the Christian faith and the denial of it." Again, Dr. Colenso, Bishop of Natal, appealed successfully against the sentence of deprivation passed upon him by his Metropolitan at Cape Town for having published certain criticisms of the Scriptures. Gladstone was watching the growth of unbelief and liberal theology with apprehension. He was never tempted to embrace it, but he was keenly alive to its influence upon existing institutions and political activity. In various directions a liberalism was in the air, and Gladstone, keenly sensitive to movements of opinion, was impelled to become the parliamentary spokesman of it, theology apart.

Circumstances helped him by unexpectedly focussing the public eye upon the franchise. All the Front Benchers were more or less committed to it, and the question really was, which group under which leader should bring it about. The rank and file were indifferent or opposed, and this opposition as usual aroused Gladstone to activity. When the Reform Bill of 1866 was defeated, and Lord Russell resigned, Gladstone uttered

his well-known saying : "Time is on our side. You
cannot fight against the future." With his responsive
sense of the political to-morrow, it is almost a statement
of his political creed. Once more out of office, he felt
the wrench again : "Finished in Downing Street;
left my keys behind me. Somehow it makes a void."
This void he invariably filled with propaganda of one
kind or another, and the dissolution itself provided the
opportunity. The working classes were suddenly convinced that they were to be deprived of a promised
privilege, and, as the spokesman of their demand, they
made Gladstone the hero of the hour. A crowd forced
its way into Carlton House Terrace and raised a cry
for Gladstone and liberty. They would not understand
that their idol was away, and in order to disperse them
the police advised his wife to appear upon the balcony.
This act annoyed the journalists, who said that the
women of his household had "courted an ovation from
persons of the lowest class." The personal intercourse
of politicians with the general public was still an innovation; even during elections Disraeli never stalked the
country, and Gladstone was already "at home" to
crowds in a way that was astonishing and new. He did,
however, decline to address a demonstration in Hyde
Park, and contented himself with the assertion that the
resignation of the Government was really a fresh step
toward success. "In the hour of defeat I have the
presentiment of victory."

During the recess, to avoid attending further celebra-
tions, Gladstone took his family to Rome. The political
pot was boiling of its own accord, and nothing practical
could be done by him until the opening of Parliament.
At the same time he promised Lord Acton not to entangle
himself in Italian grievances. "Nothing is more unlikely than that I should meddle with the prisons or
anything else of the kind." Manning was fully alive

to the propensities of the traveller, about whom probably
some uneasy curiosity was felt.   He assured the Vatican
as far as he could : " Gladstone does not come as an
enemy, and may be made friendly, or he might become
on his return most dangerous."   In the Holy City the
visitor was discreetness itself.   He spent most of his
spare time listening to sermons by Italian priests and
friars.   The only echo of previous activity was a dinner
given to him by members of the Italian Parliament, at
which his old friend Poerio made a moving speech.   On
his way home he stopped in Paris, attended the funeral
of Victor Cousin, and dined with the Emperor at the
Tuileries.   His inner eye was bent on the forthcoming
session at Westminster.

His fears that the vote would be given grudgingly were
unfounded.   The agitations, the mass meetings, the
street processions, culminating in a riot that burst the
railings in Hyde Park, were decisive arguments.   Household suffrage, like woman suffrage, was the reward of
agitation outside the House.   Nearly a million voters
were added to the register.   As it was not then known
how easily the electorate could be stampeded in any
direction by many cheap newspapers controlled by a few
hands, the dismay of the more conservative is as understandable as the false hopes of their opponents.   In a
political ode, clearly the product of genuine feeling,
Patmore spoke of the " orgies of the multitude, which
now begin."   Yet the real revolution had been economic;
the political was but the recognition of that change.
Even so, the Act of 1867 did not wholly satisfy Gladstone.
Failing to carry some of his supporters when moving an
amendment to extend the Bill, he was so much disappointed that he spoke of retiring to the back bench.
Looking back on his life, he once claimed political
insight into the state of public opinion, and he was
certainly right.   But there are more public opinions than

one, and when he seemed to fail in this discernment, it was because the determining political opinion had not yet caught up with the movement of which he was himself aware. His audience was steadily expanding with his consciousness of its existence. His sense of it now spread beyond Oxford, beyond the House of Commons. The response to which he thrilled was become the almost inarticulate movement of the masses, only limited by the political side of their desires. This was his real constituency. In 1868 he wrote to Lord Granville : " For seven years past I have been watching the sky with a strong sense of the obligation to act with the first streak of dawn."

It was the same sense which led him, publicly and in advance of other English politicians, to perceive that the Irish question was gathering to an issue. When the Fenian outbreaks spread to England in 1867 and produced the armed rescue of two Irish prisoners from the Manchester police and the explosion at Clerkenwell Prison, Gladstone said in Parliament :

> The Fenian conspiracy has had an important influence with respect to Irish policy . . . when these [recent] phenomena came home to the popular mind and produced that attitude of attention and preparedness on the part of the whole population of this country,

he was much criticised for the admission : by people, as he wittily put it, " who cannot bear to hear what they cannot fail to see." In 1869 he declared that the state of Ireland was admitted by both parties to be the question of the day. In this he was slightly exaggerating. Recognition was reluctant from first to last.

At Christmas 1867 Lord John Russell told Gladstone he did not intend to take office again, and in February 1868 Disraeli succeeded Lord Derby as Prime Minister. A month later, on a motion by an Irish Member, Gladstone said that the Church of Ireland as a Church in

alliance with the State must cease to exist. It is
characteristic that he should have approached the Irish
question through an ecclesiastical door. Lord John's
announcement left Gladstone the leader of the Liberal
party, though its strength could hardly be measured until
the next election should reveal the effect of the recent
Reform Bill. Gladstone followed his speech by framing
three resolutions concerning the Irish Church, and carried
them against the Government. The result of the
division was greeted with tremendous cheers. He wrote
to the Duchess of Sutherland :

> This is a day of excitement—almost of exultation. We
> have made a step, nay a stride, and this stride is on the pathway
> of justice and of peace, of national honour and renown.

To show the seriousness of his intentions, he at once
introduced a Bill to preclude any new appointments in the
Irish Church. This also passed the House of Commons
but was rejected by the Lords.

In the autumn Parliament was dissolved, and the issue
before the country was whether or not the Irish Church
was to be disestablished. During the election Gladstone published his *Chapter of Autobiography* to explain
how his change of view had come about. It was just
thirty years since his first book had been issued. The
Irish Church ministered to about one-eighth of the
population among whom it was State-supported, so the
question at issue had not much to do with the principle
advocated in his earlier book. Yet to most people
the sacred principle was the principle of establishment,
and Gladstone's assault on an enthroned injustice
scandalised his friends and supporters in the Church of
England. To them belief in God and belief in an
establishment were almost the same thing. His treatise
was welcomed by the public, which appreciated his desire
to take them into confidence with himself. The policy

that he now advocated was certainly just and statesman-like, though no doubt its victory at the polls was largely due to partisans who hated disestablishment as enviously as most churchmen cherished it.   Gladstone himself was elected for Greenwich after having been defeated in South Lancashire.   He was now, with a majority of 112 in the House, the head of a new party with a complicated measure to carry through.   Though not yet formally Prime Minister, he must have felt that he had earned the crown of his parliamentary career after thirty-five years in politics.

CHAPTER IV

IN AND OUT OF DOWNING STREET

I

On the afternoon of December 1, 1868, Gladstone was felling a tree at Hawarden when a messenger arrived with a telegram from the Queen. After reading the telegram he muttered, "Very significant," and continued his work. Then, resting on his axe, he turned to Mr. Evelyn Ashley and said : " My mission is to pacify Ireland." He did not speak another word till the tree was down. On his birthday a few weeks later he wrote in his diary :

> This birthday opens my sixtieth year. I descend the hill of life. It would be a truer figure to say that I ascend a steepening path with a burden ever gathering weight. The Almighty seems to sustain and spare me for some purpose of His own, deeply unworthy as I know myself to be. Glory be to His name.

With a powerful majority to sustain his own efforts, with a keen eye for the " signs of the times," and above all a sense that he was entrusted with a mission, Gladstone entered upon the most fruitful and successful period of his career. His energies indeed remained undiminished to the last, but never again did they prove so successful as during his first administration. It is true that he had been temperamentally more in accord with the serious and laborious Prince Consort than he ever managed to become with the Queen, and Albert's death in 1861 had

removed a potential ally. Whether the Prince too
would have come to dread Gladstone's propensity for
sweeping change, or been equally convinced of the
Divine approbation, is a matter for conjecture. Would
there have been room for so energetic a Minister and so
personally active a Sovereign as the Prince was becoming
at the time of his death? Many devoted friends as
Gladstone had among women, and charming as others
found him in society, he was never at ease in the royal
presence. His notion of deference was as embarrassing
to the crowned lady as her august station was to him.
With a masculine Sovereign he would have been more
at his ease. In all forms, even in forms of speech, he
was too formal to appear natural, and the mode of address
that was flattering to huge assemblies became both stiff
and constraining in private audience. Except on the
public platform Gladstone always seemed a little out of
place. That he felt this is obvious from his manner :
not even in his diaries could he contrive a personal or
spontaneous note.

To carry through his policy of disestablishment he
relied on Nonconformists in England and Wales, Scottish
Presbyterians and Irish Roman Catholics. Out of these
elements a new party was forming under Gladstone's
leadership, and he began an ascendancy in the country
that was to last, with interruptions, for twenty-five years.
In 1869 the majority for his Bill was 118, and thus introduced a new standard of quantity. The third reading
was similarly triumphant. The proceedings in the
Lords were more chequered, and were watched with
anxious interest by Gladstone's outside following. A
Roman Catholic bishop offered Mass for Gladstone, and
Mr. Spurgeon sent the assurance of his prayers.

> I think (Gladstone wrote) in these and other prayers lies
> the secret of the strength of body which has been given me
> in unusual measure during this very trying year.

Indeed his anxiety lest there should arise a conflict between the two Houses was so great that he had to lie up and to interview his colleagues from the sofa. In September he was at Walmer Castle, where Tait, the Archbishop of Canterbury, found him "lying in blankets on the ramparts eating his dinner, still looking very ill. He joined us at night full of intelligence. His fierce vigour all the better for being a little tempered." The passing of the Bill was a great triumph, and whatever his opponents have said against the measure, none has denied the skill with which it was carried through. Disraeli's admirers have professed to see in it no more than a counterstroke to the latter's Reform Bill, and no doubt, if that had not been suddenly appropriated and passed, reform would have been the issue of the election. But it is equally true that the Irish situation was becoming intolerable, and that some attempt to deal with it could not much longer be delayed. The Reform Bill itself made the Irish vote important; the Nationalist Party was extended by its means, and to Gladstone's native energy each question was one to be settled in order that another pressing matter might be attacked. He was essentially a man of action, and his susceptibility to popular movements was precisely the quality that made him disconcerting to friends and foes. Of all Irish questions the disestablishment of the minority Church was the least thorny, but, this out of the way, he turned to the much more complicated and radical problem of the land.

An agricultural nation cannot be governed successfully on the assumptions that rule an industrial state. The workman as a rule is hired and not housed, and the value of his contribution is lost in the finished product. It is not so with a worker on the land. The fields that he has drained and fenced, the roads that he has made, are permanent and visible improvements to his holding,

which may have been in the same family for years.
Has he no permanent rights in permanent improvements
like these ?   Is the landlord entitled to deprive him of all
the fruits of his labour by additions to the rent that will
leave him as badly off as before ?   Can the landlord evict
him if he refuses to pay, and on the law of supply and
demand let the holding to the highest bidder ?   The
disorders and crimes produced by these confiscations
had already been made the subject of official inquiry in
1843.   Bills had been proposed and dropped in a House
dominated by landlords, whose legislation was entirely
in favour of their own class.

In Ulster, however, custom, the natural law of agricultural communities, had enforced a rent exclusive of
tenants' improvements, and secured to the tenant the
right to transfer his lease to somebody else.   The tenant
was thus relatively protected.   Gladstone's Bill may be
roughly described as extending the benefits of custom to
areas and tenancies where it was disputed or absent.
The value of this measure has been minimised in some
Irish histories, but it was the foundation of all that
followed and began the beneficent revolution which
redistributed the land and eventually has made Southern
Ireland a country of peasant proprietors.

II

Gladstone's programme of reform was not confined
to Ireland, and the Queen was perhaps more harried
under his premiership than at any period of her reign.
Biographers of her and of Disraeli have told us how
Disraeli made complications easy by his rapid summaries
and amusing aphorisms, but the Queen, like many of her
subjects, found Gladstone's explanations even more
puzzling than his proposals.   To her it seemed that he
would leave nothing alone.   He turned to education;

he opened the Civil Service, except the Foreign Office, to competition; he abolished purchase of commissions in the Army, and when Parliament objected, he invoked the royal warrant to do so. Worse than this, he appeared to the Queen to attack the Prerogative itself when he removed the Commander-in-Chief from the Horse Guards to Whitehall and placed him directly under the control of the War Office and Parliament.

The Education Act of 1870 was partly the result of household suffrage. It was said that " we must educate our masters," and the victories of the North in America and of Prussia in the war with France were said to have been won in elementary schools. Gladstone's attitude was characteristic. He had " no fear of a secular system " of education; but it was with great reluctance that he agreed to the abolition of religious tests for Dissenters, who were admitted to degrees and endowments at the Universities in 1871. A necessary complement of the extended franchise was the Act of 1870 which secured vote by secret ballot. Abstract reasons were supposed to be against secrecy, but practical proofs of intimidation eventually prevailed. Gladstone himself was a lukewarm advocate of the change, and said characteristically :

> I have at all times given my vote in favour of open voting, but I have done so before, and do so now, with an important reservation, namely, that whether by open voting or by whatsoever means free voting must be secured.

The Lords at first threw out the Bill on the ground that secret voting would be fatal to the monarchy, which showed how little they believed in popular loyalty. Only in Ireland did the ballot make a real difference, for by it the political power of the landlords was overthrown. The political future of the Nationalist party, which had been made possible by the recent Reform Act, was now assured.

In the midst of this official activity Gladstone found

L

time to keep his eye upon the intellectual ferment at home, which Darwin's book had started among men of science and churchmen alike. In 1869, and in the hope of leading both to understand each other's position, James Knowles, then editor of the *Contemporary Review*, founded the Metaphysical Society. It resembled the Church of England in two respects. It was composed of men of very diverse views, and the majority of them were churchmen. Manning, Gladstone and Huxley were among the members. It was in order to define his own intellectual position that Huxley invented the term agnostic at this time. He did not merely mean to assert his ignorance on many matters of universal interest upon which confident assertions had been made. He also wished to distinguish himself from those who claimed personal intuitive knowledge, such as the Gnostics of old. About this date he was asked whether Gladstone was an expert in metaphysics. "An expert in metaphysics?" he replied. "He does not know the meaning of the word." Some years later Huxley said to a clergyman, "Do you still believe in Gladstone? . . . If working men were to-day to vote by a majority that two and two make five, to-morrow Gladstone would believe it, and find reasons for it that they had never dreamed of." The effect of the discussions at the Metaphysical Society on Gladstone was to make him at last distinguish between the characters of men and their opinions. He had once thought this impossible, but he never solved the mystery, and in his own political changes claimed verbal consistency to the end. He remarked to Dr. Temple, whom he made Bishop of Exeter, "The limit of possible variation between character and opinion, and between character and belief, is widening and will widen;" yet this was not, as it were, to be admitted officially until the spectacular struggle over the Bradlaugh case was fought and won.

In the autumn of 1871 Gladstone spent two days with Tennyson at the house at Blackdown which James Knowles had built for the poet.   Tennyson read aloud " The Holy Grail," and found Gladstone " a very noble fellow and perfectly unaffected."   His visitor was equally pleased :

> A very characteristic and delightful abode.   In Tennyson are singularly united true greatness, genuine simplicity, and some eccentricity.   But the latter is from habit and circumstance, the former is his nature.   His wife is excellent, and in her adaptation to him wonderful.

During this premiership he offered a peerage to Grote, and gave one to the silent historian, Acton.   He wished to give some honour to Mill.   The first Jew to become a peer received it on Gladstone's recommendation.   Now, for the first time, the years began to leave their visible mark upon him, and Phillimore observed in 1873 that Gladstone was looking well but much aged.   Troubles at home and abroad began to multiply, and he was horrified to note the growing unpopularity of the Queen.

For eleven years she had cherished her widow's weeds and her seclusion, and in the face of her retirement the fall of the French emperor and the establishment of a Republic in France produced a wave of republican feeling in England.   It took the blunt form of asking what return the nation gained from the great cost of the monarchy, and a pamphlet entitled "What does she do with it ? " attracted wide attention.   Mr. Gladstone was forced to venture on " deferential exhortations," which she began to resist and continued to dislike.   After 1872 the Queen's reserve to him increased, and his sense of awe became oppressive.   He was also alienating the support of more than one group of his mixed following in his attempt to meet the claims of the Irish Catholics for a Catholic University.   His speech of three hours upon the Irish University Bill threw the House into " a mesmeric trance," but the opposition was not quelled and his proposals were defeated.

In the sphere of foreign policy his attitude was less spectacular than Palmerston's, and the weariness which overtakes every administration took the form of asserting that England was losing the position in European councils that had been hers hitherto since the battle of Waterloo. The spectre of imperial France was replaced by the military empire of Germany, and her sensational successes in the field since 1866 were as annoying to English pride as they were dangerous to all her neighbours. Beside Bismarck, Gladstone seemed ineffective to the vulgar eye, and he was compared to his disadvantage with Palmerston. To the same eye Gladstone seemed to deserve this condemnation when Russia repudiated the limitation on her armaments in the Black Sea, imposed by the Treaty of Paris in 1856, and when our dispute with the United States over the damage caused to them during their civil war by the *Alabama*, which had been allowed to sail from a British port, was referred to arbitration and led to the imposition of heavy damages at Geneva which we agreed to pay. The vulgar notion that international arbitration is humiliating to the side that makes a sacrifice shows that nations are still in the tribal phase of public law, and it is to Gladstone's honour that he carried the arbitration through. As, moreover, the principle of an international court for Great Powers was new, the award becomes a definite achievement in foreign politics. The morality that he was accustomed to invoke for his proposals rings more truly than it often did in his vindication of this settlement :

> I regard the fine imposed on this country as dust in the balance compared with the moral value of the example set when these two great nations of England and America . . . went

in peace and concord before a judicial tribunal [rather than
resort to war].

The Americans received a third of all they asked, and
our insistence that extraneous claims must be ignored was
respected. This arbitration created an historic precedent
for the conduct of the two nations that remains worth
more to both of them than any supposed identity of
origin, speech or ideals. In foreign affairs it was Gladstone's greatest achievement.

By the autumn of 1871 the decline of his popularity
was marked, but one of his most extraordinary speeches
succeeded for a moment in restoring it. In his endeavours
for economy he always cast a jealous eye upon the Services, even apart from armaments. Florence Nightingale
complained that the improved sanitation of barracks, on
which she had set Sidney Herbert to work, found obstacles in Mr. Gladstone's anxiety to avoid expense.
The dockyard men, who were among his constituents at
Greenwich, were naturally furious at the discharges
which followed the Franco-Prussian war. France having
then to economise on her navy, advantage was taken to
follow suit at home. It was, then, with murmurs and
hostility that Gladstone was received when he went down
to Blackheath to address the largest even of his enormous
audiences in the open air. Once again the fine presence
and the beautiful voice, which carried over this vast
multitude, worked like a charm. Is there a sharper
test for an orator than to convert a murmuring crowd, a
crowd too of poor men, many of whom have been
thrown out of work by the speaker's policy? The speech
does not survive better than its fellows, but the occasion
and effect make it a crucial example of his oratory. It
was half an hour before he won a silent hearing; then
the murmurs died away, attention was riveted, and he
ceased speaking after nearly two hours in a tumult of
applause.

III

There were pinpricks nearer home, and in the Commons he was guilty of what are known as parliamentary blunders. Their only interest now is that attempts were made to found charges of favouritism upon them. A vacancy occurred upon the Judicial Committee of the Privy Council, to which four new judges were being added. After offering the position to judges who for various personal reasons declined, Gladstone, with the approval of the Cabinet, made the Attorney-General a judge in order to qualify him for the position. The proceeding was resented, and the cry raised that experience as well as status was required for the new post. The House was excited and divided in mind, and Gladstone's speech only secured a narrow majority of twenty-seven. Had he not succeeded in converting some hesitants to his side, he might have been defeated on the division. He created a worse impression by doing the same thing in another form. The living of Ewelme was vacant, and it could be given only to a member of Convocation at Oxford. A certain Mr. Harvey was on the list for promotion, but he happened to be a Cambridge man. Without objection by the college, Mr. Gladstone made him, therefore, a member of Oriel, and after six weeks' residence Mr. Harvey was admitted to Convocation. No one said a word until the appointment was criticised in Parliament. It was then suggested that the gentleman had been appointed because Gladstone had known him in the past. The proceeding seemed arbitrary, and of course this is the kind of way in which manœuvring is done. But Gladstone did not know the man, and, once again, was technically qualifying someone in other ways eligible for the post. For almost all appointments there is some technicality to be fulfilled, and the form which is a formality to the patron is easily magnified, even when innocent, into a private deal by those who have other candidates for the position. In regard to his own exercise of patronage Gladstone once said that his family had " no special cause " to thank him. His second son, Stephen, was ordained in 1870 and became eventually rector of Hawarden. The parish was very large and the stipend proportional, nominally £3,153 a year. Appropriate as the appointment was, Gladstone once declared : " the living is not in the gift of the Crown. I did not present him to the living or recommend him to be presented." If the living was in the gift of the lord of the manor, and the manor in the family, what could be more traditional or more human than that the rector should be related to the squire ? Other things being equal, some advantage would be obvious, and in country parishes, as in country estates, family ties are to the good. His fourth son, the present Viscount, was his father's private secretary, later Financial Secretary to the War Office, and Home Secretary under his father. His eldest daughter married the headmaster of Wellington, his second surviving daughter Mr. Drew, who was later rector of Hawarden, and his youngest, unmarried, became Principal of Newnham. His third son entered business, went to India, and married the daughter of Lord Rendel. The eldest son, after representing two constituencies, withdrew altogether from political life.

It has been humorously suggested that Gladstone used his power of patronage rather to rid himself of nuisances than to elevate his private friends. Writing of Gladstone's irresistible tendency to reply to interrupters in the House, Henry Lucy recorded :

> This weakness, the more notable by reason of its contrast with the imperturbability of Mr. Disraeli, made the Parliamentary fortune of many men of varying ability. When Sir W. Harcourt and Sir H. James sat together below the gangway in

the Parliament of 1868, they . . . shrewdly recognised the path-
way to promotion.   In the same way, though not in similar
degree, Mr. Ashmead Bartlett and Mr. Warton profited by Mr.
Gladstone's inability to control himself when, seated on
either of the front benches, he followed the course of acrimoni-
ous debate.   Mr. Stanley Leighton, who at one time seemed
in the running, lost his prize only because he had not staying
power.   Mr. Warton, a vulgar boorish partisan, early discovered that he could " draw " Mr. Gladstone at pleasure. . . .
To call " Oh, oh " and " Ah, ah " . . . did not require much
mental activity or seem to command prodigious recompense.
Yet it led Mr. Warton into a comfortable salaried office in the
Antipodes.   Mr. Ashmead Bartlett did better still, a minor
place in the Ministry, crowned by a knighthood, rewarded his
patriotic endeavours.   Working in the same way, though on
a higher level, Lord Randolph Churchill, Sir Henry Wolf
and Sir John Gorst first brought themselves into notice.

It is also true that the Ministery was growing stale with
time, and Disraeli gave a vivid picture of its leaders and
their worries.   In a well-known speech he said :

> The stimulus is subsiding. The paroxysms ended in
> prostration.   Some took refuge in melancholy, and their
> eminent chief alternated between a menace and a sigh.   As
> I sat opposite the Treasury bench, the Ministers reminded me
> . . . of a range of exhausted volcanoes.   Not a flame flickers
> on a single pallid crest.   But the situation is still dangerous.

This was in April 1872.   There were squabbles
among some of Gladstone's colleagues, and, comparing
a pair of them to Moloch and Belial, he complained that
they would not co-operate in Pandemonium itself.   In
the Cabinet, as elsewhere, he combined extreme deference
of manner with tenacious advocacy of his own views.
His persuasiveness was more overwhelming than the
imperiousness of blunter men.   His absences were
grudged, and his relaxations suspected.   His colleagues
would not let him attend a funeral in Scotland on the
eve of the Franco-Prussian war, and he had to correct
the public rumour that he began every day with a reading

from Homer. With the end of his Ministry in sight, he thought once again of retiring, and found convenient precedents for so doing in the thin record of most premiers after sixty years of age. He told the Queen that he did not intend to go into Opposition, and that, if the Liberal party fell into fragments with the fall of the Government, it would be the end of his political life. A little later he declared that the opposition about him could only be neutralised by his perceiving " a special cause " to remain. He loved power, but power for a purpose. He felt lonely and useless without a crusade. To lead the Opposition, unless the end of the ruling Ministry was in sight through its indifference to some question that he himself perceived to be the issue of the morrow, was not enough for him. He was like a soldier who sells out of the army in time of peace, but is never happy unless rumours of war are in the air.

When the Irish helped to defeat the University Bill which had been intended to satisfy them, Gladstone resigned. Disraeli, however, was in no hurry to succeed, so the pangs of the expiring Ministry were further drawn out. There is a note of weariness in Gladstone's comment :

> The Conservative party will never assume its natural position until Disraeli retires; and I sometimes think he and I might with advantage pair off together.

This consolation was to be denied him, however. The bond of his party was frayed in many places ; there were irregularities at the Post Office, and when he took over the Chancellorship of the Exchequer in the reconstruction that ensued, the tiresome question was raised whether he had not thereby vacated his seat. A speech against disestablishment chilled the Nonconformists, and, recalling the part that their votes were to play later in his policy, it is interesting to read that already he

" shunned the idea of entering into conflict with them."
A Gladstonian sentence follows :

> A political severance, somewhat resembling in this a change
> of religion, should at most occur not more than once in life.

Gladstone was the muscular Christian of politics;
speech remained a " religious exercise " to him; and the
widest pulpit in his day was the House of Commons.
During the middle of the nineteenth century, indeed, we
witness what can only be called the apotheosis of Parliament. Did Gladstone's moral idiom, and political
appeals to righteousness, bring this about, or was he but
a sign of the times ? Parliament was one of several
institutions to share this mysterious idealisation. The
throne intoxicated Sir Theodore Martin; the British
Constitution filled men with uncritical awe. People
read debates in the columns of *The Times* with an
interest bordering on paralysis. They received these
institutions in the spirit that overcame Mrs. Pumble-
chook so that she could only murmur " O, thou ! "
when her future husband proposed. Dr. Arnold early
attracted respectful notice for his " manner of awful
reverence when speaking of God or of the Scriptures."
Yet it is odd, but true, that, in the beautiful words of the
Prayer Book, a lively faith does not march to such a tune,
nor can all the earnestness and achievements of these
men entirely quell the suspicions aroused by their in-
temperate expressions of piety. Probably no one has
ever loved Parliament so sincerely as Gladstone, and to
be there in relatively idle opposition, for issues cannot
be invented in a moment, was to be placed almost in the
position of a rector who is compelled to sit, as one of the
congregation, in the body of his own church. He dissolved on finance, but his promise to repeal the Income
Tax, if returned to power, looked too much like a
desperate device to prove convincing.

The Conservatives were returned by a majority of forty-eight, and the Irish Nationalists, numbering fifty-eight, now publicly emerged as Home Rulers, a new independent party with an organisation of their own. The Queen, for the second time, offered Gladstone a peerage. To his brother he wrote : removal from office will be a very great change, " for I do not intend to assume the general functions of leader of the Opposition, and my great ambition or design will be to spend the remainder of my days, if it please God, in tranquillity, and at any rate in freedom from political strife."

It was the absence of any motive for activity that galled this vigorous old gentleman of sixty-five. Political repose was a kind of death to him. The formula he found for himself was therefore this : " I deeply desired an interval between Parliament and the grave." Yet was it not still possible that something might happen in that interval ? He left a door open ; he " did not formally abdicate," lest a call should come to him to arrest " some great evil or to procure for the nation some great good." The bare stage, which was enough for Disraeli, was not enough for Gladstone if there was no crusading to be done. Moreover, according to his private secretary, Algernon West, a " dislike of daily confronting Mr. Disraeli " from the Opposition side was in itself enough to explain Gladstone's withdrawal. He once went so far as to " damn " Disraeli in the hearing of Mr. West himself.

IV

Parties, like governments, however, have to be carried on even in times of tranquillity, and Gladstone's decision to exist but not to lead was awkward for everyone but himself. It promised him freedom without party responsibility, and it placed any nominal successor on a

perch from which the first stir of returning enthusiasm
in the old man would instantly unseat him.   Even his
family, perhaps, found Gladstone's self-chosen inactivity
a little disappointing and perverse.   The family attitude
is hinted in his private correspondence with his wife :

> The anti-parliamentary reaction has been stronger with me
> even than I had anticipated.   I am as far as possible from
> feeling the want of the House of Commons.   I could cheerfully
> go there to do a work; but I hope and pray to be as little there
> as possible except for such an aim. . . . I am convinced that
> the welfare of mankind does not now depend on the State or
> the world of politics; the real battle is being fought in the
> world of thought, where a deadly attack is being made with
> great tenacity of purpose over a wide field, upon the greatest
> treasure of mankind, the belief in God and the Gospel of
> Christ.

Mrs. Gladstone, like most ardent and capable women,
did not welcome even a comparatively back seat.   To
leave Downing Street from time to time was unavoidable,
but to desert the scene, perhaps to deny oneself, quite
needlessly, the chance of returning when the country
came to its senses again, that surely was almost a
betrayal of trust.   She ventured to press the claims of
duty, to remind him how many hopes were centred in
his power for good.   It was not, of course, for her to
pretend to know best, but her anxiety that he should do
the right might excuse her bothering him.   He was
gentle but inexorable to her pressure :

> I am indeed sorry that you and I have not been able to take
> the same view of this important subject, but you know that I
> am acting on convictions very long entertained, and will, I am
> sure, believe that I have probed myself deeply, and used all the
> means in my power to get at a right conclusion.   Nay, I
> think that you will be more reconciled when I tell you that
> Granville did not really see his way either to a nominal leader-
> ship, or to making any arrangement by which I could, after a
> short time, with some certainty have escaped.

There were other domestic changes that could not be

agreeable in themselves. He sold the home in Carlton House Terrace where they had lived for twenty-eight years. He sold his Wedgwood and his collection of china. The move to 73 Harley Street must have seemed the abdication of ambition, and the plea of economy always is something of a pill.

> The truth (he wrote to his wife) is that innocently and from special causes we have on the whole been housed better than according to our circumstances. All along Carlton House Terrace I think you would not find anyone with less than £20,000 a year, and most of them with much more.

He looked round on the chance of finding other excuses for political inaction, and paid a visit to Sir Andrew Clark. The doctor's entirely encouraging report on his physical condition could not be gainsaid. There was no extenuation for him there. His health was alarmingly good, and his colleagues knew it. The volcano of his energies was very far from being extinct, and Lord Granville at least was not going to preside, in doubtful ease, upon its precarious crust. The real pill was for his political lieutenants. Was ever a man so embarrassing to his friends? When one was not amazed at the tasks he was attempting, one was harassed by uncertainty over the time and place of his return. The most neutral of the epithets that rained upon him, even from admirers, was incalculable. Who should bear the the burden of representing a Jack-in-the-box, temporarily indeed withdrawn from view but liable to pop up a disconcerting head without warning at almost any moment?

His colleagues protested that he was offering them an impossible position, and looked anxiously at one another, but for the post of Jonah there were no willing volunteers. To be condemned to be hanged is bad enough, but to be reprieved on the understanding that strangulation is postponed is almost worse. On the other hand, if Gladstone would neither lead nor abdicate some solid figure-head had to be found. After Lord Granville's refusal, the thankless office was pressed upon Lord Hartington, whose weighty qualifications were two-fold. Politically he would more than " do," and personally he was inert, a man, that is to say, who would naturally prefer to be eclipsed whenever a force and a moment appeared impetuous enough to supersede him. The backwaters suited his temperament, which had little stomach for navigating storms. Lord Hartington after-wards became famous for yawning in the middle of one of his own speeches, and his yawn no doubt lent weight to the gravity for which he was admired. He was not so obtuse as to miss the disabilities of his proposed position, and Gladstone had to plead and encourage before his lethargy was overcome. There were luckily certain arguments, plausible enough in the party's present plight, against Gladstone's leadership just now. If the county Liberals were dismayed at their chief's withdrawal, and if " sunshine had gone out of politics," as the phrase went, yet there were dissenting followers, and others who regarded Gladstone with the distrust which somewhere or other his personality invariably aroused. Therefore it became possible to say that another, a more stolid, leader would be an advantage, and for the present at least Gladstone promised not to interfere. Occasionally he would enter the House, remain for half an hour, say nothing, and then glide like a silent but ominous shadow out of doors. Disraeli was enjoying his innings; the Opposition was powerless, but the end was not yet. Gladstone's eye took in the situation, and then searched the horizon. He would be here when he was wanted, and he would wait. Those followers of his who had insulted and harassed him should learn in the wilderness of their own choosing to what they and the party were reduced when the chief to whom they owed their self-importance stepped apart.

V

Withdrawal meant no more than another field of activity. " There is much to be done with the pen." Had he not always turned to literature when nothing more like action was on hand ? To-day, in particular, he had a call to write. His projects he confided to his diary :

> There is much to be done with the pen, all bearing much on high and sacred ends, for even Homeric study, as I view it, is in this very sense of high importance; and what lies beyond this is concerned directly with the great subject of belief.

There was the Metaphysical Society to attend, a discussion to have with Huxley on the immortality of the soul. Debates on such questions as these were not, unfortunately, confined to serious thinkers. The heretical inferences drawn from Darwin's book were bad enough, but more popular and more disquieting were the doubts spread by Strauss's volumes, which did not spare the fact of the Resurrection itself. A challenge become so public required an equally public reply, so while Lord Hartington was stolidly leading the shrunken Liberals in the House of Commons, Gladstone emerged at Liverpool and created much excitement towards the end of 1872 by an address with Strauss's latest notions for his theme. From the seclusion of Hawarden he descried the " strange epidemic " that was spreading, and the " temple of peace " from which he emerged to combat its ravages became in turn a beacon of light and hope in the public eye. It was a comfort to many to know that the recluse from politics was living in no idle

retirement, but was aware of all that was passing in the outer world, and that in this time of doubt and question his intellect was grappling with the enemies of all that true Englishmen ought to hold dear. He was hale enough, they read in the papers, to continue to fell trees, and, if he worked at Greek mythology, the educated could remember that Homer was a subject for reverent study second only to the Bible itself.

Discussions of metaphysical or abstract questions were not, however, the natural pasture of his mind. It was the conduct based on them, or the practical questions that their adoption or rejection involved, that really roused his energies. A matter had to touch the world of immediate politics before it was properly within his grasp. His political sense was considerably more subtle than his intellectual acumen, and he was somewhat at a loss amid movements of opinion which left nothing immediate to be done. The Syllabus of the Principal Errors of our Age, issued by Pius IX in 1864, had, he noticed, challenged modern society in the entire range of its ideas. He had foreseen the Papal reaction that was preparing. The fate of the Papal States, which had been lost and won in 1850, made the Pope more determined to reassert his spiritual supremacy. Having already in 1854 promulgated by bull the dogma of the Immaculate Conception, the Pope now summoned an Œcumenical Council, which met at Rome at the end of 1869 to consider, and eventually to approve, the dogma of Papal Infallibility. Liberalism in the wide sense was being attacked anew, and surely this might raise questions of conscience among Roman Catholics in different countries, and in some emergency might even raise problems of statesmanship. In January 1870 Gladstone wrote:

> For the first time in my life I shall now be obliged to talk about popery; for it would be a scandal to call the religion they are manufacturing at Rome by the same name as that of

Pascal, or of Bossuet, or of Ganganelli. The truth is that Ultramontanism is an anti-social power, and never has it more undisguisedly assumed that character than in the Syllabus.

When the minority at Rome withdrew from the Vatican Council, and the definition of Infallibility was proclaimed by 533 to 2, Gladstone said that the fanaticism of the Middle Ages was more sober. As things fell, war between France and Prussia was declared the very day after the dogma of Infallibility had been promulgated, and the loss of the temporal power which it hastened was, to the Pope himself, an almost mortal blow. The Vatican decrees were not accepted by Dr. Döllinger, who was excommunicated, and, no doubt encouraged by a visit to him at Munich in 1874, Gladstone himself determined to write upon the question, though mainly confining himself to the political problem which, he thought, the Decrees might raise among English Romanists at home. The *Vatican Decrees in their bearing on Civil Allegiance : a Political Expostulation*, appeared in the autumn of 1874. Nearly 150,000 copies were sold, and replies were made, among others, by Newman. Gladstone told Lord Granville that his main idea was " to place impediments " in the way of the " party which means to have a war in Europe for the restoration of the temporal power." He also felt that " the high place assigned to liberty in the counsels of Providence " was endangered by the Decrees, and one cannot but wonder what would have happened to his faith had he previously become a Roman Catholic. Would he have joined the Old Catholics in the interests of liberalism ?

In 1873 a curious incident occurred. A movement was on foot to raise a public memorial to John Stuart Mill, whom Gladstone, from personal acquaintance, had once called " the saint of rationalism." Gladstone, invited to subscribe to this memorial, declined on the dubious ground that people could not agree whether Mill had

M

advocated birth control or not. The withdrawal of his name looked very much like condemnation, and, as Morley remarks, decided the question for the general public. Since Gladstone had grown accustomed to distinguish the character of men from their opinions, and since Mill's opinion on this matter was not clear, it was not very generous to refuse him the benefit of the doubt. Should this doubt have weighed in Gladstone's mind against the claims to public gratitude of the author of the essay on *Liberty*? His opinion on any topical question was of great influence in his day, which made the politician in him careful; and authors found that their fortunes were made if he could be induced to review their books favourably. Young writers of both sexes continually pestered him with requests. He replied to all gravely and often at length, even when he was not to be drawn by their productions. He must also have made the fortunes of many magazines when his essays did not run to complete pamphlets, and is said to have received larger fees than any other contributor. He took a certain interest in the earnings of his pen, and once noted with satisfaction that he had made £1,000 from his writings in the preceding twelve months. In 1874, when ritualism was beginning to disturb the public mind, he gave his views in one of these magazine articles.

The matter became political when Archbishop Tait introduced in this year his Public Worship Bill, and the Government of Disraeli offered facilities for putting down Mass in masquerade, as that arch-masquerader termed it. Gladstone returned to the House of Commons to oppose the Bill, and immediately dominated the scene. He defended the use of moderate ritual, and startled Sir William Harcourt by quoting the canonist Van Espen, and citing, later in the debate, Ayliffe's *Parergon Juris Canonici Anglicani*. In spite of his researches, the Bill was passed, to remain a dead letter. He answered his critics in another article entitled *Is the Church of England worth Preserving?* declaring that we must preserve it more by moral forces than by penalising measures. It was plain to any of his party that he could resume the leadership whenever he chose, and that whenever he should appear he would be personally irresistible.

None the less, even in 1868, Gladstone was far from being accepted as a full member of the family party of aristocratic big Whigs and big Tories who still regarded government as their inherited preserve. Their attitude of reluctant respect for his personal predominance is well preserved in a statement recorded by Sir Algernon West, who was Gladstone's private secretary from 1868 to 1872 : " If Mr. Gladstone thinks [a Whig magnate is quoted] that he can lead the House of Commons with the force of the millions without the goodwill of the ten thousand he will find his mistake." It is still the ten thousand, now of industrialists and financiers, who control Parliament to-day. From the same source we learn that Gladstone was regarded as an outsider, and, in the words of a Yorkshire squire, as " not having been bred in their kennel." West adds that Gladstone's famous Budget was said by an old Whig to be " Oxford on the surface and Liverpool below." The great Parliamentarian, in his virtues and weaknesses, was a typical middle-class product, and he seemed more because the magnates of commerce, whose social conscience was uneasy, and therefore open to suggestion, when they had any consciences at all, were invading the peerage and politics, and, as it happened, represented mentally upon the throne. Provided that Gladstone ran along accustomed paths, he was acceptable to the oligarchy, but they foresaw a time when his following in the country at large might lead him to make proposals that they would be determined to resist. It would then appear

what were the inevitable limits to be imposed on all
popular initiative. New cries were inevitable in party
politics from time to time, but there was an unwritten
understanding that the old order was not to be trifled
with at bottom. It might always become necessary to
remind Gladstone that "outsiders" were only privileged
so far. Such people, when successful, were liable to
swollen heads, and the curious fact remained that
physically Gladstone did require a larger hat every year,
and that its present size was bigger than any worn by
more than two established political leaders.

VI

If Gladstone had wished to forget his place and
stature in the public eye, he must have found it difficult,
even in moments of political retirement, from the daily
reminders that he received by post alone. Presents,
advice, applications for assistance, assurances of trust,
news that he was regarded as a saint by the family of his
correspondent, daily piled themselves upon his desk.
In his "temple of peace" they surrounded him.
Generous in money matters, he was a miser of his
papers. Each had to be answered, filed and docketed,
and stored away. Even so, it was possible that sufficient had not been preserved. Past activities were
open to misunderstanding, and what could be more
valuable than the record of the chief actor himself? He
therefore added to the papers which he stored minute
and elaborate memoranda of his own. With an egoism
disarming in its ingenuousness, he preserved, as far as
possible, a written record of every moment in his life.
Everything must be made as easy as possible for the
future biographer. The same record must extend to
everyone who came in contact with him. When his
baby girl died in 1850 at the age of four, his daughter

tells us that Gladstone " put on paper a record of her little life." When his sister, who had joined the Church of Rome, died at Cologne, he wrote a memorandum on the evidence he found of the ultimate state of her beliefs. Even half-sheets of blank note-paper must not be wasted; everything must be used and everything preserved. The acquisitive instinct, typical of the middle class, which leads some men to amass property, others to form collections of manuscripts, books or pictures, led Gladstone to accumulate papers concerning himself.

No doubt the itch for activity was responsible for a good deal of his own writing. It explains the answer which he dispatched to every letter, the postcards that he sent in numbers, the innumerable letters that he wrote to newspapers on every subject, from the value of egg-flip to important questions of the day. But it does not explain the value that he set upon preserving every record. He was perhaps one of those unfortunate creatures who are not naturally at home in the world, and increase with pathetic ardour every tie that binds their memory to it. " To live always on the brink of the grave and looking in " might, as he had once phrased it after attending a funeral, be his ideal of human duty, but resignation was easier if one left a record of endeavour nearly full. He had the evangelical's passion for funerals. They were the human ceremony that carried on human importance for a space beyond death, and added a new memory and a new tie to the survivors. A funeral gave even to the humblest some public importance, and the occasion itself could be recorded as a public event after the grave had closed. To preserve the memorials of life was something won from the dark enemy of mankind, and the fuller the record the greater chance there was for the ego to linger with posterity. Whatever duty or resignation might enforce him to respect, there can be no doubt that, to a man of Glad-

stone's immense vitality, the thought of death must have
been unusually depressing.   Taking himself with extreme
seriousness, desiring above all things to pursue some
high calling, and to make the loftiest principles apply to
every act of daily life, he was somewhere conscious of
an emptiness.   What was this mysterious void that the
utmost expenditure of energy could not remove?

Activity enabled one to forget while it lasted, but
however occupied the day, there was always some
pause, a pause like a precipice, when the inner void
reappeared.   No inner light, no interior assurance!   Of
that lack from the first he had complained, and not even
the invariable practice of attending church twice every
Sunday had supplied it.   There was more than this to
be done.   One could lead the responses; one could read
the lessons; one could thereby play an active part.   A
part?   Was it only a part, a visible rather than an
intimate self-offering?   Identification with the object of
worship was his desire, and this was mysteriously denied
to him.   In its absence, or incompleteness rather, one
could only fall back upon the support of one's fellows,
and receive from them the support withheld from on
high.   Perhaps such questionings themselves were sinful,
a sign of incomplete surrender of the human will.   One
could escape them only by renewed endeavour, by still
more strenuous activity, and so the old man returned to
his memoranda and his papers, to build with them a
buttress against the void yawning within.   Sometimes
he would look up, through the open window, or scan
his correspondence and the newspapers for the signs
of political change.   That fellow Disraeli would be sure
to make a moral blunder one of these days.

VII

In the absence of more promising questions, Gladstone
began to consider the subject of Future Retribution.
Morality was bound up with the prospect of a terrible
wrath to come, and surely the sceptics themselves must
be aware that the foundations of morality would be
sapped if this promise of retribution were neglected.
Did Disraeli believe in it ? One could be far from sure,
and England under his leadership would be likely to
commit or countenance some enormity. It was well to
keep an eye on foreign policy, for Disraeli was flirting
with the idea of Imperialism, and Imperialism always
meant making war upon some people " rightly struggling
to be free."

Once again victims of foreign oppression at last cried
out for succour, as the prisoners at Naples had done,
in a former interlude, when there was no Englishman to
heed their cry but he. This time it was in one of the
provinces of Turkey—Turkey ever countenanced by
Disraeli because she was more complacent than Russia
to the Jews. Pogroms are not a Mahommedan amusement. Moreover, now in 1876, Disraeli's Government
in due course was nearing its term, and public as well as
moral reasons must be found to prevent its re-election.
This Mahommedan Power had slipped out of the general
view since the Crimean War, when England and France
combined had secured to her twenty years of undisturbed
external freedom. The way that she had spent this
interval within her borders, her treatment of her
Christian subjects, was suddenly apparent to the world
when revolt occurred in Bosnia and Herzegovina. The
rising spread to Bulgaria, and was repressed, according
to a British agent on the spot, with a cruelty that
" stained the history of the century." The gravity and

horror were brought directly to the attention of the
Powers when the French and German Consuls at
Salonica were murdered by the Turkish rabble, and
Serbia and Montenegro took to arms. Eastern politics
were clearly once more a peril to Europe, and the tension
did not lessen when Russia, Austria and Germany
decided to impose reforms. The other Powers could not
be neglected, and England, France and Italy were
invited to support the plan. When Disraeli's Cabinet
refused, the Turks hoped that they might find in Great
Britain support, and perhaps arms, against Russia.

If his race led Disraeli to sympathise with the Turk
against Russia and her Jewish pogroms, Gladstone was
equally drawn to the country of Eastern Christianity.
He remembered our obligations to the subject races in
the East, as they might be inferred from the Treaty of
Paris. As a statesman he was concerned at our apparent
withdrawal from the Concert of Europe, and his compassionate nature was stirred by the reports of the
atrocities that had occurred. They had been, perhaps
were still being, inflicted too upon our fellow-Christians.
The moral case for protest was clearly very strong. Yet
for the moment Gladstone did not move. What was
Lord Hartington doing ? Would not that stolid figure
move when the moment, however delayed, was ripe ?
Mr. Forster, Gladstone noticed, was alive to the emergency. " I suffered others," he wrote in the retrospect,
" Forster in particular, to go far ahead of me." Meantime the British public listened to reports and to denials,
to accusations and to charges of exaggeration, with
British bewilderment. What was it that suddenly
decided Mr. Gladstone to be up and doing ? The
explanation he has left on record himself :

> I went into the country, and had mentally postponed all
> further action till the opening of the next session, when I
> learnt from the announcement of a popular meeting to be held

in Hyde Park that the question was alive.   So at once I wrote
and published on the Bulgarian case.   From that time onward
till the final consummation in 1879–80, I made the Eastern
Question the main business of my life.   I acted under a strong
sense of individual duty without a thought of leadership;
none the less it made me again leader whether I would or no.

The sincerity of this is unquestionable.   While Mr.
Forster was the first to move, it is Gladstone's movements that are remembered.   His sixth sense, as we have
called it, for a rising tide of feeling did not fail him.
His strong sense of individual duty was quickened to
strenuous enterprise by the popular excitement of others.
He learnt, from a popular meeting, that the question was
alive!   The born crusader's retreat was over.   An army
was offered to his leadership, and he was the only
politician who fully recognised the popular call.   His
instinct swept him forward.   The personal consequences
to himself, and to his party, were not to be weighed.
He was acting as a private individual.   If he became
more, it was because he was voicing the feelings of his
countrymen.   It was not his fault to be more energetic
than his colleagues.   Any ambition that he felt was but
to voice the wishes of the people.   Of the people, not
the classes, we may observe.

> The nation nobly responded to the call of justice, and
> recognised the brotherhood of man.   But it was the nation,
> not the classes.   When, at the close of the session of 1876,
> there was the usual dispersion in pursuit of recreation, I
> thought the occasion was bad.   It was good, for the nation
> did not disperse, and the human heart was still beating.   When
> the clubs refilled in October, the Turkish cause began again to
> make head.   Then came a chequered period, and I do not
> recollect to have received much assistance from the Front
> Bench.   Even Granville had been a little startled at my
> proceedings, and wished me to leave out the " bag and
> baggage " from my pamphlet.

This phrase, that the Turks should be made to clear
out of Europe, with their pashas and their muftis, bag

and baggage, is the single phrase that Gladstone contributed to everyday speech. Few men, writers or
speakers, contribute so much as one, but a single example
from Gladstone is niggardly compared to the extent, and
immediate effect, of his oratory. It happens, incidentally,
that Touchstone was the original coiner of it. Shakespeare makes him say : " Come, shepherd, let us make
an honourable retreat, though not with bag and baggage."
To have eclipsed Shakespeare in the popular authorship
of a phrase is more than has been accomplished hitherto
by Bacon himself. Disraeli, the dandy of words, who is
credited with several phrases, was very unhappy in his
attempts to pour ridicule upon Gladstone's efforts at this
time. The first reports of the atrocities, which he dismissed as coffee-house babble, were soon confirmed, and
made him look foolish as a Minister. His foreign policy
was destined to become, through Gladstone's efforts, the
issue of the next election, and Gladstone's extraordinary
tenacity never slackened for the four intervening years.
Before we follow them, let us recall that toward the end
of the session Disraeli left the Commons to take his seat
as Earl of Beaconsfield in the House of Lords. Gladstone wrote to the Duke of Argyll :

> Disraeli is not quite such a Turk as I thought. . . and his
> fleet is at Besika Bay, I feel pretty sure, to be ready to lay hold
> of Egypt as his share; so he may end as Duke of Memphis yet.

Two things were clear : Disraeli was become an
Imperialist, and neither Disraeli nor Imperialism had any
moral principles to recommend them. Both were showy
and selfish; both desired glittering earthly prizes for
themselves. The brink of the grave attracted them not.
Once convinced that the Eastern Question was
" alive " in the popular mind, Gladstone did not lose a
moment of the August holiday in preparing his account
of the atrocities and writing his indictment of the Govern-

ment's foreign policy. When Front Benchers were looking forward to the twelfth and the gun-rooms of the country houses were busy with insensitive sportsmen, he was to be found working away at his brief in the Reading Room of the British Museum, where he completed the draft that he had begun to compose while in bed. *The Bulgarian Horrors and the Question of the East* was issued without delay, and its effect reached even sportsmen at their shooting. Within three or four days of publication 40,000 copies were sold, and aroused enthusiastic indignation in many parts of the country. On September 9 there was an enormous demonstration at Blackheath, the first of many. It only remained for Gladstone to fan the congenial flames. He was again the hero of the crowd, which anxiously awaited him to appear in person on the platform.

In October he began to find an improvised platform wherever he was recognised in public. At Hawarden itself, where so many pilgrims came to hear him read the lessons that in time they threatened to oust the parishioners from the church, or in the park where he might be seen felling a tree and perchance a chip be borne away by the daring visitor, Gladstone was scarcely safe. In October he started to pay some country visits to " escape a little from the turmoil of our time."

The experiment proved a revelation.

> Through Cheshire and Lancashire (he wrote) we accomplished the first stage of our journey to Derby without any particular indication of public sentiment; and this rather encouraged our extending a little the circle of our visits, which I am now half-tempted to regret. For at every part I have had the greatest difficulty in maintaining any show of privacy, and avoiding stray manifestations. I never saw such keen exhibitions of the popular feeling, appearing so to pervade all ranks and places. A Tory county Member said to my wife two days ago, " if there were a dissolution now, I should not get a vote." This may be in some degree peculiar to the Northerners with their strong character and deep emotions.

That character was Gladstone's own, and the eager
crowds recognised their spokesman, the man who could
present public matters to them in their own way, with
solemn earnestness, moral appeal, and emotional fervour,
above all in a style approaching an eloquent sermon. To
them, as to his kindred, he was inevitably drawn. Disraeli's wit and sarcasm might be well enough at sophis-
ticated Westminster, where audiences met in the hope
of being amused over affairs, but half the country preferred edification to amusement, and did not like grave
public questions to be treated, still less to be dismissed,
in a flippant way. We have already heard the opinion
of the upper ten thousand upon him. Here is Gladstone's experience of them, as he put it in a letter to that
curious bird of passage, believed to be a private emissary
of the Tsar, Madame Novikoff :

> From this body (the upper ten thousand) there has never
> on any occasion within my memory proceeded the impulse
> that has prompted, and finally achieved, any of the great
> measures which in the last half-century have contributed so
> much to the fame and happiness of England.

Lord Hartington might be as English as an oak, and as
steady as the bench on which he sank, but neither he nor
Lord Granville had ever initiated anything : favourable
specimens these, and trustworthy, of course, but not
inspiring. To be dull and reliable at the same time is the
English taste in public men. If Gladstone was too vital
to be dull, he was too imposing to be lively. He was
the epitome of all that was serious in the middle class.
The combination of their attitude with his physical
qualities was irresistible.

Towards the end of October he returned to Hawarden,
where Tennyson soon joined him. The poet read
Harold, which occupied over two hours. They discussed
theology, but on the important question of retribution the
poet did not display much " spontaneous thought."

Gladstone then turned again to the Eastern Question in a further pamphlet. He expected some reply from Disraeli, and at the Lord Mayor's banquet it was made. In some generalised remarks the Prime Minister " uttered a hardly veiled threat to Russia," which Gladstone explained by his " Judaic feeling, in which he is both consistent and conscientious." This threat was not allowed to pass without protest, and a meeting of all the eminent was called at St. James's Hall to make any declaration of war impossible. Gladstone, of course, attended, and must have recorded the impression of his hearers when he described the demonstration as " great, noble, and almost historical." His qualification would out even here! Soon afterwards the Foreign Office proposed a Conference at Constantinople, but it broke up with the refusal of the Turks to the demands.

Clearly the agitation must be kept alive, for Disraeli's Government had no real heart in the business. How could they, if they had no moral principles themselves ? Gladstone therefore produced yet another pamphlet under the title of *Lessons in Massacre*, but the sale was disappointing, not more than seven thousand. Plainly his efforts were indispensable, but it was possible that he had accomplished enough, if far from all that he had hoped. He could say that the Concert had been restored, and, having been roused so far, the Government could hardly go back. How Gladstone appeared to the more educated of his admirers is revealed in a passage that Morley quotes from the letters of J. R. Green :

> The aspirations of nationalities after freedom and independence *are* real political forces ; and it is just because Gladstone owns them as forces, and Disraeli disowns them, that the one has been on the right side and the other in the wrong in parallel questions such as the upbuilding of Germany or Italy. I think it will be so in this upbuilding of the Sclav.

The delighted historian met his hero, and found " a modesty that touched us more than all his power." He met Darwin and Huxley in the autumn, and their comments have survived. Darwin found it wonderful that so great a man should visit him. Huxley said that " if you put Gladstone in the middle of a moor, with nothing in the world but his shirt, you could not prevent him from becoming anything he liked." So far, he had shaken the Government's popularity, and forced their foreign policy into the public gaze. Thus ended the first round after his partial return to politics.

VIII

When Russia declared war on Turkey in the spring of 1877, it was evident that any pretence of official indifference was at an end. Excitement at last invaded Westminster; the question was alive, even there. Lord Hartington's strength could be no longer to sit still. Those who wished to do so and those who did not threatened to split the Liberal Party between them. Such a split had been not improbable from the first. That at least could not be called Gladstone's doing, but he increased embarrassment in his party by giving notice of resolutions without delay. The letters of approval that he received were not arriving from politicians. He felt his political loneliness, but he would not fail the populace without. Three days after war was declared, that is to say, on April 27th, Gladstone's mind was made up :

> This day I took my decision, a severe one, in face of my not having a single approver in the upper official circle. But had I in the first days of September asked the same body whether I ought to write my pamphlet, I believe the unanimous answer would have been No.

In a House both impatient and hostile, for there were several preliminary skirmishes, he rose at length, and his diary is terser than usual :

> For over two hours I was assaulted from every quarter except the Opposition bench, which was virtually silent. Such a sense of solitary struggle I never remember.   At last I rose on the main question nearly in despair as to the result, but resolved not to fail through want of effort.   I spoke two and a half hours, voice lasting well.   House subsequently came round, and at last was more than good.

Lord Balfour has called this speech unequalled in parliamentary courage, skill, endurance and eloquence, and another listener declared that at its close Gladstone looked like " an inspired man."   One of the most admired passages ran as follows :

> There is now before the world a glorious prize.   A portion of those unhappy people are still as yet making an effort to retrieve what they have lost so long but have not ceased to love and desire.   I speak of those in Bosnia and Herzegovina. Another portion—a band of heroes such as the world has rarely seen—stand on the rocks of Montenegro, and are ready now, as they have ever been during the four hundred years of their exile from their fertile plains, to sweep down from their fastnesses and meet the Turks at any odds for the re-establishment of justice and of peace in those countries. . . . It is not yet too late, I say, to become competitors for that prize; but be assured that whether you mean to claim for yourselves even a single leaf in that immortal chaplet of renown; which will be the reward of true labour in that cause; or whether you turn your backs upon your duty, I believe, for one, that the knell of Turkish tyranny in these provinces has sounded.

Look for a moment at the last sentence.   It is seven lines long, and if one reads it sympathetically, one can hear the orator pausing to take breath.   Put yourself beside him in imagination, and you will understand that, to those of his listeners critical enough to study the speaker's technique, one of the pleasures of listening to

Gladstone was to observe the resolution of sentences filled with relative clauses and alternative propositions such as these. By this time, with his long practice, the coils seemed to unravel themselves of their own volition, and the anticipated knot never occurred. Behind it all was the force of a man simple-minded enough to believe the truth of what he said, and that is necessarily a rare simplicity in the House of Commons. On this occasion, in a full House, Gladstone's resolutions were defeated by no more than 131. The second round was finished, but the forces of time, on which he generally relied, were marshalling under his direction, if he could prevent them from dispersing before the next election arrived.

Beaten in Parliament, therefore, Gladstone returned to the platform to hold the Government up to odium in the provinces. It was never very difficult to coax him to speak, and the pilgrims now flocking to Hawarden would sometimes bring an axe with them. The old gentleman in his shirt-sleeves in the park could not accept the present without a few words of thanks in return. If so, the burning theme would issue, even in a few words, with the result that more pilgrims were encouraged in the hope of further speeches. His enthusiasm, at first infectious, began to take even his admirers' breath away. The pilgrims and their reception became a regular chronicle in the newspapers. A new spectacle was added to English life, and, like most spectacles of the kind, it threatened to become a bore to cooler people. Was the man's whole existence, they asked, to be lived in a blaze of publicity? Could he not even go to church without attracting a crowd? Was his reading of the lessons to become one of the sights of England? As a hostile politician put it:

There appear continually in the newspapers announcements with which the public have been for years familiar, to the effect that Mr. Gladstone went to "early morning communion," that he "read the lessons" in a clear (or husky) voice, and that he made a point of walking to the church through the snow or rain.

After the felling of a tree, says the same writer, "chips were sometimes served round by Mr. Herbert Gladstone." It was certainly an extraordinary atmosphere, more congenial to American notions than to ours. Reuter must have retained a correspondent at Hawarden, if Mr. Gladstone's private devotions were "news items" of public interest. If not, how did they reach the newspapers? If it is not suggested that Gladstone sent them himself, it is also not suggested that he discouraged them. There are characters which thrive on boundless exhibition; not deep, not reflective, naturally ambitious, and not always without a sense of humour : actors and actresses, popular preachers, dandies like Disraeli, wits like Wilde. All these enjoy the display of their persons, the gaze of the multitude, the paragraph in print. The exhibitionist is of many kinds. From the physically indecent to the egotistically vain, they take pleasure in making a spectacle of themselves. The latter, whose emotions may lead him to confess his sins at revival meetings, or to publish his doubts or scruples to the world, often takes himself extremely seriously, and believes in lofty reasons for his acts. He may set up as an example or a warning. He may need the countenance of others to maintain belief in himself : his sincerest moments, his very inner life, may only be lived upon the platform. What privacy and "recollection" are to others, publicity may give to him. With the obvious exception of the man who is locked up, most of these elements contributed to Gladstone's ardent character.

The less inner light a vital being has, the more necessary will the countenance of outer illumination be to him. If he is a simple-minded person as well, it will hardly occur to him that his behaviour seems incongruous

N

to other people. He will argue, with pained surprise, that his is a good example, that the possibility of a crowd of strangers does not free a man from the duty of going to church; and when you tell him that the example can not be separated from its surroundings, that literal rightness is never the criterion of good taste, he will be puzzled, for his instinct is for public prayers, even if confined to the family prayers in his own dining-room. His belief in communal activity is as far as he can reach by experience towards the Communion of Saints. Yet those whom we think of as having attained to that mystery have been the solitaries of religion, and the lonely voices of poetry. That Gladstone was never for a moment idle shows that the communion of contemplation was not possible for him. He was busy like Martha, and like Martha much troubled whenever he had to sit still. The bounds to his spiritual perception were as rigid as his energies were full. The energies provided a public spectacle. The limits prevented him from seeing that he was beginning to appear absurd. Had there been no display of public impatience, Gladstone would not have been aware of anything excessive in all this.

After a sea-trip in one of Sir Donald Currie's steamers from London to Dartmouth in July, and an Irish visit strictly confined to the Pale in October, he experienced the fickleness of popularity. In January 1878 the Russians reached the Sea of Marmora, entered Adrianople, and created nervous excitement in England. As the British fleet passed the Dardanelles, jingoism raised its ugly head, and the apostle of a righteous foreign policy became vulgarly transformed into an unpopular pacifist. An excited crowd made its way into Harley Street, broke windows, and was only dispersed with the aid of two lines of mounted police. Gladstone remained unmoved in his opposition to a war. On the brink of hostilities, the fleet was halted, and a truce was granted at Adrianople which led to the Treaty of San Stefano. Turkey recognised the independence of Montenegro, Serbia and Roumania, and Bulgaria became a tributary Principality with a national militia and a Christian government. The European interests involved in these and other changes, notably the plan whereby Russia received Bessarabia in exchange, were admittedly to be settled by a European Conference, which met at Berlin, from which Disraeli returned bringing " peace with honour." He did not accomplish this until he had called out the reserves, brought troops from India, and, by one of many arrangements, had taken over the island of Cyprus on the understanding that we would protect Turkey from Russian aggression in Asia. So far as Turkey in Europe was concerned, she had virtually been made to quit it " bag and baggage " after all.

Gladstone did not at all approve of the tortuous arrangements by which this had been brought about, and regarded our acquisition of Cyprus as the real object of the negotiations : a sop to Imperialist opinion, he might have said, not differing much, in appearance, from the sop of the abolished income tax which he had offered to the electors on the eve of his party's defeat. We undertook, he said, vast and indeterminate obligations to Turkey in return for a territorial bribe, and the whole thing was damaging to our reputation for justice in Europe. The arrangement was an " insane convention," bad in itself and in morality, a criticism which led Disraeli to refer to " a sophistical rhetorician, inebriated with the exuberance of his own verbosity." In the popular mind Cyprus wiped away the " humiliation " of Geneva, and an island in the hand was worth any peaceful arbitration. As soon as the House rose, Gladstone wrote on *England's Mission*, and on other

more or less kindred themes.   Such papers and addresses
fill the *Gleanings from Past Years*, which he first now collected from periodicals.   His autumn was comparatively
studious.   He worked at his *Homeric Primer ;* he started
to rearrange his books, and found seven hundred volumes
of poetry among them.

> [He] read *Maud* once more, and aided by Doyle's criticism
> wrote my note of apology and partial retractation.   The fact
> is that I am wanting in that higher poetical sense which
> distinguishes the true artist.

The first and favourite of Millais' three portraits of
Gladstone was painted during the summer of 1879, and
Gladstone left a note upon it :

> It was at his own suggestion, and for his own account, that
> he undertook to paint me, while I rather undertook to dissuade
> him from wasting his labour in an unpromising subject.

Convention demands that no Englishman should seem
anxious to have his portrait painted, yet few gifts are
more popular than a presentation portrait.   No man
can profess to judge whether or no his face is promising
artistically, and there is no disgrace to feel curious about
the obvious feature that we never see.   Gladstone was
conventional in assuming reluctance, and equally conventional in sitting after all.   If the second part of the
convention is human and natural, the first part is deemed
meritorious.   In whatever age convention was nearer
to human feeling Gladstone would have appeared more
sympathetic than in his day.   It is when he is least decorous,
in his sudden enthusiasms, his ardent oratory, his willing-
ness to be human with the outcasts of the street, the
egoism that leavened his display of recreation and
devotion, that he becomes most nearly a man among
men.   In many respects he was an animated mask, a
man who wished, without question, to be the embodiment of everything considered correct.   Luckily he was

too explosive a creature to become entirely what he desired, and the explosiveness that disconcerted his contemporaries, not the formality in which this was disguised, is the vital quality in his character. Nothing so ardent has ever been subdued to such a generalised shape, and how the new wine contrived to lie contented in the old bottle is the paradox of his queer personality.

His political view of his own nature, and his opinion of the state of affairs at Westminster, are contained in two comments that he made at the time. When Ruskin visited Hawarden in the autumn of 1878, Gladstone denied that he was " a leveller," and declared : " I am a firm believer in the aristocratic principle—the rule of the best. I am an out-and-out inequalitarian," a statement which made Ruskin laugh. Yet, if the best be procurable under a system of universal suffrage, Gladstone was right about himself; and who doubted the sufficiency of the system since John Stuart Mill had expressly stated, in his famous essay on the subject, that " from accumulated considerations . . . it follows that the ideal type of a perfect government must be representative." After studying the syllogism that led up to this conclusion, there was plainly nothing more to be said. Representative government implied representative institutions, and the time had hardly arrived to inquire whether in huge constituencies, electing by bare majorities, the representative machinery does not defeat itself. We now know that the larger the community and the wider the electorate, of less use is a vote to anyone. Men gave the vote to women after they had proved it valueless to themselves. The advocates of proportional representation or the second ballot will probably be indulged eventually, but it still remains doubtful whether any system of voting can be devised really representative of large communities, or with more than nominal value as an index of popular consent. How far, in the autumn of 1878, this consent was still with Disraeli became uncertain to the wary watcher in Wales. Madame Novikoff received a letter which revealed Gladstone's preoccupation with the morrow :

> My opinion is that this Government is hastening to its doom. . . . It is not to be desired that this take place at once. The people want a little more experience of Beaconsfield toryism.

IX

Five years had gone by, and the approach of the elections was foreshadowed in an invitation which Gladstone received to stand for Midlothian, the metropolitan county of Scotland. It was a timely call, for he had already decided not to offer himself to his constituents at Greenwich again. By this time publicity had attended him so long that his halo threatened to become a ring about his neck. If he could not go to church as a private citizen, or walk unobserved in his own park, any public decision of his became a matter for inflated discussion. To accept the invitation from Midlothian was, therefore, received by opponents as " a monstrous piece of vanity," and by his admirers as the timely return of the hero to his native heath. What message should he bring upon his lips? To pulverise the Government was not enough. Some glimpse must be added of a Liberal promised land.

The wily old politician was in no doubt what tactics to pursue, or how the enemy would attempt to evade his condemnation : as he wrote to Lord Granville :

> For several reasons I should believe that they intend sailing on the quiet tack. Having proved their spirit, they will now prove their moderation. In other words, they want all the past proceedings to be in the main " stale fish " at the elections. Except financial shuffling they will very likely

commit no new enormity before the election. In my view
that means that they will not supply any new matter of such
severe condemnation as what they have already furnished.
Therefore my idea is that we should keep the old alive and
warm.

He would forget nothing; the whole displeasing
record was itching at his fingers' ends. After five years,
discontent and blunders there were bound to be, and he
would remind the public of the excellent reasons they
had for their vague petulance. With this invigorating
object he left Liverpool on November 24, 1879, accompanied by his wife and daughter. If the attention that
he had aroused from the beacon light of Hawarden had
been misinterpreted, the enormous effect of his personality should now be put in train. The numbers that
had flocked to collect chips from his axe, and to hear
him at the lectern, argued that he would be waylaid as
soon as he emerged to public view. If this prospect
could not be hidden from his mind, even he must have
been startled by its inadequacy. Hardly had he left his
home when, in his own words, a triumphal procession
began. The country was amazed at a spectacle such as
England had never seen before. Not a monarch, not a
preacher, not a heroine, not a saint, had evoked anything
resembling Gladstone's popular reception.

Meanwhile another pilgrim, Charles Stewart Parnell,
who had been elected Member for Meath in 1876 and
had sat for two years a silent observer of parliamentary
procedure, was on his way to America, where his task
was as difficult and his reception by the Clan-na-Gael
as dubious as Gladstone's was secure. Yet in two
months he had achieved his object, and, hating the public
platform and the making of speeches, Parnell visited a
city a day, was invited to address Congress and reported
that "the enthusiasm increases . . . military guards and
salvoes of artillery salute our coming." The man who

said " I hate public assemblies, I dislike crowds," was preparing to meet the happy pilgrim through Midlothian. The astonishing diary of the latter is what we have to follow here. If one factor can be distinguished from another in the whole pageant, then the memory of Gladstone's own speeches is less remarkable than the enthusiasm which his presence aroused.

When the train paused at Carlisle, public addresses were presented, and the pilgrim made his first speech. Another opportunity occurred at Hawick, and a third at Galashiels. To the crowd that had collected, sometimes after long journeys on foot from remote hamlets and distant towns, he began to state his case against Disraeli's Government. They must not suppose that he was moved to this indictment by a measure or two, however open to objection; it was a system of unrighteous government that the election would sustain or condemn. To himself it did not occur that the natural person to raise the issue would be the leader of the Liberal party, which he still refused to be officially. In his own mysterious eye he was but an individual who, having recognised the popular feeling against the Bulgarian atrocities, was now continuing the protest against a government whose indifference to them had corresponded with an unrighteous foreign policy in Egypt, Afghanistan and South Africa. No wonder politicians, even among Liberal ranks, were exasperated at his spectacular proceedings. Here was a venerable man who would not lead his party, but was quite willing to make leadership impossible for anyone else; an incalculable fountain of activity owing no allegiance beyond the capricious enthusiasm of his own mind. Whatever his motive might be, no sooner did he start on one of his progresses than Parliament was eclipsed; and the centre of debate upon public affairs was transferred to railway stations and public halls, where the enthusiasm was the more dangerous because it could lead to nothing but the embarrassment of the elected representatives of the nation. Whatever else this extraordinary being might accomplish, his personal ascendancy grew from day to day.

The three speeches that he had delivered during his journey of nine hours to Edinburgh were but the prelude to the demonstration that greeted him at night. The impressive space of Princes Street was crammed with a vast multitude, recruited then or during the ensuing fortnight by pilgrims from the Hebrides and the loneliest corners of Scotland. It seemed as if a displacement of population were taking place, and that Dalmeny, where he lodged, was become the Mecca of multitudes. At the end of his journey, unaffected by fatigue, he wrote in his diary : " I have never gone through a more extra-ordinary day."

He had been seen but not heard by this throng, and it was chiefly to hear him that they had journeyed. The question then arose, what hall was vast enough to accommodate a city ? and it proved unanswerable. A building designed to hold six thousand received forty thousand applications for admission. All that could be done was for Mr. Gladstone to speak in as many places as possible, with intervals only for his conveyance and for meals. The energy that he retained on the eve of his seventieth birthday proved equal to this task, and his voice was no less reliable. Indeed an irreverent person declared that its endurance was " a danger to the commonwealth." The record of a single day must suffice to indicate his occupations. On December 5th he began with a breakfast party. After this he retired to make notes for the inaugural Address which, as Lord Rector of Glasgow University, he was to deliver at midday. At the ensuing luncheon he spoke again, and the function lasted till four. Before six he reappeared and made a political speech to six thousand. The speech lasted for an hour and a half. This done, he went off to dine before arriving at the City Hall, where an immense audience was assembled to hear him. He calls this, however, " an overpowering day." The students he delighted with an academic discourse, the merchants in the Corn Exchange with " formidable statistics," the mass of his hearers with a political exhortation, to which an added piquancy was given by thrusts at a well-known antagonist easily recognised but scarcely named.

Only one of these speeches is now resurrected, that delivered at Edinburgh the day after he had set forth, at the opening of the Midlothian campaign. To say that it does not survive the test of reading is, with an important qualification, to admit the quality of his homilies. To his presence, his voice, his transparent fervour, he now added the impressiveness of age, of years too passed almost uninterruptedly under the eyes of his fellow-countrymen. They came desiring to be impressed, and Gladstone represented to them everything that was impressive : his mien, his manner, his sentiments, his experience, his position, his vocation for public affairs, his education, his wealth. His personal power of emphasising all this by his beautiful voice and personal vigour was an entrancing spectacle which made no unexpected demand upon his hearers, but was rather an idealised image of themselves. There was no reason, in the nature of things, save that he was pre-eminent in qualities common to the whole middle class, why each man among them should not achieve similar eminence. The bare sight of him was a flattery to his audience, for he was the realisation of all that they held in esteem, the living proof that their ideal was not only majestic but obtainable. Whose sentiments were more lofty, whose career more successful, whose capacity better proved, whose fame, even beyond our shores, more undeniable ?

Beside being an effective statesman, he was understood to be a man of thought also, and his thoughts and feelings and prejudices conflicted at no vital point with theirs. Such advantages as he had had in youth were not those of a privileged class as privilege had been understood hitherto. If he had enjoyed the best education, he had made the most of it, and had won the highest honours at the University. Since he became a man he had made his own way. That was a fact which they richly appreciated. It kept him, even when he had become their Prime Minister, one of themselves, and their world was one in which a man who did not make his own way was punished by failure, perhaps by the workhouse. Commercial competition knows no mercy. It was a strife in which self-reliance and industry were the only ultimate securities in the welter of effort, which balanced the gross gains of success by the chance of bankruptcy.

The attitude to life that this social confusion engendered had already produced, if late in the day, its written gospel a quarter of a century before. Then another north countryman, Samuel Smiles, had published his *Self-Help*, a book more successful even than George Eliot's novels. It thus became the first of a series of evangels on Character, Thrift, Duty, and the lives of eminent industrialists in whom these virtues were to be found. The Gladstones had been magnates of Liverpool, and had produced a son who brought these desirable qualities into the exalted field of politics. Now this industrial world was still so new to human experience that it had no intellectual or humane traditions either in theory or in civic life. It was, and remains, to put it mildly, an entirely secular existence. All energy was absorbed in the struggle for material success, and such emotional needs as were left unexhausted turned for satisfaction to civic banquets, chapel or church. The latter alone had survived from the humaner society that had perished. They were, however, like an organism which has lost the use of its limbs. The industrial world acknowledged on Sundays, at places of worship, the graces that attend a more abundant life than it lived during the rest of the week; but the contradiction between the moral theory and the moral practice was a fact, and a fact, to those who paused to remark it, that seemed inevitable, and even salutary, to the successful. The effect of this contradiction paralysed such reflective power as remained unabsorbed by business in Gladstone's hearers. Their critical faculty was blunted by it. Facts stared them in the face, and the facts were overwhelming. Consequently ideas dwindled to the pale reflections of themselves in such copy-book maxims or sentiments from hymns as might not irk the active life, in competition with one's fellows, which was the imperious reality of existence. Self-help, character, duty, the whole activity of conduct, at last was coming to monopolise their limited capacity for reflection, criticism, thought.

All these ideals Gladstone accepted and exemplified. Religion had shrunk for many to expression of faith in a Book, a Book about which active inquiry was unseemly; and more than respectful attention to it when read aloud by an appointed person at an appointed time was in doubtful taste. With this for their intellectual background, his public audiences met to hear Gladstone, assured of the fare that he would offer them, and they were never disappointed. Public affairs, the public platform, when such a man was the speaker, had all the dignity of a pulpit with the added interest of a sermon on affairs. Politics, being the most exalted form of public struggle, was the revered sphere of conduct in the minds of men for whom struggle was the necessity and fulfilment of life. To be pre-eminent in this was to become their hero, their own hero in a sense which an aristocratic Prime Minister, for all his wonder, could never be. In other words, the eloquence of Gladstone could hardly have enthralled vast audiences so completely if its substance had been capable of surviving. A critical or original strain in it would have disturbed their attention. This desired to be soothed by the superlative echo of itself. He was the greatest common measure of their intelligence, and the highest multiple of their vitality. A style less impersonal than his own would have been as disturbing as an individual note in a leading article. The editorial " we " flatters the newspaper-reader, because he is exalted by a plural which is the imaginary multiplication of a narrow self. If we care to consider Gladstone's writings, we shall find that, from his earliest days, and before he became a practised orator, the plural style and the literal sentiment were instinctively his. He remains a dull orator on paper, because the wonderful voice, and its topical message, were, from the beginning, the superlative echo of the crowd. Apart from his voice, the individuality of his speeches resided in the unique power of a single man to embrace and give back of his own volition the sentiments and energies of a multitude. The generalisation was consummated in an individual. The rule thus issued with the wonder of a perfect representation, and, the voice apart, nothing but his representativeness is astonishing in his words. Gladstone was an extraordinary being because he was the consummate expression of his type and age. A living Average Man would be inconceivable, as an entity, were it not the prodigy of Gladstone to have made the abstraction a single and expansive fact.

A being so vital but so generalised carried all before him through his overwhelming fortnight in Midlothian, which ended, literally for once, in a regal departure from Glasgow. This was on December 8, 1879, and three

weeks later, on the evening before his birthday, he looks
back on his career :

> And now I am writing in the last minutes of the seventh
> decade of my life. This closing is a great event. . . . For
> the last three and a half years I have been passing thro' a
> political experience which is, I believe, without example in
> Parliamentary history. I profess to believe it has been an
> occasion when the battle to be fought was a battle of justice,
> honour, freedom, law, all in their first elements from the very
> root, and all on a gigantic scale. The word spoken was a
> word for millions, and for millions who themselves cannot
> speak. If I really believe in this, then I should regard my
> having been morally forced into this work as a great and high
> election of God. And certainly I cannot but believe that He
> has given me special gifts of strength on the late occasion,
> especially in Scotland. Three things I would ask of God over
> and above all the bounty which surrounds me.
>
> This first, that I may escape into retirement.
>
> This second, that I may speedily be enabled to divest myself
> of everything resembling wealth.
>
> And the third—if I may—that when God calls me He may
> call me speedily. To die in church appears to be a great
> euthanasia, but not at a time to disturb the worshippers.

He goes on, " such are some of an old man's thoughts,
in whom there is still something that consents not to be
old." How touchingly sincere he was ! How very
little he understood himself ! But how poor too would
be an interpretation that sees no more than the irony of
the contrast. If this page from the diary of his age be
compared with the enormous letter that he wrote to
his father from Oxford, the letter in which he pleaded
to be allowed to answer the call of the Church and be
ordained, we observe a remarkable similarity. The old
man, for all his experience and intense desire to see
aright, knows himself no better than before. There is
the same excellent intention, the same ardour, the same
egoism, the same humble-mindedness, the same curious
ignorance of himself; for death as in life the same desire
for a public connection with the Church. To die in

church is a public act, even if one dies in an interval
between the services, and to die there is an euthanasia,
because one dies in a sacred building with, therefore,
such exterior support as the surroundings of an official
institution may afford.   Almost everyone desires to die
at home; but was not an august public building the
spiritual home of him who had confessed on the verge of
manhood that, in himself, he was " utterly blind " ?
The wish that he might " escape into retirement " is a
curious wish to crown the end of a triumphal campaign
for turning the existing Government out of office.   But
he had a departmental mind ; each of his moods absorbed
him severally.   If the promise of Midlothian were fulfilled,
it would force, by his efforts of yesterday, the political
leadership upon himself.   The wish that he be " speedily
enabled to divest himself of everything resembling
worldly wealth," understandable in so far that he had
already made over Hawarden Castle to his son subject to
his wife's occupation during life, is a way of verbally
reconciling the Christian monastic ideal with the use
and enjoyment of a background necessary to the public
work that called him.   It is possible enough that he had
no passion for accumulating other property except
papers referring to himself, yet he could not be both
poor and political.   He did not die a poor man.   These
papers themselves were so multitudinous that in the
very year beginning after the above words were written,
he added to Hawarden a special fire-proof, octagon room
to lodge them in permanent safety.

This was the celebrated Octagon, built at the north-
west corner of his " temple of peace."   He estimated,
Morley tells us, the " selected letters " addressed to himself at 60,000, and, his official biographer goes on, " the
rest, with his copies of his own to other people, run to
several tens of thousands more."   Poor Morley's comment was : " probably no single human being ever

received 60,000 letters worth keeping, and of these it is
safe to say that three-quarters of them might as well have
been destroyed as soon as read, including a certain
portion that might just as well have been neither written
nor read." Besides this accumulated correspondence
there were Gladstone's own innumerable and lengthy
memoranda, covering the smallest as the major doings
of his and his family's life. Morley estimates that a
quarter of a million papers passed his hands, a mass
almost impossible for one biographer to have digested.
Now this was the species of property that Gladstone
particularly prized, and it did not occur to him that the
vanity of human possessions is nowhere more ostensible.
It was indeed that vanity, using the word in its various
shades of meaning, for which he prized them : they
were the most personal, and the most public, property
he possessed. The vaster the surviving evidence of his
activity, the greater the hope of filling the void round
which his ego revolved. His copious flow of act and
word resembled a whirlpool in which the greater the flow
of water the hollower is the centre of its circle. That
inner void which distinguished him from his fellows he
was desperately anxious to fill, but by the very law of
its nature the more energy a whirlpool expends the more
rounded is its inner emptiness. The insufficiency of good
works and of activity to satisfy the soul which is not
content with natural existence, is exquisitely indicated
by Gladstone's character. The more he did, the less
satisfied he was, and he had not Florence Nightingale's
occasional glimpses of the richness of passivity and contemplation. In the theological classification, where a
mine of psychological truths is to be found, Gladstone
was neither a once- nor twice-born man. He was
spiritually a perhapser. To borrow an admirable paradox, he was "an egoist without an ego." He resembled
a circle of immense activity without a centre. The more

he strained to discover that centre, for a vacancy is contrary to nature, the wider his circumference grew. He was a centrifugal force passionately desirous of reversing a tendency the true direction of which he felt but never understood. This was the pathos of his position, that he was drawn to dominate others because he could not fill his inner self. The more he tried to serve them, the greater his predominance became, and without belittling his achievements it is nevertheless true that he accomplished nothing comparable for human wonder to the pinnacle that he personally reached. At one moment he thought that God had blessed his efforts, at another he was amazed by his prestige. The certainty that he could not find was the peace of knowing God to be within him. The desire, but not the Comforter, was in his heart.

X

On his return from Midlothian, however, he was not given much time for reflection, but was soon writing to his son :

> They are beginning to ask *who* is to succeed if Beaconsfield is displaced. Voices are coming up here and there, some of them very confident, that the people will call for me. Nothing, however, but a very general and nearly unanimous call from the Liberals, with the approbation of a sort of national will, could bring this demand to a form in which it could or ought to be obeyed. The reasons against my coming forward are of immense force; those against my indicating any shadow of desire or willingness to come forward are conclusive.

While he must have known himself the indispensable alternative to Disraeli, he had admitted when he went into " retirement " that he had not an easy course to steer. At the same time he was anxious to be completely fair to Hartington and to Granville. The real embarrassment remained with them. He left on careful

o

record his determination to respect their nominal leadership of the party. Would the rank and file and the populace insist on Gladstone's return to power? The answer seemed obvious, but Granville and Hartington were to be the judges. It would be easy here again to argue that Gladstone had, from whatever motives or none, manœuvred them into a position which gave the predominance to himself. His verbal respect was perfect, but what had his activities been? His private conduct here resembled the qualifications that accompanied his statements; his activities the statements themselves. To those who would justify him the evidence is ready, but so is the evidence of his previous acts. The decisive fact, which governs both, however, is that he had not taken the field over Bulgaria or scoured Midlothian only from personal ambition or from motives of personal aggrandisement. The latter was the effect rather than the cause of his campaigns. If he must be charged with selfishness, which is not the same as self-seeking, the charge would lie against his withdrawal. It would rest on his refusal to bear the burden of Opposition, to meet Disraeli from the inferior side, and to continue in spite of some disaffection of his party. These decisions can hardly be defended on impersonal grounds. His return can, even if the opportunity to do so with *réclame* was the reward of his previous tactics. The weakness that leads most men to shrink from great responsibility led Gladstone to shrink from the disagreeable burden of party leadership, below Disraeli, in the House of Commons. Without the assurance of active sympathy beyond or within his party the horrid inner void tormented him, and he could escape it only by activity, and in company with supporters not for the moment available. The countenance of others was a necessity for his nature, and his weakness was betrayed whenever this was denied.

A thankless task to Gladstone was one which did not promise deferred popular support, so he had turned his back on the Commons, and left Hartington and Granville to keep the disunited Liberals together as well as they could. He knew very well that they received thereby a claim to scrupulous consideration, though a finer scrupulosity, a richer nature, might have preferred to spare them the thanklessness rather than to defer to a nominal leadership that his recent activities had made it impossible for them to maintain. The revelation of a man's character is more important than any opinion we may form of its weaknesses. At the moment he was anxious above all to respect the formalities of his " retirement," yet, as we shall see in a moment, at the crucial minute he rejected a personal sacrifice that would have given to his leaders the substance of the position that was theirs. It was they, he insisted, who should relieve him of embarrassment at the start :

> My ears are shut against all the world, except it were Gran-ville and Hartington. . . . Were they to speak now, and as I have defined above, I should then say, let us have nothing more than a formula, and let the substance of it be that by the nature of things no man in my position could make beforehand an absolute renunciation, and that the leadership in the next Parliament must, like everything else, be con-sidered in connection with what may appear at the dissolution to be the sense of the country, but that my action individually has been and will continue to be that of a follower of Lord Granville and Lord Hartington.

The position of these two gentlemen was certainly embarrassing. Notwithstanding the Midlothian cam-paign, and the popular enthusiasm in the north, they knew, like everyone else, that, in some mysterious way, the personality of Gladstone continued to arouse per-sistent antagonism. If he filled crowds with adulation, distrust was still excited by his name in many hearts. At this very moment it lived in the breasts of Liberals even. It was not certain, even now, that his detractors were negligible, until his return to London, where he addressed two enthusiastic gatherings, showed that the disaffected were few.

Parliament was dissolved on March 8, 1880, and Disraeli tried to make the English hatred of Home Rule the issue of the election. Gladstone made a royal progress to Edinburgh, and was returned for the constituency of Midlothian, despite the creation of " faggot " votes against which he had protested in his original opening speech in the autumn. It is interesting to read that these votes, given to those for whom houses were run up in the constituency, were not, according to Mr. R. H. Gretton, neglected by Gladstone's supporters, but, in the excitement of a contest, the candidate is often in the dark over the precise stones which have been turned by his agent and organisers. His own triumph and that of the Liberals was complete. They had a majority of 107 over the Conservatives, and of 42 over the Conservatives and the Irish added together. The new Premier, whoever he might prove, would be apparently irresistible in Parliament.

As soon as the results were known, Gladstone wrote to the Duke of Argyll :

> All our heads are still in a whirl from the great events of the last fortnight, which have given joy, I am convinced, to the large majority of the civilised world. The downfall of Beaconsfieldism is like the vanishing of some vast magnificent castle in an Italian romance. It is too big, however, to be taken in all at once. . . . But the outlook is tremendous ! The gradual unravelling of the tangled knots of the foreign and Indian policy will indeed be a task for skilled and strong hands, if they can be found.

If they can be found ! The two peers were summoned by the Queen, only too anxious to admit their claims, and not too anxious to substitute Gladstone for dear Lord Beaconsfield as her adviser. The unfortunate gentlemen could not comply. If they did, what was to happen to Mr. Gladstone ? The Queen must have been even more eager than her subjects to know this. She was not left in doubt for long. Let us share her suspense by following Gladstone's diary. On the day after the declaration of the poll in his constituency, Gladstone with his wife and daughter hurried home. At Hawarden the results elsewhere made thrilling news :

> 7th. The triumph grows and grows. To God be the praise.
> 9th. Wolverton . . . threatens a request from Granville and Hartington. Again I am stunned, but God will provide.
> 12th. Wrote some Memoranda of names applicable to this occasion.
> 13th. Read *Guy Mannering*, and that most heavenly poet, George Herbert.
> 19th. Reluctant good-bye before 1. London 6.30.
> 20th. This blank day is, I think, probably due to the Queen's hesitation or reluctance, which the Ministers have to find means for [overcoming].

There were comings and goings in the clubs and political offices. The Liberal majority and even his opponents agreed that, if Gladstone would not really retire, it was better that he should be active openly. What place in the Ministry would he accept ? On that point at least he would not yield. The Queen's hesitation and reluctance were at last overpowered when she learnt that Gladstone refused to serve in any capacity except that of Prime Minister.

The leader of the Opposition to Disraeli, having now fulfilled his function, could secure the essential services of Gladstone in the Cabinet on these terms alone. God had " provided," and every scruple, except one, had held Gladstone back.

CHAPTER V

THE MORROW OF MIDLOTHIAN

I

WHEN Gladstone went down to the House of Commons on May 20, 1880, the enthusiasm of the crowd which awaited him in Palace Yard seemed to be the first-fruits of his great victory. Accustomed as he now was to ovations of this kind, he was not insensible to its meaning. In a characteristic fragment he says :

> It almost overpowered me, as I thought by what deep and hidden agencies I have been brought back into the midst of the vortex of political action and contention. . . . Looking calmly on this course of experience, I do believe that the Almighty has employed me for His purposes in a manner larger and more special than before, and has strengthened me and led me on accordingly, though I must not forget the admirable saying of Hooker, that even ministers of good things are like torches, a light to others, waste and destruction to themselves.

Reflection was soon to show, if it had not shown already, that the complications of Gladstone's recent tackings were by no means at an end with his electoral success and resumption of leadership. Though it was true that his parliamentary rival, Disraeli, was no longer a disagreeable presence in the Commons, which he had left for the House of Lords in 1876, his policy remained "a tangle" not quickly or easily to be unravelled. The legacy of Beaconsfieldism had to be liquidated before Gladstonian principles could be replaced, and

as the legacy concerned chiefly complex questions of
foreign policy, it is very hard, in this phase of Gladstone's life, not to lose the man in the mass of European
and international foreign politics.   Gladstone had quitted
political life at a time when restiveness had become
apparent in his own party.   His " retirement " none
the less had filled many Liberals with dismay; his
sudden and unofficial resumption of activity made confusion worse confounded, and whatever the elections
might have shown, it remained to be proved how far
his personal ascendancy would be reflected even on his
own side in the Commons.   He could not return as if
nothing had happened in the interval.   It could not
be as if he had never left, and his conduct in having
gone, in having led an unofficial campaign when out
of responsibility, and in having resumed the leadership,
did not set a good example of party discipline.   If he
had been content to shoulder the burden of Opposition
to Disraeli, in that dusty strife he might have earned a
confidence in his party that he had deliberately endangered.   The party would have been inclined to
obey in the moment of victory the leader who had still
led through long and unprofitable days.   He had chosen
to disappear, and to appeal over their heads to platform
audiences.   He had temporarily exchanged a parliamentary for a popular ascendancy.   How far would he
be able to recover the control in the Commons that he
had found too burdensome to keep ?

It was at least an open question, and restiveness
immediately reappeared.   Indeed one of the earliest
impressions of the Speaker was unfavourable to the
apparently resistless old man.   The Liberal party seemed
to the Chair " not only strong, but determined to have
their own way in spite of Mr. Gladstone.   He has a
difficult team to drive."   An added complication, for
which he was not responsible, was a little group of four,

headed by Lord Randolph Churchill, which emerged
during the session of 1880, and was to cause much
annoyance to everyone except themselves. The kind
of criticism which Gladstone was to receive at their
hands was new to his experience, and the style which
lent point to the attack was a new style in parliamentary
speaking. It really marks the end of Gladstone's
oratorical epoch, and reflected more aptly than his own
the popular presentment of subjects and personalities
which he had done so much to inaugurate. The 'eighties
too were the period of what was called the new journalism, and we see how the same levity that was to enliven
at its best, and at worst to cheapen, popular discussion
of public affairs, had its counterpart also in debate.
Lord Randolph and Mr. Labouchere, a journalist himself, were excellent exponents, of the new manner, and
though we shall be anticipating, an example from the
former's well-known speech of 1884 is not only an
admirable specimen of the new manner, but it crystallises
the reaction. Gladstone's habit of publicity, as we have
seen, irritated and annoyed those who were not prostrated
by him.

> The Prime Minister (said Lord Randolph) is the greatest
> living master of the art of personal political advertisement.
> Holloway, Colman and Horniman are nothing compared
> with him. Every act of his, whether it be for the purpose
> of health or of recreation or of religious devotion, is spread
> before the eyes of every man, woman and child in the United
> Kingdom on large and glaring placards. . . . For the purpose
> of recreation he has selected the felling of trees. Every
> afternoon the whole world is invited to assist at the crashing
> fall of some beech or oak. The forest laments that Mr.
> Gladstone may perspire, and full accounts of these proceed-
> ings are forwarded by special correspondents to every daily
> paper every recurring morning. For the purpose of religious
> devotion the advertisements grow larger. The parish church
> of Hawarden is insufficient to contain the thronging multi-
> tudes of fly-catchers who flock to hear Mr. Gladstone read

the lessons for the day, and the humble parishioners are banished to hospitable Nonconformist tabernacles in order that mankind may be present at the Prime Minister's rendering of Isaiah or Jeremiah or the Book of Job.

The peculiar note by which we recognise the knocking of the younger generation is unmistakable in these words, and the sting, which was wit to the juniors and bad taste to the seniors, then, as always, marked the turn of a chapter. The criticisms could not have been made except from one detached from the ideal which had occasioned them, for ideals of behaviour only seem ridiculous to those for whom they are out of date. With the collars and the bag and the four-wheeled carriage for two hung between the driver's seat and a dickey, the Gladstonian deportment in public was a convention passing away. The day was not far distant when the importance of being earnest should be the title of one of the wittiest comedies in English. Lord Randolph himself was a young man of promise, heralding the new order, but he was not to live long enough to dominate it.

Another of the restive ones was Mr. Joseph Chamberlain, who had begun to make a name for himself in the active municipality of Birmingham, and was to cause trouble by indiscretions much more blasphemous than these. He was understood, at this time, to be a Radical, and Mr. Gladstone once defined a Radical as " a Liberal in earnest." This might be true with two provisos, to which, however, the young Chamberlain paid little verbal heed. The provisos were that the aristocrats must never be twitted with laziness, and that not a word must be breathed against even the largest unearned income. When, therefore, Chamberlain described the Lord Salisbury of his day as belonging to the class of beings " who toil not, neither do they spin," who " levy an unearned share on all that other men have done," and, still speaking as a Cabinet Minister, went on to ask the dangerous question : " What ransom will property pay for the security it enjoys ? " Mr. Gladstone was seriously inconvenienced. The Queen was perturbed, and wrote vehement remonstrances, so that between the orchid of Birmingham and the briar-rose of Windsor the Premier had uncomfortable hours. His own Cabinet was not too harmonious, nor particularly anxious to agree, because it lacked, according to Morley, the binding dough of mediocrity.

Once more we must remind ourselves that Gladstone himself had set the example of this platform discussion of questions not officially engaging the Government of the day, but the idiom which he used was less disturbing because in the conventional, if declining, canon of taste. Thus, in September of this year, 1880, he wrote to Lord Rosebery :

> What is outside Parliament seems to me to be fast mounting, nay, to have already mounted, to an importance much exceeding what is inside. . . . I always admired Mr. Grote's saying that politics and theology were the only two great subjects.

Gladstonism was a blend of both, and if only his colleagues had been content with the old gospel it would not have mattered much. As agriculture had been sacrificed to trade, the landed interests to middleclass manufacturers, the pocket borough to a wide franchise embracing most of the teeming population of the towns, so, in their turn, questions of a livable existence for the multitude of wage-earners, in other words, some redistribution of property, were demanding political attention. It was on this congenial field that Chamberlain was welcomed by his audiences. As he was a Cabinet Minister, he was understood to be setting the pace for Gladstone, much as Gladstone, during his "retirement," had set the pace for his nominal chief, the official leader of the Opposition, a few years before. The embarrassment thus created quickly led the Duke of Argyll to resign, and after the fall of Gladstone's Government in 1885 he gave an excellent summary of the position :

> From the moment our Government was fairly on the way I saw and felt that speeches *outside* were allowed to affect opinion, and politically to commit the Cabinet in a direction which was not determined by you deliberately, or by the Government as a whole, but by the audacity . . . of our new associates. . . . Your amiability to your colleagues . . . has enabled men playing their own game . . . to take out of your hands the *formation* of opinion.

His amiability was carried so far that he is said to have counted heads on disputed points in the Cabinet itself. If opinion was divided within, were not the prospects of the apparently invincible Government dubious when difficult questions in the Commons should present themselves ? Had they but known, those outsiders who thought that Gladstone's personal ascendancy in the country deserved a nemesis, would have found it here. The malice of fate, with infernal cunning, was harassing Gladstone just where he was most tender, by personal contentions, and unreliability in the House. Ministers would absent themselves from divisions, or abstain from voting, or even move amendments against the proposals of their leaders, and the first two months were a time of agitation for the Government whips. On one motion indeed the Prime Minister found himself voting in the minority. Gladstone himself was extremely patient and forbearing, but persuasiveness, which may be effective with a crowd, was not enough in Cabinet or Parliament. He could manage mobs better than men. The note of authority was too faint.

II

Thus hampered, the tangle of foreign affairs left by Beaconsfield awaited unravelment. The death of the Prince Imperial in Zululand, followed by the defeat of Gladstone's proposal for the vote of a memorial to him, was not an auspicious introduction to these affairs. Then the whole party suffered a shock when the expectation that Sir Bartle Frere would be recalled from South Africa was disappointed. He was a favourite with the Queen, and Gladstone's attitude was only maintained against remonstrances with the utmost difficulty. Once in office, he was as assiduous as ever, but the strain of controlling an unruly following was revealed during the summer, when with ungrateful dismay it became known that he was ill. As soon as he was convalescent he went for a cruise in the *Grantully Castle*, and returned just in time to deliver a speech on the Eastern Question before the session ended early in September.

We must now turn to the tangle that awaited him in Afghanistan, South Africa, Montenegro, Egypt, the Soudan, before we see him in the immediate trouble of the Bradlaugh case and under the heavy cloud of Ireland, the last of his great crusades. So that he may not be lost in a mass of historical events, each will be confined as far as possible to his immediate share in the handling of their difficulties.

Though Gladstone's father was untouched by the idea, his own youth belonged to the generation in which liberty was a lively political creed, and he was only a little late in embracing it. Thus in foreign politics his essential attitude was one of sympathy for peoples " rightly struggling to be free," and he was not of those who took it for a truism that to be free meant to be incorporated in the British Empire. He held that we were bound to safeguard our existing possessions, giving to them as much local self-government as possible, but he was without the desire for expansion or aggrandisement in foreign policy, and had viewed with misgiving the new Imperialism which had lent a gilt and glamour to the activities of Beaconsfield. A particularly dangerous corner has always been the North-West Frontier of India, with the dubious buffer of Afghanistan between Russia and ourselves. There the old cautious policy had been abandoned; an English agent had been placed at Cabul, and his violent death there had been followed by the annexation of Candahar; this might easily occasion further trouble. Here the recent forward policy was definitely reversed. Gladstone, for once in agreement with his colleagues, determined to evacuate the place, and, though the Lords gave an adverse vote to the decision, it was carried in the Commons. Aggressive Imperialism received a set-back.

In South Africa matters were unfortunately incapable of such a simple solution as this. Sir Bartle Frere has already been mentioned, and he was responsible for the Zulu war, which Gladstone had condemned in his Midlothian speeches. The party held that it was pledged to his recall, and apart from the Queen, who would hardly have been permitted to overrule Gladstone's own feelings, Gladstone's reasons for not recalling Frere are worth examination. The policy of Gladstone was one of confederation, towards which it was thought that the Parliament at the Cape was moving, and the idea was to retain Frere until this was realised. When this hope was disappointed Frere was recalled, as early, in fact, as July 1880. On taking office the situation that Gladstone found was briefly this : In 1877, through fear that a recent success of the natives against the Boers of the Transvaal would lead to a general upheaval, the sovereignty of the Queen had been proclaimed, on the express assumption, which was speedily disproved, that the Boers desired to become British subjects. An Assembly and other legislative privileges were promised, but Kruger came to England to protest on behalf of the Boers. Despite this, in 1879 Sir Garnet Wolseley, the Administrator of the Transvaal, announced that the country must remain permanently part of the Queen's dominions. Gladstone was averse to annexation here, as he had been to that of Candahar, but was cautious in his words. Yet, on taking office, he was advised that the situation was improving, and that the Transvaal Boers might accept the accomplished fact as the Boers at the Cape had done. The Cabinet were urged to make a definite announcement of their policy, and eventually, in spite of some of Gladstone's previous utterances, endorsed the policy of the late Government. The angry Boers persuaded the Cape Parliament against confederation; disturbances occurred, and a general revolt followed. At the end of January 1881 the British received their first check, and certain overtures might have led to a settlement if only the British had not moved to occupy Majuba Hill. From this we were promptly driven with heavy loss. The sensation and dismay produced at home raised the question whether negotiations were to be cancelled. As a matter of fact agreement to a meeting was on its way at the time of the provocative assault on Majuba. This may serve as a general indication of the confusion on the spot which accorded so ill with the policy of Gladstone's Government. Sir Evelyn Wood, now in command, recommended military action, but was forbidden to take the offensive. The tangle of cross purposes and divided counsels can be gauged from the fact that some military authorities favoured further fighting in order that our soldiers might learn confidence in the breech-loading rifle that had been lately introduced! The Boers dispersed, and a joint commission was refused to them.

A convention made at Pretoria in 1881, which recognised
the semi-independence of the Transvaal, was followed
by another in 1884 which restored the former title of
the South African Republic. The Government was
thus attacked for not having prevented the rising, and
for having yielded to force what had been refused to
muddled negotiations. All through Gladstone was on
the side of agreement, but he was badly served on the
spot, where nervousness led to provocative action, and
mischance played a certain part. Such failure as occurred
was rather due to the agents of the home executive
than to Gladstone himself. He showed courage in persisting throughout the muddle to restrict the mischief
and the bloodshed as far as he could in the presence of
a bewildered and impatient House and country.

The fortune which had proved malign for his policy
in South Africa was amusingly indulgent to him over
the unfulfilled clauses in the Treaty of Berlin which
affected Greece, Montenegro and Turkey. The Sultan
was nodding at the critical moment and, by a lucky
misunderstanding of the circumstances, gave way. Both
these smaller states were entitled by the Treaty to some
extension of territory, and Gladstone's policy was to
bring pressure upon Turkey by the joint action of the
Powers. He proposed a common demonstration off
the coast of Albania on behalf of Montenegro; and
when Austria and Germany virtually backed out, to
send the joint fleet to Smyrna in order to take from
Turkey the customs duties of that port, which were too
valuable for her to lose. The proposal came from us,
but the Sultan, in ignorance that the other Powers were
not likely to agree, gave way. Montenegro, to whom
Gladstone had made a burning reference in his Midlothian speeches, received Dulcigno, and Greece was
almost restored to her Homeric size. With pardonable
satisfaction, Gladstone remarked :

> The whole of this extraordinary *volte-face* has been effected within six days; and it was entirely due not to a threat of coercion from Europe, but to the knowledge that Great Britain had asked Europe to coerce.

This distinction is characteristic, but he had proceeded by agreement, and had proved what partial agreement, in a lucky moment, could gain in foreign affairs. There, as at home, he abhorred domination, and placed persuasiveness and joint action at the basis of his policy.

Another branch of the ubiquitous Eastern Question concerned Egypt, where, at first, all seemed to be well. On this Gladstone had indulged in what proved to be a remarkable prophecy as far back as 1877. In the August number of the *Nineteenth Century* he had then written :

> Our first site in Egypt, be it by larceny or be it by emption, will be the almost certain egg of a North African empire, that will grow and grow . . . till we finally join hands across the equator with Natal and Cape Town, to say nothing of the Transvaal and the Orange River on the south, or of Abyssinia or Zanzibar to be swallowed by way of viaticum on our journey.

Here, again, he inherited a situation that pointed to the path which he did not wish to tread. France and England in 1879 had imposed two controllers upon Egypt, and thus brought what Gladstone described as foreign intervention into the midst of that country. Then came Beaconsfield's purchase of the Suez Canal shares, which sealed our interest, a purchase which Gladstone, ever cautious of future entanglements, had deemed " hazardous and ill-advised." Egypt had administrative independence under the Sultan, whose viceroy was the Khedive, and the whole position was obviously unsatisfactory and unstable.

When the leaders of the latter's army, whose grievances were neglected, revolted under Arabi in January 1881, and the disorders spread to the civil population and led to the appearance of a Nationalist party in the Chamber, the Sultan saw a chance of diplomatically reasserting his shadowy authority. This complexity of events brought France and England into the matter. France was opposed to Turkish interferences, and the Sultan, to whom the Cabinet looked as the least objectionable source of restored order, had been made odious to English opinion by the hero of Midlothian himself. Under the momentary ascendancy of Gambetta at the end of 1881, the French view prevailed, and some common action between the two controlling European Powers was vaguely agreed to. The effect of their Joint Note was to make the Khedive appear the creature of France and England; he was encouraged to oppose reforms; and everyone else, the Sultan, the Nationalists, and the other Powers, were exasperated. The army became the master of the Government, and the sending of an Anglo-French fleet to Alexandria was followed by the bombardment of the forts which commanded it by the British ships only.

Before this happened Gladstone had sought in vain the co-operation of the Powers, and now declared that Egypt must be rescued from anarchy by us alone, if such co-operation was impossible. France was more afraid of Germany than of Gladstone, and therefore was unwilling to send troops to Egypt. The Cabinet therefore sent Wolseley to Egypt, and he defeated Arabi at Tel-el-Kebir in September 1882. The bombardment of Alexandria lost Bright to Gladstone, who laboured in vain to persuade him that a situation of force had been created by Arabi which only force could meet, and that the pillage which followed was due to the same cause. Gladstone added that none of the Powers had disapproved, and that the blow struck at violence had "greatly advanced the Egyptian question towards a permanent and peaceful solution." It also advanced

P

the English occupation of Egypt and prepared the tragic episode of Gordon. To this, pursuing the foreign difficulties of Gladstone's Government to their end, we may now turn, since it is impossible to follow a series of different entanglements, as they appeared, simultaneously. We have seen enough to show that Gladstone did not disapprove of force when all other means had failed him, and he even took a severe view of Arabi's claim to clemency when his fate came to be discussed. He was tried for rebellion and sentenced to death, but the sentence was commuted to banishment to Ceylon.

Once in Egypt the theoretical choice between annexation and withdrawal hardly existed, and yet annexation was not desired by the Cabinet or public opinion. A military victory seemed, for once, to arouse small enthusiasm at home, and the nation had not forgotten its repudiation of expansion at the time of the defeat of Beaconsfield. Endless and intricate negotiations culminated in the London Convention of 1885, by which the financial complexities were settled by European agreement. The margin of empire remains, however, as intractable as the desire of a man to own all land adjacent to his own, and now that we were planted in Egypt, trouble occurred on its southern border, the Soudan.

Four years before the London Convention was signed, in 1881, a self-proclaimed Mahdi, or Moslem Messiah, appeared in that distracted country. It had been, of course, atrociously misgoverned by Egyptian pashas, and Gladstone was once more confronted with a people "rightly struggling to be free." Egypt could not plunder her dependency for ever without having to pay the penalty. Troops were sent to Khartoum, and their success encouraged an advance which the Cabinet ought to have forbidden, and would have done but for a wish not to interfere with the authority of the Egyptian Government. Our status and responsibility were so ill defined that the Cabinet, as in South Africa, was once more at the mercy of a distant administration, which in turn was weak before the opinions of its soldiers on the spot. The advancing general and his forces were completely defeated by the dervishes, who under the Mahdi now threatened Khartoum. The remedy seemed to be to evacuate the Soudan, but this meant the difficult task of extricating the Egyptian garrisons. To this end the Cabinet, with Gladstone dissenting, decided to send a force to Suakin, the eastern port of the Soudan on the Red Sea, yet despite much bloodshed the Mahdi was as triumphant as ever. This was early in 1883, and our failure produced the inevitable wave of excited criticism. It was at last decided to send General Gordon with express instructions to complete the withdrawal of the Egyptian garrisons from the Soudan as quickly as possible. His personal influence was thought capable of persuading the tribes to allow the garrison at Khartoum to depart, and to let him conduct the other garrisons to safety.

For such a difficult and delicate task plainly much depended upon the character of our emissary, and events proved that Gordon was too wayward a person to send. The first mistake had been to allow Hicks to advance beyond Khartoum into Kordofan. The second was to rely on Gordon sticking to the letter of his instructions. An incalculable creature, he was wayward and impulsive; and his personal heroism and mysticism were more likely to create trouble than to lay it. His instructions were to " consider and report on the best mode of effecting the evacuation " of the Soudan, a mission extended at Cairo to carrying it out himself. Some of his instructions, added to in Egypt, were loosely worded, and when he arrived he found that evacuation was entangled with other questions. Discovering that he was not welcomed at Khartoum, he suddenly decided that the Mahdi must be

smashed, and that the British must control the Soudanese
administration, which should be placed under Zobeir
as their governor-general.   He was concerned with the
fate of the outlying garrisons and proposed to undertake to relieve them by military force.   When this
change of policy was known in London, Gladstone was
anxious for Gordon's recall.   After many heart-searchings the sending of Zobeir was refused, and the refusal
was made certain when Gordon revealed his plan to a
newspaper correspondent.   The result was that public
opinion made the appointment of that " slave-holder "
impossible.   If Gordon's idea was to force the Government to do what he wanted, he miscalculated badly.
Meantime the Mahdi's forces surrounded Khartoum,
and within a month of Gordon's arrival its line of
communications was cut.

Gladstone's summary of these events is quoted by
Morley as follows :

> When Gordon left this country and when he arrived in
> Egypt, he declared it to be, and I have not the smallest doubt
> that it was—a fixed portion of his policy that no British
> force should be employed in aid of his mission.

Then came his assertion that we should have to
smash up the Mahdi, lastly the declaration that to
leave the outlying garrisons to their fate would be an
" indelible disgrace."   Mr. Lytton Strachey says that
Gladstone read this message for the first time in a newspaper while on a visit to a country house, and then
goes on to quote from an unnamed observer the following
description of the scene :

> He took up the paper; his eye instantly fell on the tele-
> gram, and he read it through.   As he read, his face hardened
> and whitened, the eyes burned as I have seen them once or
> twice in the House of Commons when he was angered—
> burned with a deep fire, as if they would have consumed the
> sheet on which Gordon's message was printed, or as if

Gordon's words had burnt into his soul, which was looking out in wrath and flame. He said not a word. For perhaps two or three minutes he sat still, his face all the while like the face you may read of in Milton—like none other I ever saw. Then he rose without a word, and was seen no more that morning.

It is an unforgettable description, one in which a certain mood or aspect of Gladstone's physiognomy is imprinted on the reader's eyes. One is glad to have it, because a few observers, though a minority, have recorded something sinister in his expression. Some, at least of the later portraits, bear this out, particularly perhaps the one by Millais at Christchurch, Oxford. In her life of her husband Mrs. Charles Stewart Parnell closed the opening volume with this visual memory :

> Always as I stood face to face with this Grand Old Man on leaving, and looked into his slate-coloured eyes, so like those of an eagle, I experienced a sudden uneasy feeling, in spite of his gracious courtesy, of how like to a beautiful bird of prey this old man was : with the piercing cruel eyes belying the tender courteous smile. . . .

Gladstone's impressive face was one of his many ambiguities. The contradiction, which was part of his strange character, lurking in his expression gave there too an excuse for the diverse feelings and estimates that he inspired. To refuse to surrender to either of the extreme views concerning him is to keep closer to the truth. That face, in which a radiant light could be blent so mysteriously with the expression " you may read of in Milton," masked, at this moment, the belief that though Gordon might be hemmed in, he was not surrounded, the contrasting terms passing over the situation like sunlight and cloud over a hillside. Not through Gordon's pressure would Gladstone budge.

Gordon's view was that " if you do not send Zobeir, you have no chance of getting the garrisons away."

If there was no chance of his mission being successful, what was Gordon's next move to be? The centre of interest now shifted from the garrisons to Gordon himself. Was the rescuer to be rescued? The initiative was supposed to lie with him, the man on the spot, and there was now no news concerning him. No one wanted to send a relief expedition to Khartoum if it could be avoided, and in the absence of definite news it was not certain, in spite of growing public concern for the fate of Gordon, that it could not. In these doubts and hesitations the spring and summer of 1884 drifted along. At last, in the beginning of August, a vote of credit for an expedition was demanded. In August Lord Wolseley was given the command, and on September 9th he arrived at Cairo. On that very evening one of Gordon's steamers, taking advantage of the rising Nile, with the English and French Consul and Gordon's own second in command on board, set out for Egypt. He could have joined them, but he chose to remain. Even so, Fate had a trick in store, as if she would not be cheated of her tragedy. The ship struck a rock, and the Consul and Colonel Stewart were murdered; the official papers also fell into the Mahdi's hands. They revealed the precarious condition of Khartoum, and the Mahdi decided to wait no longer. On January the 28th, 1885, the expedition at last arrived, to find that Khartoum had fallen two days before.

The news of Gordon's death produced a terrible outcry in England. Gordon, who had been a hero, was proclaimed a martyr, and Gladstone became the public villain of the piece. He is never more interesting than in these recurring, if short-lived, moments of public odium or unpopularity. If he had refused, as he suspected, to allow his hand to be forced before, he would refuse now. So far from bowing to popular clamour, he confronted it. He would not make the failure of

the relief expedition an excuse for proceeding to punish
the false Mahdi and to conquer the Soudan.   Luckily a
cloud on the Afghan frontier called for the withdrawal
of Wolseley and his forces from Egypt.   Mr. Gladstone
stood firm.   His original policy of abandoning the
Soudan was not to be deflected by unforeseen circumstances and popular passion.   His judgment, here at
least, was not influenced by the personal unpopularity
that it created.

His mature opinion of the whole matter was as
follows :

> Gordon was a hero, and a hero of heroes ; but we ought
> to have known that a hero of heroes is not the proper person
> to give effect at a distant point, and in most difficult circum-
> stances, to the views of ordinary men.   It was unfortunate
> that he should claim the hero's privilege by turning upside
> down and inside out every idea and intention with which he
> had left England, and for which he had obtained our approval.
> . . . My own opinion is that it is harder to justify our doing
> so much to rescue him, than our not doing more.   Had the
> party reached Khartoum in time, he would not have come
> away (as I suppose), and the dilemma would have arisen in
> another form.

The tangle of cross purposes is too apparent to cover
any of the protagonists in the famous and debated
story with praise or blame.   Every time we read it we
feel that all are caught in a web stronger than themselves.   It is this sense of the inevitable that makes the
tragedy a lively issue still.

III

The above bird's-eye view of foreign affairs might
seem to have provided ample worries enough for a
harassed administration, but fortune was equally unkind
at home, where a press of difficulties could not be
palliated by calling them a legacy from Beaconsfield.

Before turning to these embarrassments we may notice a gleam of light at the Exchequer, where, once again, Gladstone devised an admirable Budget. He put heart into his colleagues by a speech which delighted the House, and more particularly by finding a way of repealing the malt duty, irksome to farmers and apparently beyond the skill of the Conservatives to remove. Gladstone changed the malt tax into a duty on beer, the finished product. He also reduced the duties on light wines, and safeguarded the Exchequer by adding a penny to the income tax. He wove all these dry proposals into " an animated narrative " with his accustomed skill and enthusiasm.

The domestic storm which arose lasted for five years. It touched one of those questions bordering upon religion and liberty which might seem specially fitted for Gladstone to solve; and, had he not had a recalcitrant and prejudiced House of Commons to handle, he would soon have solved it himself. The new Member for Northampton was Charles Bradlaugh, who had been making himself difficult, and therefore unpopular, in a variety of ways. He was a secularist, a free-thinker, a republican. He had attacked the House of Brunswick (Windsor) without attracting much attention, but he created much noise by republishing, in the interest of liberty of discussion, an American pamphlet on birth control, called the *Fruits of Philosophy*, the original printer of which had been prosecuted for indecency, but lightly sentenced. For coming to the vindication of free speech in this way, Bradlaugh and his friend Mrs. Besant were the heroes, and the victims, of a scandal, only escaping a heavy sentence by a technicality which saved them on appeal. Bradlaugh had several times figured in the courts, where his opinions were held, unfairly, to disqualify him from taking the oath and to justify juries in refusing him protection for attacks that might be made on his character. Indeed, his refusal to take the oath in court had led to the law of 1869, which entitled a witness to affirm in place of it.

On his election to the Parliament of 1880, Bradlaugh was anxious to carry the principle that he had established into the House of Commons. Instead of taking the oath of allegiance, without which he could not occupy his seat, he claimed the right to affirm under the Parliamentary Oaths Act. A select committee was appointed, and the claim, by a majority of one, refused. The violent prejudice aroused against Bradlaugh is apparent from the fact that, when he now said that he was ready to swear, this was refused also. The disgraceful attempts, of which this was the first, to deprive a duly elected Member of his seat are too tedious to relate except in so far as they reveal Gladstone's own position. They show him now converted to the view, which he had once repudiated (p. 38), that disbelief in revealed religion should not disqualify a man for election to Parliament. His immediate business was to extricate the House from the discreditable morass into which its vindictiveness had thrown it. Gladstone wrote to the Queen that his " own view is that the House has no jurisdiction for the purpose of excluding any one willing to qualify when he has been duly elected." When the House decided by a majority that Bradlaugh should neither be allowed to affirm nor to swear, because he was a declared atheist, Gladstone reported that the " ecstatic transport exceeded anything " which he remembered to have witnessed. It showed, he added dryly, the unfitness of the House for the office it had chosen to assume. Morley also finds in it " the first stroke of revenge for Midlothian." Bradlaugh reappeared at the bar, asked to be heard, and challenged the legality of the decision, a challenge which Gladstone, in rather ambiguous words, endorsed to the Queen. Bradlaugh's

speech, of course, made no difference to the excited
Members, and Bradlaugh was removed by the Serjeant-
at-Arms. He returned, and was again removed by
force. When someone then moved that Bradlaugh
should be committed, Gladstone refused to advise, but
declined to object to the proposal. In fact he supported
it with his vote, to the annoyance of the Speaker, who
virtually held that what he supported it was due to his
position to have proposed.

The only solution was to prepare an Affirmation Bill,
but the temper of the House did not desire a solution.
On the contrary, it desired to victimise Bradlaugh and
to embarrass Gladstone in every way. Party feeling
was pleased to hear him christened a " patron of blas-
phemy." Not till 1883 was an Affirmation Bill introduced with a serious chance of acceptance, and then it
was defeated by a majority of three. Nonconformists,
those historic champions of the right of private judgment, were among the majority. Throughout this
Parliament the electors of Northampton were denied
their representative, but when he reappeared after the
election of 1885 to take the oath, the Speaker refused
any interference, and in 1888 Bradlaugh himself attained
his end with the passing of an Affirmation Act. On his
death-bed in 1891 the House repented, too late for him
to know, and expunged from its records the resolution
that had been passed with ecstasy ten years before.

From Gladstone's own speeches throughout these
troubled years we may glean a few sentences which
show how far he had travelled from the narrow tenets
of his youth.

> I have no fear of Atheism in this House (he said when
> moving the Bill of 1883). Truth is the expression of the
> Divine mind . . . and we may be sure that a firm and
> courageous application of every principle of equity and of
> justice is the best method we can adopt for the preservation
> and influence of Truth.

This, we may note in passing, is an ethical rather than an intellectual principle, very characteristic of a man who was taught by circumstances rather than by insight to believe in toleration, and to believe in it rather because the absence of toleration creates impossible situations than because the principle of toleration is excellent in itself. His inspiration was to overcome difficulties, to satisfy unmistakable aspirations, to meet troubles as they arose. The stubborn facts were recognised by this eager, active nature more quickly than by most Englishmen. He had a genuine love of accommodating differences. It was from facts and public movements that he learned. Ideas to the last rarely penetrated his mind until they created movements of practical bearing. Then, with his natural fervour, he would appeal to high principles in support of their satisfaction, and the principles of liberty and of justice suited him best because both are elastic, and themselves come into view most clearly in the sphere of immediate affairs. The bias is sufficient for a statesman, and if, unlike most able men, he began by being conservative, his distinction lies in not allowing his first ardour for his adopted principles to fade, but in maintaining, and indeed increasing, its vigour as he grew older.

IV

Whatever his difficulties in Parliament might be, his public following continued to idolise him. He succeeded in convincing his audiences in the country that, however puzzled they might sometimes be at his proceedings, and however little they might be able to follow his reasonings, yet in some mysterious manner he was on their side, and, unlike other official persons, was not an aloof being, but one of themselves set in a lofty place. Thus his previous ovations were repeated when

he visited Leeds in October 1881 to return thanks for
his success in the General Election. Threatened with
four days of continuous effort, he pleaded only that no
progress through the streets should precede any mass
meeting :

> I see no difficulty but one—a procession through the
> principal thoroughfares is one of the most exhausting pro-
> cesses I know as a preliminary to addressing a mass meeting.
> A mass meeting requires the physical powers to be in their
> best and freshest state, as far as anything can be fresh in a
> man near seventy-two. . . . It would certainly be most desir-
> able to have the mass meeting first, and then I have not any
> fear at all of the procession through whatever thoroughfares
> you think fit.

Four days later he repeats his request, explaining :

> I should be very sorry to put aside any of the opportunities
> of vision at Leeds which the public may care to use.

The number of addresses presented must have been
too numerous to be read, and one wonders whether a
public luncheon may not prove almost as ill a prelude
to a mass meeting as a public progress through the
streets. At the mass meeting he addressed an audience
of twenty-five thousand, and his days ended with torch-
light processions, public dinners and a final departure
by night. It was on this occasion that he coined one
of his few familiar phrases, a vaguely ominous, if in-
tangible, threat to Parnell, who was applying test cases
to the new Land Act, that " the resources of civilisation
against its enemies are not yet exhausted." We all
know how dear vague phrases are to politicians, to
journalists, and to the audiences to whom they are
addressed, but Gladstone's reputation for resource and
for mystery gave a histrionic value to this expression
which probably impressed everybody except the coolest
of men, Parnell himself. The relations of Gladstone to
Parnell and to Ireland deserve a chapter to themselves.

They were the last, most difficult, and most honourable of Gladstone's crusades, which extended beyond the five years of his second premiership, and indeed terminated only with his final retirement from the political scene. Before glancing at this historic page, let us turn to more personal events. They include his political jubilee and a northern cruise on which Tennyson accompanied him.

In December 1882, the month in which he was born, and at the age of seventy-three, he completed fifty years of parliamentary life. His opinions indeed had changed, but on the whole we may say that there had been more expansion than development. He had begun by appealing to principles, and his first political principle had been to identify reform with revolution. In this he was echoing the opinions of his preceptors in his family, in the Church, at Oxford. His entry into politics at Westminster had brought him under the influence of no new theory, but of undeniable political facts. One of these facts was the movement for reform. It was the practical application of the faith in liberty that lay at the basis of all the political movements of the nineteenth century. His instinct for accommodating differences, his keen eye for tendencies that would not be denied, quickly convinced him that these tendencies, when duly presented, must be respected. He needed, therefore, a larger principle to include them in his own ideals. Just as he had believed implicitly whatever he was told authoritatively in his youth, so later the evidence of his eyes convinced him. That which theoretic argument in favour of liberty had failed to impress upon his mind, the facts of immediate experience proved conclusively. From facts he was always ready and eager to learn, and the popular demands in which they generally came to him gradually received the idealisation originally represented for him by ecclesiastical teaching. He was

a minister still : not in Holy Orders, but as spokesman
and representative of popular movements, and the
recognition which his political jubilee received showed
that he was so regarded in many countries besides
England. A subscription was raised in Athens to place
a statue of him in the city, and the Greeks also made
him a splendid personal gift. He had become, among
living statesmen, an international symbol for Europe,
and in his seventies he seemed to be still in the plenitude
of his powers. Just because his vitality was extraordinary, in one or two practical matters he was beyond,
instead of abreast of, the political trend of his time.
The most significant instance of this so far, had been his
settlement of the Alabama claims by arbitration. If he
had reorganised the tariff to suit the inevitable victory
of free trade, he had also at the Exchequer laid the
basis of future financial policy, and some of his achievements for civil administration are now only obscured
because they are taken as a matter of course. So much
industry and fervour promised no term beyond his
natural powers, and already in his seventies he appeared
to be younger than his political contemporaries. The
Queen, nervously anxious that his activities might be
curtailed (she had been disturbed to learn that he had
contemplated another visit to Midlothian, which Sir
Andrew Clark came to her rescue by forbidding), hoped
that he would accept a peerage. He was not to be
tempted. The House of Commons was his arena and
his home. For a rest he spent the first month of 1883
at Cannes, and soon after his return was invited to
Sandringham, where " the Prince bade me read the
lessons." His constant self-deception, that he wanted
to retire, persisted to the end, and we find him now
writing to Manning : " I trust it may not be long ere
I escape into some position better suited to declining
years." The explanation is familiar. He was in the

thick of those personal questions that harassed him, including Cabinet reconstruction and the utterances of Chamberlain that gave offence at Court. We are reminded of his difficulties in his confession to Lord Granville:

> Every extravagance of this kind puts weapons into the hands of opponents, and weakens the authority of Government, which is hardly ever too strong, and is often too weak already.

Many personal embarrassments with the Queen, with the House of Lords, with colleagues, not to mention the Irish Members, made the year 1883 an exhausting one for him. In September, therefore, he went for a northern cruise on the *Pembroke Castle*, as Sir Donald Currie's guest. The account of his journey is contained in three letters to the Queen, to whom he had to apologise for a breach of etiquette :

> Mr. Gladstone presents his humble duty to your Majesty, and has to offer his humble apology for not having sought from your Majesty the usual gracious permission before setting foot on a foreign shore.

He had intended to visit only the Western Isles, but the ship seemed so seaworthy that the party, of whom Tennyson was one, decided to cross the North Sea and to run over to Christiansand and Copenhagen. It was a brief trip, but something occurred even more exciting than the bevy of royalties who were entertained at Copenhagen, where Tennyson read some of his poems aloud to them. We have a glimpse of the affair from the point of view of Tennyson's son, in his life of his father :

> Mr. Gladstone caught sight of me reading by the bulwarks of the *Pembroke Castle* one day, and beckoned me to walk with him. He said that literature was one of the noblest callings he knew, that he honoured my father greatly, and

that for the sake of literature he would like to offer him a
distinction from the Queen—about which he had been in
correspondence with Lord Granville—a barony. "Do you
think that your father would accept it?" I replied that the
offer was so startling that I did not know how he would
take it, but I thought that he might accept it for the sake of
literature (remembering how various literary men had cried
"shame upon him" when he did not take the baronetcy
offered three successive times). The only difficulty in Gladstone's mind was that my father might insist on wearing his
wideawake in the House of Lords.

The difficulty of the wideawake was overcome, and
no objection arose from Tennyson's pipe, despite Gladstone's undying horror of tobacco. He expected his
private secretaries, if they smoked themselves, to change
their clothes before they entered his presence. Even
distinguished visitors to Hawarden are said to have made
conditions, or to have smoked clandestinely in their
bedrooms like boys at school. After accepting a royal
invitation to dine at Fredensborg, Gladstone reported
to the Queen that he found there:

the entire circle of illustrious personages who have been
gathered for some time in a family party, with a very few
exceptions. The singularly domestic character of this remarkable assemblage, and the affectionate intimacy which appeared
to pervade it made an impression on him. . . . Nor must
Mr. Gladstone allow himself to omit another striking feature
of the remarkable picture, in the unrestrained and unbounded
happiness of the royal children, nineteen in number, who
appeared like a single family under a single roof.

The crowned heads of Russia, Denmark and Greece
all visited the vessel. In reply to the King of Denmark's
toast of his health, Gladstone observed that "perhaps
the most vigorous and remarkable portion of the British
nation" had been drawn from Scandinavian countries.
After luncheon Tennyson read two of his poems, with
the royal children "clustering round the doors."

On his return Gladstone thanked the Queen for

"'giving him full credit for not having reflected at the time' when he decided, as your Majesty believes, to extend his recent cruise to Norway and Denmark." It is amusing to see him, in this small matter, spinning his habitual web of explanation, and pointing out that he had, in the course of his trip, extended his views rather than his voyage, and pleading guilty only to not having foreseen everything which had occurred. He denies the report in certain foreign newspapers that there had been any discussion of public affairs, and is consoled to find that suspicion in England had been confined to two secondary journals which have never found " in any act of his anything but guilt and folly." On the voyage out they had landed at Kirkwall, where Gladstone proposed the health of Tennyson. After remarking that their careers had been contemporaneous, he went on to say that the work of the poet would prove more enduring than his own :

> We public men play a part which places us much in view of our countrymen, but the words which we speak have wings and fly away and disappear. . . . The Poet Laureate has written his own song on the hearts of his countrymen that can never die.

The humorous reflection that "fame has no present and popularity no future" is hardly true of either man. No statesman has been more personally successful than Gladstone, and Tennyson was the most successful of our fine poets. The office of Laureate perhaps will never again be so appropriately filled. Tennyson's verse on official occasions is the masterpiece of its difficult kind, and if his success was necessarily due rather to the quality that belonged to his age than to the virtue which was above it, still, as poet and as Laureate, Tennyson's position is secure. Gladstone worked in much more perishable material, and if he is finally remembered as a prodigy of energy rather than for any special dis-

Q

tinction of mind, of who else can it be said that a century
of political life was garnered and expressed in a single
career and public character?

V

One final matter of domestic importance was the
question of extending the borough franchise of 1867 to
country householders, and Gladstone knew that his
term of office could not be allowed to expire without
taking virtually the final step towards manhood suffrage.
It is always the last move that a Government makes, if
only because it is the natural precursor to a General
Election. The Bill that became an Act in 1885 is
important to Gladstone's story, not because of the bitter
controversy over the redistribution of seats that accompanied it, but because it provided the means whereby
the national voice of Ireland could be unmistakably
heard, and so gave to Gladstone his overwhelming
argument in favour of the Irish proposals. The Opposition, virtually the House of Lords, which twice rejected
the measure in spite of the technically unanimous consent
of the Lower House, feared that if the new franchise
was granted without a redistribution of seats, the Conservative party would be condemned indefinitely to a
minority. Gladstone held that the two changes should
indeed arrive together, but that if the two Bills were
presented simultaneously the franchise would be defeated.
The difficulty between the two Houses was so great
that, if the possibility of a creation of peers was to be
avoided, it became necessary for Gladstone to secure
every vote in the Lords that was open to his persuasiveness. He approached the Archbishop of Canterbury;
he even wrote to Tennyson : " You are the only peer,
so far as I know, associated with Liberal ideas or the
Liberal party, who hesitates to vote against Lord Salis-

bury." With tireless patience and tenacity, and with his usual endeavours to be accommodating without sacrificing anything essential, Gladstone declared himself ready to produce his redistribution scheme once the passage of the Franchise Bill was guaranteed. As a last resort, the chiefs of both parties met privately to discuss the official scheme before it was introduced into the House, a very unusual proceeding, needless to say. These discussions produced at last a settlement, and the new Reform Bill added about a million and a quarter voters to the register in England, and nearly half a million Irishmen.

Parnell told his countrymen that the Nationalists and the Irish in England now had the power of determining at the next General Election whether the Liberals or the Tories should return to power. This influence, he added, had secured the inclusion of Ireland in the Franchise Bill, and he prophesied, with calm assurance, that his party would come back ninety strong. The important fact was that, whether the Irish Members rose to ninety or remained at seventy-five, they held the balance, and that balance made him indifferent which English party was in office. The power that he could throw into the scale would suffice to defeat any Government which denied the Irish claims. The endeavour to satisfy them is the last, most chequered, and dramatic chapter in Gladstone's extraordinary career.

VI

Before we look backward and forward into this tremendous story, we must follow the fortunes of Gladstone's second administration to its end, and confine ourselves to the strenuous year that preceded the elections. At the close of 1884 he had been sleeping badly. This rare visitation invariably pointed to harassed days.

There is a touch of pathos in his birthday note : " a little woodcraft for helping sleep," and on New Year's Eve, " only an hour and a half of sleep, which will hardly do to work upon." The approaching elections were disturbing because they raised once more the inevitable possibility of his retirement, and the immediate prospect of a split in his party, which that retirement was held certain to foreshadow. Yet few welcomed the withdrawal of Gladstone's experienced and restraining hand at the moment when the extension of the franchise held unforeseeable possibilities. Conservative-minded people were apprehensive, the rest excited, and the presence of Gladstone, even should he be left in opposition, was regarded as a valuable bridge over the currents of change. The few months that remained before the fall of the Government included the news of the fall of Khartoum, which was nearly fatal, for the Government escaped a vote of censure by the bare majority of fourteen. Gladstone determined to remain, despite a divided Cabinet, until the Redistribution Bill was passed. The condition of affairs in the Cabinet itself may be judged from one of his comments : " A very fair Cabinet to-day—only three resignations." As he wrote to his wife :

> All the later history of this ministry, which is now entering on its sixth year, has been a wild romance of politics, with a continual succession of hairbreadth escapes and strange accidents pressing upon one another, and it is only from the number of dangers we have passed through already that one can be bold enough to hope we may pass also through what yet remain. . . . Russia and Ireland are the two great dangers remaining.

The Russian danger in Afghanistan passed, and on the evening of the following day, which happened to be a Sunday, Gladstone dined at Marlborough House, which, though otherwise charming, he found " un-

Sundaylike and unrestful." Ireland was quieter. One could hardly say more.

In August 1885 the Crimes Act was to expire, and with a General Election in sight, it became a matter of party interest whether or not it should be renewed. In May Gladstone proposed to renew certain of its clauses. Thereupon it was obvious that Parnell's support might be gained and the elections won if the Conservatives offered to drop coercion. Without official information upon the actual condition of affairs in Ireland, they could hardly promise this, but they went as far as they could and allowed their attitude to be known. The Liberals were divided on the question of coercion. Some favoured an increased degree of local self-government, others the creation of a central board with administrative functions for the whole country. Gladstone preserved a memorandum of his own attitude at this time :

> I looked upon the extension of a strong measure of local government like this to Ireland, now that the question is effectually revived by the Crimes Act, as invaluable itself, and as the only hopeful means of securing Crown and State from an ignominious surrender in the next Parliament after a mischievous and painful struggle.

He goes on to say that he did not contemplate opening the Irish question in connection with his resignation, should he resign. " It would come antecedently to any parliamentary treatment of that problem." If the Cabinet was then broken up, he felt, as he looked round upon the virtual settlement of the Russian and Egyptian difficulties, that " it would leave behind it an excellent record at home and abroad."

Despite the approval of Parnell, the plan for a central board failed to carry the whole Cabinet. Gladstone was disappointed, and his comment was : " Ah, they will rue this day "; and again, " Within six years, if it

please God to spare their lives, they will be repenting
in sackcloth and ashes." Refusing to be depressed,
Gladstone spent Whitsun at Hawarden, and found
refreshment in *Cooper on the Atonement*, some congenial
visitors, and other books. On June 4, 1885, he returned
to London, and four days later the Irish Nationalists
combined with the Conservatives to defeat the Government upon the Budget proposals. This new alliance
showed that Parnell's already quoted words were true,
and that, having failed in spite of Gladstone to gain
what he wanted from the Liberals, he now proposed to
put the Tories to the test, by placing them immediately
under an obligation to him.

So ended the long struggle against unsuspected difficulties which filled these five precarious years. Even
apart from Ireland, they were perhaps the most exacting
of Gladstone's political life. After accepting his resignation, the Queen offered him an earldom, adding that
while the country would " doubtless " be pleased, she
believed " that it would be beneficial to his health—no
longer exposing him to the pressure from without, for
more active work than he ought to undertake." She
went on :

> Only the other day—without reference to the present
> events—the Queen mentioned to Mrs. Gladstone at Windsor
> the advantage to Mr. Gladstone's health of a removal from
> one House to the other, in which she seemed to agree. The
> Queen trusts, therefore, that Mr. Gladstone will accept the
> offer of an earldom, which would be very gratifying to her.

He replied that, while he prized every word of her
letter, he ought not to accept, and that any services he
could yet render would be greater in the Commons
than the Lords. " It has never formed part of his
views to enter that historic chamber." He coveted
rather " that interval between an active career and death,
which the profession of politics has always seemed to

him especially to require." To Lord Granville he is more personal.

> I send you herewith a letter from the Queen which moves and almost upsets me. It must have cost her much to write, and it is really a pearl of great price.

Gladstone, more than most people who do not take a courtier's view of life, must have felt the lack of intimacy between himself and his sovereign. Perhaps, after all, it did *not* cost her much to offer the customary recognition that would incidentally curtail his future activities in politics. That he felt otherwise, however, is the last pin-prick of his second term of office. We have now to go back to the part of Ireland in these years, that we may trace without interruption the last of Gladstone's crusades. It involved an effort in which even changes of government were but episodes. It was his one domestic struggle that deserves the name of drama. It is perhaps the only one which the future cannot help following with unabated interest, though the prime hero is not Gladstone but Parnell, the most arresting political personality of the century.

CHAPTER VI

HIS LAST CRUSADE

I

THE election which had followed the Midlothian campaign had not turned, as we have seen, upon Irish affairs, and it is not really necessary to examine Gladstone's previous utterances in order to determine precisely when and why he became convinced that the settlement of the Irish claims was both just and inevitable. Once again it was the facts of the situation that taught him, and English politicians have never had a sterner schoolmaster than Parnell. The distinction of Gladstone is to have been the first responsible English politician to admit the facts, and to refuse to pretend any longer to ignore them. He never had axiomatic objections to permanent settlements of burning controversies. He was not a man who would shut his eyes to a situation, and our treatment of Ireland in the past would seem to exalt this into an English characteristic. He was thus alone, and in the position of having to fight against his own side. There was no popularity to be won in England by meeting Irish aspirations. Here he was unquestionably disinterested, and he was carried forward by his innate desire to clear difficulties out of the way, and to overtake arrears rather than to make innovations. He could admit movements beyond the Channel.

There was no reference to Ireland in the Queen's Speech, and Gladstone thought that the Church Act of

1869 and the Land Act of 1870 had settled the question.
He and the country were soon undeceived. Distress in
Ireland, in circumstances which could not have been
foreseen, were leading to the wanton eviction of many
tenants, and to the defeat of the objects of the Act of
1870 itself. A Bill to compensate evicted tenants, on
certain conditions, was passed by the Commons but
rejected by the House of Lords. In one of his innumerable memoranda Gladstone wrote :

> The rapid and vast extension of agrarian disturbance
> followed, as was to be expected, this wild excess of landlord-
> ism, and the Irish Government proceeded to warn the Cabinet
> that coercive legislation would be necessary. Forster allowed
> himself to be persuaded by the governmental agents in Ire-
> land that the root of the evil lay within small compass. . . . I
> must say I never fell into this extraordinary illusion of Forster's
> about his " village ruffian."

Gladstone was anxious that there should be an attempt
to try the ordinary law before seeking special powers,
and was opposed to the suspension of the Habeas Corpus
Act. He did not like the imprisonment of men before
they had been tried. In these early days of his Government, however, he was much occupied with foreign
affairs, and he gave way upon both points for fear of
breaking up his new Government, the first duty and
" special commission " of which was to reconstruct the
foreign policy of the country. Meantime, after the
rejection of the Compensation for Disturbance Bill, the
condition of Ireland became alarming. Evictions were
followed by riots, and any who dared to accept the farms
of evicted tenants were attacked, their cattle maimed,
and their ricks set on fire. Parnell declared that the
Land League must give the protection which the Government had failed to supply, and in one of those cool,
direct speeches, which make exciting reading even
to-day, he said :

Depend upon it that the measure of the Land Bill next session will be the measure of your activity and energy this winter. It will be the measure of your determination not to pay unjust rents; it will be the measure of your determination to keep a firm grip on your homesteads. . . . Now what are you to do to a tenant who bids for a farm from which his neighbour has been evicted? I think I heard somebody say, Shoot him! but I wish to point out to you a very much better way. When a man takes a farm from which another has been evicted, you must show him on the roadside when you meet him, you must show him in the streets of the town, you must show him at the shop counter, you must show him in the fair and in the market-place, and even in the house of worship, by leaving him severely alone, by putting him into a moral Coventry, by isolating him from his kind as if he were a leper of old, you must show him your detestation of the crime he has committed and you may depend upon it that there will be no man . . . to transgress your unwritten code of laws.

In this speech the policy was launched which gave the word boycott to the language. With the wonderful faculty of the Irish for acting together, Captain Boycott was the first of a line of victims to the triumphant policy of Parnell. It reminds us that the real difficulty was the virtual expropriation of the peasants from the land by a system of law devised by the landlords for their own benefit, and that the political movement for Home Rule, though reasonable in itself, became the extension of agrarian hatred to landlords who were also political masters. There were two strands to a common aspiration, but the land was the question of the hour. Gladstone was placed in the difficulty of having to devise a new Land Bill while meeting the immediate disturbances with a renewed resort to coercion.

II

With this harassing prospect the session of 1881 opened, and Parnell's answer to coercion was to bring

obstruction into full play. Mr. Forster's Bill, summarised by Morley as enabling the Viceroy to lock up
anybody he pleased, gave the Irish Members the excuse
to make parliamentary business impossible. By a continuous sitting of twenty-four hours Gladstone tried to
force the measure through. The Speaker felt that it
rested with him to extricate the House from the defeat
of its wishes by a minority, and offered to closure discussion of his own authority. After an all-night sitting
the inexhaustible Biggar was still on his feet when the
Speaker returned to take the place of his deputy and put
the question. It was the climax of the debate, and the
Irish retired under protest on the second division. By
this means Westminster was forcibly reminded of the
happenings beyond the Irish Sea, where during the
previous year over ten thousand tenants had been
evicted. The evicting landlords found graves dug
before their doors when they crossed their own thresholds
in the morning. In a word, coercion was the only
alternative to the refusal of the House of Lords to grant
any concessions to the peasantry.

It is remarkable that, even before this manifestation of
Irish power to impede English legislation, in fact in the
previous autumn, Parnell was under no illusion over the
permanence of his tactics or the independence of his party.
As the most detached observer that the House has
numbered among its active Members, Parnell's opinion
of the atmosphere of Westminster is worth recording.
From time to time the doubt that he expressed revives,
and its force is not confined to the minority of Irishmen
whom he was contemplating. On receiving the freedom
of Limerick he told his audience :

> I am not one of those who believe in the permanence of an
> Irish party in the English Parliament. I feel convinced that,
> sooner or later, the influence which every English Government
> has at its command—the powerful and demoralising influence

—sooner or later will sap the best party you can return to the
House of Commons. . . . But I think it possible to maintain
the independence of our party by great exertions . . . while
we are making a short, sharp, and I trust decisive, struggle for
the restoration of our legislative independence.

Gladstone believed in the parliamentary atmosphere
which Parnell distrusted, and the contrast between the
two men is too distinct to be emphasised.   A piquancy
is added to their struggle from the fact that the cool,
imperturbable Parnell represented Ireland with what
Englishmen believe to be English qualities, while the
eloquent master of persuasive rhetoric was not the Irish
but the Englishman.   Though Parnell could not prevent
the passing of a Coercion Bill, he fulfilled his determination that the struggle against it should be " such as
never has been seen within the walls of Parliament."
If, for example, the Speaker had closed the debate on
Wednesday morning, the Irish succeeded in spending the
whole of the rest of the day till the adjournment dis-
cussing the question that he should search for precedents
to justify what he had done.

The result of this was to lead Gladstone to propose
certain changes in procedure which would render the
repetition of these tactics impossible.   Thereupon Mr.
Parnell rose in a scene of indescribable uproar to move
that the right hon. member be no longer heard.   The
comedy of the situation, for the terms of the motion were
inconceivable to the House and to the country, is obvious,
and Parnell and thirty-two Irish Members were suspended
before Gladstone was allowed to speak.   Despite the
revised procedure, the Coercion Bill was not passed until
March 2, and though Kilmainham Gaol became full of
Land Leaguers, the agitation did not cease.

III

The next step was to introduce a Land Bill, and if it was not received in a spirit of conciliation, it was admitted by Irishmen themselves to be " a sweeping measure of reform." Gladstone himself called it " the most difficult measure he had ever known to come under the detailed consideration of a Cabinet." It removed the exceptions and limitations which had robbed the Act of 1870 of its effect. Land courts were formed to fix rents, and the right of the tenant to dispose of the good-will of his holding was secured to him. The principal demands of the Land League were granted. It was the reward of agitation. As Gladstone said in 1893, " without the Land League the Act of 1881 would not now be on the Statute Book "

Parnell, convinced that the Bill was safe, was anxious not to be responsible for it, and advised his followers not to vote for the second reading, though some of them were carried away by feelings of gratitude. In committee, therefore, whenever the Bill was in danger, Parnell came to the Government's support. Whenever it was safe, he suggested improvements. Gladstone must have watched these parliamentary tactics with eager interest, for they showed a mastery as unmistakable as it was different from his own. If Parnell forced his hand by means of the Land League, and kept the same pressure on the land courts by discouraging the tenants from recourse to them until certain test cases had been submitted, yet it is also true that Gladstone was the sole responsible English statesman who desired to see existing abuses settled equitably. He had to deal also with English opinion; he too was ultimately dependent upon it, and he cannot be blamed for making English opinion the limit of reforms that it was possible for him to

propose. It should be enough to recall that the Land
Act of 1881 is one of the two or three measures which
have been regarded as Gladstone's best achievements of
statesmanship. Yet its embodiment of fair rent, fixity
of tenure, and free disposal—the Three F's—had seemed
incredible to him when recommended by the Bess-
borough commission a few months before.

It was on October 7, 1881, that Gladstone, as we saw,
threatened Parnell with "the resources of civilisation,"
and Parnell's reply, characteristically defiant, is interesting for a certain familiar criticism that it contains.
After describing Gladstone, in one of his few personalities,
as "this pretending champion of the rights of every other
nation except those of the Irish nation," Parnell continued :

> He says the late Isaac Butt was a most estimable man and a
> true patriot. When we in Ireland were following Isaac Butt
> into the lobbies, endeavouring to obtain the very Act which
> William Ewart Gladstone, having stolen the idea from Isaac
> Butt, passed last session, William Ewart Gladstone and his
> ex-Government officials were following Sir Stafford Northcote
> and Benjamin Disraeli into the other lobby.

While it is extraordinary that Gladstone had no immediate insight into rights or principles, though apparently
preoccupied with nothing else, it is no less extraordinary
that he was quicker than any of his countrymen to accept
unpalatable facts, and, having learnt from them, to work
harder and more tenaciously than his colleagues to con-
vince his countrymen of the remedy. Difficulties for
Gladstone existed to be solved, though he needed jogging
to become aware of their existence. Indeed it may be
said that the combination of Parnell, that relentless goad,
and Gladstone, that indefatigible steer, was the only one
imaginable to settle the Irish question in a nineteenth-
century English Parliament.

Parnell anticipated arrest after making this speech.

When asked who would take his place, if this happened, he replied in one of those terse phrases that are still moving for their point, " Captain Moonlight will take my place." He meant that, after all, he was the brake that held back disorder, and his phrase is worth quoting as the shortest instance of an electric force of words that belies Morley's distinction between the immediate effects of oratory and the abiding effect of literature. Parnell and Gladstone were both almost worshipped by their audiences, yet the speeches of Parnell still made excellent reading. There is a grip upon reality about them which is as effective now as it was at the moment when he spoke. From Kilmainham Gaol he sent this message :

> I shall take it as evidence that the people of the country did not do their duty if I am speedily released.

Gladstone was answered.

This was in the autumn of 1881, and by the following April Gladstone's own attitude was as follows. In a letter to Forster he wrote :

> In truth I should say (differing perhaps from many) that for the Ireland of to-day the first question is the rectification of the relations between landlord and tenant, which happily is going on; the next is to relieve Great Britain from the enormous weight of the government of Ireland unaided by the people, and from the hopeless contradiction in which we stand while we give a parliamentary representation, hardly effective for anything but mischief, without the local institutions of self-government which it presupposes, and on which alone it can have a sound and healthy basis.

He had advanced far, but in the meantime, as the prisoner had predicted, Captain Moonlight at large was more dangerous than the Parnell whose place he had taken. In despair, Gladstone appealed to Newman on the chance that the Pope might be able to intervene. Nothing came of the Errington mission, as it was called, except that to the Irish it seemed a backstairs attempt

which they much resented. The matter is only interesting as showing how warily, as Newman had
remarked, the Pope must proceed in political affairs
which affect others besides the priests.

From this just quoted letter to Forster another sentence
must be detached to show an unusually clear example of
development on Gladstone's part. Speaking of local
self-government for Ireland, Gladstone said :

> If we must postpone the question till the state of the country
> is more fit for it, I should answer that the least danger is in
> going forward at once. It is liberty alone which fits men for
> liberty. This proposition, like every other in politics, has its
> bounds; but it is far safer than the counter-doctrine, wait till
> they are fit.

He had not thought so in his youth when he declared
that moral must precede the physical emancipation of
the slaves, but experience had enlightened him. The
problem was how to apply this principle to the present
state of Ireland. Since the last Coercion Act and the
imprisonment of Parnell, conditions in Ireland were
worse than before. Statistics showed that murders and
crimes had either doubled or trebled. Parnell was in
gaol, but what was to be done ? The failure of the
repressive policy was hopeless. Gladstone had resorted
to coercion with dislike, and had acted on the advice
of the Irish executive. Since the policy must be altered,
he could not but think of Parnell. Even the Conservatives declared that " the present measures of coercion
have entirely failed to restore order." It seemed to some
of the Irishmen that the Conservatives were going to pose
as the friends of their country at Gladstone's expense.
From Parnell's point of view there was a risk that the
country would soon pass beyond his control. His
active control became, therefore, a matter of concern to
both nations. He and Gladstone were thinking of each
other. Released on parole to visit his sister, whose son

was dying in Paris, Parnell saw Captain O'Shea, who was
in touch with the Government, and told him that the
present anarchy was due to the numerous small tenants
who, unable to pay their rents, were intimidating the
richer ones; and that, while the eviction of the former
would intensify crime, an Arrears Bill, to relieve those
who could not pay, would tranquillise the country.
Parnell held that if the arrears question were settled, as
he proposed, he and his colleagues would be able to
check further outrages. It is true that, if set at liberty,
they would be better able to control events, but the
position of the imprisoned leaders was never discussed,
nor were they concerned with anything but to explain to
the Government how to relieve the appalling situation
in Ireland.

Rumours of these exchanges spread abroad, and,
not liking the proposals, Lord Cowper resigned the
Viceroyalty and Mr. Forster the Chief Secretaryship.
Parnell was released. There has been a tiresome discussion whether there was a Kilmainham treaty or not.
Gladstone strenuously denied it. Negotiations there
certainly were, but there was no consideration. Parnell
volunteered the opinion that, if a satisfactory Arrears
Bill was introduced, the country would be tranquillised
and he would be in a position to slow down agitation.
In this he was stating a fact rather than laying down a
condition, but his release gave colour to the suggestion,
which he and Gladstone both denied, truly enough, in
Parliament, that his release was part of an arrangement.
Further colour was given to the fiction because it was
over Parnell's release that Forster had resigned. Everyone recognised that Parnell was a controlling influence,
and his release was only a matter of time. Coming when
it did, however, and followed as it was by Forster's
resignation, it looked like part of a bargain, and this it
certainly was not.

R

IV

To fill the vacant offices Gladstone chose Lord Frederick Cavendish, who had married one of Mrs. Gladstone's nieces, for the Chief-Secretaryship, and Lord Spencer for the new Viceroy. On the evening of his arrival, Lord Frederick Cavendish and Mr. Burke, the Under-Secretary, were murdered in Phœnix Park by a group of assassins. They called themselves the Invincibles, and had sprung up under Forster's administration. Mr. Burke was their object, and Lord Frederick, who was an innocent stranger, was murdered by mistake. They did not know who he was. The horror that the crime occasioned was felt throughout Ireland as well. Not only was Gladstone stunned by the news, but so was Parnell. " How can I," he cried, " carry on a public agitation if I am stabbed in the back in this way ? " It arrested the new policy of conciliation at the moment of its birth. Parnell offered to resign his seat, a proposal Gladstone refused to entertain, though he said that he was deeply sensible of the honourable motives which had prompted the proposal. Gladstone wrote to Lord Granville : " If Parnell goes, no restraining influence will remain." Meantime English opinion demanded a new Coercion Act, which was shortly passed in 1882. The Irish did what they could to oppose the measure, but they could not disguise that the Phœnix Park murders had weakened their hands. Parnell was sympathetic to Gladstone himself :

> We have been contending against the right hon. gentleman for two years. We have found him to be a great man and a strong man. I even think it is no dishonour to admit that we should not wish to be fought again in the same way by anybody in the future. I regret that the event in the Phœnix Park has prevented him continuing the course of conciliation that we had expected from him. I regret that owing to the exigencies

of his party, of his position in the country, he has felt himself compelled to turn from that course of conciliation and concession into the horrible path of coercion.

After eighteen Irish Members had been suspended, they retired, protesting that important parts of the measure, having been passed in their enforced absence, the new law would be devoid of moral force. Gladstone immediately brought in an Arrears Bill, which practically embodied the suggestions made by Parnell himself in Kilmainham. He was thereupon true to his word. With the question of arrears settled, he proceeded to suppress the Ladies' Land League, which had been extremely active during his imprisonment, and generally to secure such quiet in the country as would fulfil his intentions and prepare the way for a new move at a more seasonable time. In October 1882 the National League was formed, which made political agitation for Home Rule, and not the land, its principal concern.

The next event of importance was the Reform Act of 1884, which extended household suffrage to Ireland. Mr. Gladstone's difficult part in conducting this measure through both Houses we have already seen. The electorate of Ireland was trebled, and if some thought that the new Act would make Ireland Liberal they were rudely undeceived. With the help of the Irish vote the Conservatives returned to power, and Lord Salisbury became Prime Minister in 1885. The idea perhaps was that the Conservatives would do something which, having made the question of Home Rule an English party matter, in time would encourage Gladstone and the Liberals to do more. Parnell once said to his biographer, Mr. R. Barry O'Brien : " You do not know what it is to fight Mr. Gladstone. I am no match for him. I could not explain to you what it is to have to fight him. I know it. I have fought him, and am ready to fight him again ; but he knows more moves on the board than

I do." He thought Gladstone the most useful ally that he could have in England, but he also thought that the Liberals were less likely than the Conservatives to conduct a Home Rule Bill through the House of Lords. By exercising relentless pressure upon both the English parties, Parnell believed that in the end Gladstone would take the lead. In the meantime, therefore, he had to set the pace for him by proving the influence of the Irish vote at Gladstone's expense.

The first-fruits of this punishment of the Liberals and instalment of the Conservatives were promising. Lord Carnarvon, the new Viceroy, announced the abandonment of coercion and his intention to rule by the customary law. Other Conservatives, including Lord Salisbury and Lord Randolph Churchill, struck the same note so forcibly that the rank and file of the party and its papers were shocked. The conciliation of Parnell seemed to them to be going too far. It was the Conservatives now who were pledging themselves to an alternative policy. After practically forty years of misgovernment by exceptional legislation, Ireland was surely entitled to a change. Coercion was thus described as the Liberal policy, and the impression made by the change of front was stronger on no one than Gladstone himself. Did it not now seem that *both* the English parties might combine for the solution of the Irish question ? In the elections the voice of united Ireland had been unmistakably pronounced. This was the deciding factor to Gladstone, who looked forward hopefully to the future.

Parnell's motion for an inquiry into certain capital convictions carried out under Lord Spencer was received sympathetically. Indeed some of the speeches condemning the policy of the late Government were so strong that they produced remonstrances, and it was not difficult even for Conservatives to argue that Ministers were acting against their known convictions for party reasons. It was at least a complete somersault. Gladstone's view of it must be given in his own words :

> Within the last two or three weeks (he wrote to Lord Derby) the situation has undergone important changes. I am not fully informed, but what I know looks as if the Irish party, so called in Parliament, excited by the high biddings of Lord Randolph, had changed what was undoubtedly Parnell's ground until within a very short time back. It is now said that a central board will not suffice, and that there must be a parliament. This, I suppose, may mean the repeal of the Act of Union, or may mean an Austro-Hungarian scheme, or may mean that Ireland is to be like a great colony such as Canada. Of all or any of these schemes I will now only say that, of course, they constitute an entirely new point of departure. . . .

He followed this up by writing to Granville :

> For my own part I have seen my way pretty well as to the particulars of the minor and rejected plan, but the idea of the wider one puzzles me much. At the same time, *if* the election gives a return of a decisive character, the sooner the subject is dealt with the better.

This was in August 1885. The wary old statesman was watching the shifting sands of opinion to see if it might not now be possible to build on them an Irish parliamentary house. Parnell was the reality close at hand, and it remained to be seen whether the ministerialists on both sides were not going in advance of the country, and whether their followers would remain docile to leadership of this kind. It may still be said that Gladstone was almost the only responsible English statesman who took the Irish question seriously, and desired that it should be settled permanently. It was old and thorny, and English affairs could not wait for ever for their turn.

Two days after the above note was written, Gladstone, whose throat was proving troublesome, joined Sir Thomas and Lady Brassey on a cruise to Norway, during which he astonished the party by a walk of eighteen miles. Though now past his seventy-fifth birthday, no one who saw Mr. Gladstone, Lady Brassey recorded, " could feel much anxiety on the score of the failure of his strength." He meditated on spiritual matters, and began to draft notes for his next election address to Midlothian. The draft, completed after his return and in view of the approaching dissolution, was " written with my best care to avoid treading on the toes of either the right or the left wing." Has anyone else so combined the art of ambiguity in expression with the same practical power of carrying matters through ? On this occasion he was discursive to an extreme even for him, and many fell into the temptation of judging the result without weighing the innumerable qualifications. To write papers incapable of exact summary, and too long to remember, was Gladstone's way of reserving his freedom. The final emphasis of meaning would only fall upon the right clause when all the practical circumstances were known. His sincerity lay in the tenacity with which, through devious expressions and in doubtful circumstances, he pursued his way towards the best solution available at the moment. His material was the changing current of opinion, and his object was to devise a policy which should satisfy Ireland without dividing the Liberals at his back. If he was trying to unite incompatibles, it was his fate and not his fault. The sincerity of his attempt was the one permanent fact upon which Parnell could now rely in English politics. The following words, written to Lord Granville early in October 1885, are surely convincing and characteristic :

> I remain at present in the leadership of the party, first with a view to the election, and secondly with a view to being, by a bare possibility, of use afterwards in the Irish question if it should take a favourable turn, but [not] . . . should the question be merely one of Liberal v. Conservative, and not

one of commanding imperial necessity, such as that of the Irish Government may come to be after the dissolution.

The attempted settlement of the Irish question, but nothing less, would encourage Gladstone to take office. This put the party, in the person of Lord Granville, in a dilemma. As long as Gladstone was available he was the indispensable leader, but his insistence on a Home Rule policy made the indispensable a possible source of disunion. After a visit from Chamberlain to Hawarden matters seemed brighter, and agreement with that decided gentleman within reach. Of this conversation Gladstone wrote to Lord Granville :

> I told him . . . that if a big Irish question should arise, and arise in such a form as to promise a possibility of settlement, that would be a crisis with a beginning and an end, and perhaps one in which from age and circumstances I might be able to supply aid and service such as could not be exactly had without me.

He would not remain for other questions or for party reasons, least of all as a nominal head. Certainly if the last of his crusades could be carried to success, it would be an appropriate end to his career, the most appropriate imaginable. Can we infer that, this achieved, he would really have retired at last ? It is unusually rash to prophesy, at any time of Gladstone's life, of the fulfilment of this recurrent, pious aspiration. But we are safe in assuming that the settlement of an outstanding difficulty was the strongest of motives with him, and that, if it could be gained, at his time of life he might conceivably withdraw, provided that no fresh incentive should appeal to his energies. At the moment his venerable age might lend to him an authority unique for his cherished purpose, and there was the added thought that his power to exert it was matched against time.

V

Gladstone's attitude, of course, was not the only factor in a mysterious situation. With the approval of Lord Salisbury, Lord Carnarvon, the sympathetic Viceroy, had had a conversation with Parnell, which Parnell left " believing that I was in complete accord with him regarding the main outlines of a settlement conferring a legislature upon Ireland." Parnell naturally inferred that such a conversation could not have been held unless the Government was also favourable. In the controversy that followed, Carnarvon, in effect, denied no more than having stated that the Conservatives intended, if they were returned after the election, to create an Irish Parliament. To surmise something of the kind was surely but to believe that the recent alliance between the Irish and the Conservatives was bearing fruit. It is true that this was a larger expectation than Parnell had expressed before, but then his power had grown in the meantime, and his party would certainly be stronger after the approaching election. He was setting one English party in the scales against the other. He was bidding high. In thinking of the value of the Irish vote to either, he must presume that the English leaders knew how far opinion in this country would support them. It was not for him to worry whether they were thinking too little of their followers and too much of him. His business was to keep them strictly to the level by insisting upon the utmost value for his support.

When Parnell's attitude was known, the division in the ranks of the Liberals began to appear. The explicit demand led Lord Hartington to reject it, and Chamberlain to go back on his words. He had compared the administration of Dublin Castle to " that with which Russia governs Poland, or that which prevailed in Venice under Austrian rule." That was in June 1885. In August Parnell had spoken. In September Chamberlain had replied : " If these are the terms on which Mr. Parnell's support is to be obtained, I will not enter into the compact." It is hardly to be wondered that Parnell put no faith in English professions, and maintained to the last his attitude that the English would give what they could be made to give and no more. Mr. Gladstone, aware of these contradictions in the men behind him, remained. He was naturally wary and non-committal, seeking, as his custom was, for words that should imply the greatest common measure of agreement and committing himself as little as possible beyond. The wish of his colleague, Mr. Childers, to announce to his electors a virtual scheme of Home Rule seemed to Gladstone " a great step in advance," but he begged his adherent not to go beyond a readiness to consider an Irish Parliament for Irish purposes. In September, therefore, he made a speech, saying :

> I believe history and posterity will consign to disgrace the name and memory of every man, be he who he may, and on whichever side of the Channel he may dwell, that, having the power to aid in an equitable settlement between Ireland and Great Britain, shall use that power not to aid, but to prevent or to retard it.

Here we see him at his work of education, implying the solution that he did not state, and using moral pleas to persuade his readers that it was the right one. A little later, in November 1885, with an emphasis that had been slowly gathering in the meantime, he told his constituents in Midlothian that " it will be a vital danger to the country and to the empire if, at a time when a demand from Ireland for larger powers of self-government is to be dealt with, there is not in Parliament a party totally independent of the Irish vote." He pleaded for an independent majority of Liberals. The worst, because

the most unreliable, prospect was one in which the Irish
should still hold the balance.   It would allow no margin,
and give every opportunity to hesitants and to intrigue.

Parnell had tried to draw Mr. Gladstone into stating his
plan, but he was too wary, finding the convenient
excuse that it was not the province of an Opposition
leader to produce such schemes.   This enabled him to
place the onus on the Conservative Government, which
he was afraid would simply make a point of opposing
anything that came personally from himself.   Lord
Salisbury, on his side, was hardly more committal in the
usual idiom of ministers, though it is possible to find
contradictory passages in his speeches, because he had
not Gladstone's mastery of elusiveness.   It is given to
few men to make no definite statements at all.   With
Gladstone's latest utterance before him Parnell, deeming
it to be inexcusable hedging, decided to throw the Irish
vote on the Conservative side.   If he could maintain
them, the feebler party, in office, he could expect from
them the better terms.   So he argued, forgetting perhaps
that the Liberal party was not united on the Irish
question, and that every Liberal seat lost by the opposition of Irish voters must divide them more and make
Ireland an odious word to them.

Parnell's refusal to give either party any rope at all
cost Gladstone about twenty seats at the election.
Parnell was inclined to blame himself later for his decision,
which, events were to prove, overlooked the fact that it
was not Mr. Gladstone who remained unconverted but
his colleagues.   How could the doubters adopt the
cause of an Irish party which voted against their own
members at a critical time ?   But how could Gladstone
be explicit, and how could Parnell be sure that he would
go as far as he dared ?   The issue of the election turned
upon this miserable balance of considerations, which
reveal humanity confronted by difficulties that only

omniscience could solve. We may wish that Gladstone
had been a shade more explicit, and Parnell a shade more
patient. We can sympathise with both. It is not so
easy to sympathise with Lord Salisbury, who, more
definite in words than Gladstone, was really trifling with
the issue more than he.

VI

In October Gladstone was at home, reading and
writing on exalted themes. In November he was in
Midlothian, and was received once more with vast
enthusiasm in Edinburgh. The result of the election
was to give to the Liberals a majority of 82 over the
Conservatives, while Parnell came back with 86. He
still held the balance, but he had made an enemy of many
Liberals on the way, and had shown Lord Salisbury that
his aid was worth little to the Conservative party. He
had also shown that he and his party did represent an
overwhelming national demand. Out of 89 contests the
Nationalists had won 85, and their majorities left the
Tories nowhere. Not a single Liberal in Ireland was
returned. Ireland had spoken with as nearly unanimous
a voice as a nation can speak.

This to Mr. Gladstone was the vital fact of the election.
He comes before us as a statesman nowhere more clearly
than here. He did not want to make the Irish settlement
a party question. He had offered, and was to offer
again, to put no hindrances in the way of the Conservatives if they would deal with it. During the
autumn he had also tried to educate the country by
encouraging an Irish writer to publish two articles :
on " Irish Wrongs and English Remedies," which
appeared in November, and another on " A Federal
Union with Ireland," which appeared in January 1886.

He neglected none of his characteristic arts of persuasion, and if, in the light of subsequent history, we question the tactics of the Irish and the Liberal leaders, we are asking them to be other than themselves.

The alliance between the Conservatives and the Irish left the former in power, with a nominal surplus, despite the result of the elections, and until Parliament should reassemble no one knew what the position really was. On December 10 Gladstone was endeavouring to persuade the Conservative Government to take up the Irish question, and offering informally his co-operation in such a plan. Salisbury had good party reasons for hesitation, and the difference between him and Gladstone was that he could not see the matter in any other light. Uncertainty and excitement were turned into commotion when Gladstone's silence led to rumours in the papers purporting to contain his scheme, the establishment of an Irish Parliament. Gladstone's son was in London. There he formed the opinion that, unless some pronouncement was made, the Liberal party would be split. He therefore gave in an interview his idea of his father's opinions to a journalist who declared that the party needed a lead. Into the announcement the words a Parliament in Dublin crept. Gladstone explained in a telegram that the statement was unauthorised, and " not an accurate representation of my views, but, I presume, a speculation upon them." The result of this well-intentional effort was unfortunate. It was a premature announcement, at a time when Gladstone held silence to be golden, and in truth his precise scheme had not yet formed in his mind. His denial was not satisfactory to the public, for it was a moment when ambiguity was of no avail. It also forced him into utterance at the moment when he held that the Government was the authority to speak. We may perhaps note in passing that there is no hint that Gladstone showed any sign of resentment. If his magnanimity to individuals is ever questioned, surely we may quote this instance in reply.

The ensuing mischief was revealed when Lord Harting-ton publicly declared that he had received no proposals of Liberal policy for meeting the Irish demand, and that he stuck to what he had said during the elections. It meant that he and his Liberal followers would resist any new policy in Ireland. Chamberlain said that the Irish claim was now unmistakable, and that " we ourselves by our public declarations and by our Liberal principles are pledged to acknowledge the justice of this claim." He added that it was for Parnell to " settle accounts with his new friends. . . . If he finds that he has been deceived, he will approach the Liberal party in a spirit of reason and conciliation." The idea of leaving the Conservative minority in power till they had satisfied Parnell was not agreeable to the new Liberal Members of Parliament. Gladstone received many letters of protest against any such course. What, then, was he to do ? In a private memorandum to Lord Granville, written at the end of December, the farthest point to which he would go was this:

> If from any cause the alliance of the Tories and the Nation-alists which did exist, and presumably does exist, should be known to be dissolved, I do not see how it is possible for what would then be the Liberal majority to shrink from the duty appertaining to it as such, and to leave the business of govern-ment to the 250 men whom it was elected to oppose. . . . The case supposed is, the motion made—carried—Ministers resign—Queen sends for me. Might I go so far as to say, I should only accept the trust if assured of the adequate, that is, of the general support of the party to a plan of duly guarded home rule ? If that support were withheld it would be my duty to stand aside.

At the end of the same month Parnell decided that there was nothing to hope from the Conservatives now that his aid had only reduced the number of Liberals at

the elections. The reason why Gladstone was so
anxious not to be drawn is clear from Parnell's remark:
" Whatever chance there was [of the Conservatives acting]
disappeared when the seemingly authoritative statements
of Mr. Gladstone's intention to deal with the question
were published." Yet the Liberals were identified with
coercion in the Irish mind, and therefore for the moment
he left the Conservatives in office. Yet only a combination of the Irish and the Liberals would give either a
majority.

The interval before the meeting of Parliament on
January 12, 1886, was spent by Gladstone at Hawarden
in many matters of personal interest. His second daughter
became engaged; he felled trees, he attended church
punctually; he wrote many letters, and prepared an
article on Huxley for publication; he read Dicey and
Maine, and among other light volumes Rider Haggard's
King Solomon's Mines. He made extracts from Burke,
whom he found " sometimes almost divine." He
renewed friendly correspondence with Manning. On his
birthday seven hundred letters and parcels arrived.

> It was a day for intense thankfulness, but, alas, not for
> recollection and detachment. When will that day come?
> Until then, why string together the commonplaces and
> generalities of great things, really unfelt?

In all this pressure upon him, which included the
weight of the Irish question, what beyond immediate
circumstances had he time to feel, or was he constitu-
tionally capable of feeling? He is certain, he says, of a
keen and deep desire to be extricated from the life of
contention, but was not the life of contention for political
aims his truly inward life? He would change indeed
from political to literary activity, but he could not sit
still, could not even walk slowly, or saunter, or climb
steps less than two at a time. A Martha aspiring in

himself to be a Mary is the shortest accurate description
of this veteran at the beginning of his seventy-seventh
year.

A few days after Parliament assembled, Hartington
told Gladstone that he was determined to maintain the
union; " that is, [so Gladstone understood the phrase]
to proclaim a policy of absolute resistance without
examination to the demand made by Ireland through
five-sixths of her Members. That is, to play the Tory
game with a vengeance. They are now, most rashly
not to say more, working the Irish question to split the
Liberal party."

This naturally seemed to Gladstone to make his own
position impossible, first by hindering him from working
for a settlement, and secondly by assuring the party
split which he had done everything to avoid. In Parliament itself the speech from the throne hinted at the
revival of coercion and referred to the legislative union
of the two countries. By the middle of the month it
was known that Lord Carnarvon and the Chief Secretary
had resigned. Mr. Gladstone's refusal to commit himself was interpreted to mean sympathy for the Irish
claim, and there was no demur to be heard from the
benches behind him. This led the Conservative leaders
to regard the Irish claim as a Liberal party question. As
the recent alliance with the Nationalists had done their
party little good, they were ready enough to repudiate
it now.

On January 26, therefore, the Government announced
a Bill for the suppression of the National League, to be
followed by another Land Bill on the lines of the Ash-
bourne Act of the previous year. The effect on Parnell
was to describe this as " an unscrupulous *volte-face* by
the Tory party when they found that our vote was not
numerous enough to keep them in office." That party
policy, when pursued to the neglect of grave national

interests, leads to these disgraces, one cannot but agree. The objection to the Conservatives over their treatment of the Irish at this time was and remains this : they treated a subject nation as a pawn in party manœuvres. Parnell's reply was not long delayed. The Irish supported an amendment to the Address, and the Government was defeated by 79.

VII

Gladstone protested against the proposed resort to coercion, which seemed to him a miserable answer to the unanimous declaration that Ireland had practically made at the polls. If Lord Carnarvon had nothing to hope from the Tories, no one else could hope at all. Gladstone therefore welcomed the first chance of turning out the Government. When he told Harcourt of his intention, and was met with the question, Are you ready to proceed without either Hartington or Chamberlain? Gladstone replied, Yes.

> I believe it was in my mind to say, if I did not actually say it, that I was prepared to go forward without anybody. That is to say, without any known and positive assurance of support. This was one of the great imperial occasions which call for such resolutions.

If we remember that, though this passage was retrospective, yet that Gladstone when he wrote it was not speaking from the vantage of success, that indeed he died long before this, the most exacting of his crusades, was within sight of accomplishment, there is something moving in these words. The circumstance just stated enables us for once to stand in his shoes, and to feel the call as he felt it.

Who will deny that this was an occasion when he was bigger than the men about him because he was prepared, alone if need be in the effective sense, to undertake a task that promised nothing to the party man, though glory to the statesman who would accept it. In spite of the high-sounding appeals that were so impressive in his day and have become so tedious in ours, there were occasions, and this was one, when the generous and lofty impulse that he named undoubtedly possessed him. The risk now is that they may be overlooked in the monotony of moral tone with which he was over-familiar.

The Government resigned, and on February 1, 1886, Gladstone for the third time became Prime Minister. How many of his colleagues, whether Ministers or not, could he carry with him on this dangerous voyage? Hartington not, and Chamberlain probably not, for the latter was in favour of a large measure of local self-government for Ireland, whereas Gladstone had been led by Parnell to desire an Irish Parliament for Irish affairs. He also wanted to exclude the Irish Members from Westminister, as did Parnell, to mark the independence of the Irish Parliament. Chamberlain wanted to retain them, and, if necessary, on this point Parnell was willing to yield. Apart from these two, we must remember that, while 18 Liberals had voted with the late Government on the crucial amendment, 76 Liberals were away. No more than 257 had, apart from the Nationalists, helped to throw the Government out. Morley and Lord Spencer were with him, but the prevailing opinion was that, without Chamberlain, Gladstone would not be able to carry Home Rule. Of the new Cabinet Chamberlain was from the first a reluctant member. Still, in spite of difficulties, it was formed, and Gladstone wrote to one of his sons that, on the whole, he was satisfied with its composition. "Yet," he added, "short as the Salisbury Government has been, it would not at all surprise me if this were to be shorter still, such are the difficulties that bristle round the Irish question. But the great thing is to be right; and as far as matters have

s

yet advanced I see no reason to be apprehensive in this capital respect."

There was little or no time for delay, and on April 8th Gladstone moved the first reading of his Home Rule Bill. It proposed an Irish Parliament and an Irish executive for Irish affairs, reserving to the Crown imperial matters of defence, foreign policy, trade and the post office. The Dublin police for two years, and the constabulary for an indefinite time were likewise excluded, though a concession altered this. The Irish Members were also excluded from Westminster. A Land Bill accompanied the measure, which was read a first time without a division, though Chamberlain objected to the provisos that the Irish Parliament should be forbidden to touch such questions as, for example, religious endowment, or customs and excise. Both measures have been summed up as giving to Ireland an Irish Parliament and a peasant proprietary.

Mr. Chamberlain and Mr. Trevelyan soon resigned, and were followed by others outside the Cabinet. Parnell and Morley had many discussions, especially on finance, for if the Irish were not to control the customs Parnell thought their contribution to Imperial expenditure should be, not a fifteenth, but a twentieth part. On the day of the introduction of the Bill Gladstone wrote in his diary :

> Extraordinary scenes outside the House and in. My speech, which I have sometimes thought could never end, lasted nearly three and a half hours. Voice and strength and freedom were granted to me in a degree beyond what I could have hoped. But many a prayer had gone up for me, and not, I believe, in vain.

It was an assembly, we are told, such as no Minister had ever before addressed in the historic chamber, and the packed audience began to arrive at cockcrow. Every motive, including curiosity, was present to see and hear what the famous orator would unfold.   It was a wonderful day for the Irishmen and for the imperturbable leader who had achieved his impossible promise of hearing his country's claim supported by the most venerable English statesman living.   Gladstone's speech was persuasive and explanatory; only the speaker's animation and personal qualities of voice and eye added a glow of fire.   On the second reading it was Lord Hartington who moved the rejection of the Bill.   While the discussion lasted from May 10th to June 7th, Gladstone did his utmost to conciliate the dissentients, and implored them to accept the principle of the measure since he was willing to reconsider every point besides. Since the Irish landlords offered no welcome to the Land Bill, which proposed to buy them out, Gladstone was ready to sacrifice it.   On that evening Parnell made a conciliatory speech, in which, however, he told the House that the rejection of the Bill would lead to renewed disturbance in Ireland which even the most drastic coercion, already a proved failure, could not quell.   He hoped that the division would show that " England and her Parliament, in this nineteenth century, were wise enough, brave enough, and generous enough to close the strife of centuries, and to give peace and prosperity to suffering Ireland."

The tension in the House was reflected to an extraordinary degree elsewhere, at least in London.   The provinces were less excitable, as they often are, but London hostesses did not know whom they could dare to ask to dinner, and Gladstone was in the same difficulty over his annual dinner on the royal birthday.   There were virtually no aristocratic Whigs left in his party, and if his seceding colleagues had declined, as he half expected, to attend, the Prince of Wales might have been aghast at the people who were not there to meet him.   It became a question whether to hide or retain a

portrait of Gladstone if one happened to have one in
the house.   It was a bad time to stand for election to
any club.   People who drifted through Mayfair dining-
rooms and country houses suddenly found that invita-
tions ceased, and that they were left dinnerless on week-
days and homeless at week-ends.   In this turmoil of
feeling, execration, excitement and lobbying, Gladstone
remained firm.   He had encouragement from the con-
fines if he had little near at hand.   Though some Liberals
seceded, the party associations held firm.   We need not
further follow the see-saw of chances and opinion.   The
issue was virtually certain when Gladstone, very pale
but in his finest form, made his last speech.   We have
glanced at Parnell's concluding words :   here are
Gladstone's :

> Ireland stands at your bar expectant, hopeful, almost
> suppliant.   You have been asked to-night to abide by the
> traditions of which you are the heirs.   What traditions ?   By
> the Irish traditions.   No, they are a sad exception to the glory
> of our country.   What we want to do is to stand by the tradi-
> tions of which we are the heirs in all matters except our
> relations with Ireland.   She asks also a boon for the future.
> Think, I beseech you, think well, think wisely, think, not for
> the moment, but for the years that are to come, before you
> reject this Bill.

The Bill was rejected, in a full House, by 30 votes,
and the majority included 93 Liberals in opposition.
Gladstone, we are told, for the first time seemed bent
under his load, but his tenacity, his patience, his spirit
even, were unexhausted.   He decided, not to resign, but
to dissolve and appeal to the country.

VIII

It was almost like another Midlothian campaign,
except that, this time, far more was at stake than the
personality and fervour of a man on the rebound from a

self-exile from Parliament. All issues were not now
subsumed in the person of an eloquent and incalculable
pleader. He was now the pleader of a domestic national
cause, and that live reality set him off better than the
customary festoons which accompanied whatever, small
or political, matter might engage him. Parnell had won
Gladstone : Gladstone had almost won a party. It was
now for Gladstone to induce England to return that
party to power. Hitherto Parnell had neglected most
of the English constituencies in the belief that the
English would only listen to an Englishman, and that
it was for him to bring that Englishman to the scratch.
Having performed this miracle, he consented to address
some English meetings. Meantime Gladstone went to
Edinburgh on June 17, and met " wonderful demon-
strations all along the road." He indulged them with
little wayside speeches in his now familiar manner.
Despite the tone of the newspapers, he found the feeling
in Edinburgh " truly wonderful." On the 22nd he was
at Glasgow and addressed a meeting there. From
Glasgow to Hawarden more speeches by the way : "the
whole scene a triumph. God help us, His poor creatures." In a few days he was at Manchester : " great
meeting in the Free Trade Hall. Strain excessive.
Five miles through the streets to Mr. Agnew's; a
wonderful spectacle half the way." The suffocating
heat of this meeting was almost too much for his endurance, but a characteristic spurt of energy carried him
through. The tour ended with a culminating address at
Liverpool :

> Worked up the Irish question for my last function. Seven
> or eight hours of processional uproar, and a speech of an hour
> and forty minutes to five or six thousand people in Hengler's
> Circus. Few buildings give so noble a presentation of an
> audience. Once more my voice held out in a wonderful
> manner. I went in bitterness, in the heat of my spirit, but
> the hand of the Lord was strong upon me.

What amazing activity for a man of over seventy-six !
Parnell could have had no better canvasser, for Gladstone
was now an institution, almost the walking embodiment
of the Constitution itself, and the measure of his influence
is the measure of one man's power to persuade an at
bottom indifferent people.   This indifference is shown by
the fact that even now, after all these years, the Irish
claim seemed surprising and strange to the average
voter in the country.   It may be remarked that the
English have been governed aristocratically or by an
oligarchy for so long that they have no political initiative
in them.   They look for guidance to accredited leaders,
and the whole of Gladstone's strength at the moment lay
precisely in this fact.

He had to create in England the very support to which
he was appealing, for the unsurpassed testimony of
Ireland at the previous election was lost on a nation with
no political initiative themselves.   Mr. Gladstone had
the unique gift of representing to his audiences the
popular movement which he purported to be aiding.   He
spoke with a *vox populi*, and the people were persuaded
that their own voice was speaking through him.   In
principle, therefore, from this point of view, he was a
national Illusion, and this was his last and finest attempt
to make it a reality in the minds of his hearers.   Here,
however, he touched upon their sense of property, of
property in a subject nation; for when we say that
England has no political sense, we mean that she has no
faculty for recognising that instinct in others when it
conflicts with her possessive ideas.   Gladstone's present
plea was to cost them an interference and a supremacy
that they valued.   He was, in fact, appealing to their
genuine disinterestedness for the first time.   Sympathy
with Bulgaria was easy, because Bulgaria was remote, and
the burden of reparation was not to lie upon our own
shoulders.   But Ireland was " ours."   Mr. Gladstone's

influence, potent though it was, here was matching
itself, at last, against the British sense of property.

To him all things were possible, except inactivity.
When, therefore, the Queen renewed her expressions of
distaste for his campaigning outside the bounds of his
constituency, and he had long become a public figure
that seemed to overshadow the throne with welcomes
and processions that made her rare appearances look
official merely, Gladstone was not content with quoting
precedents :

> Your Majesty will be the first to perceive that, even if it had
> been possible for him to decline this great contest, it was not
> possible for him, having entered upon it, to conduct it in a
> half-hearted manner, or to omit the use of any means requisite
> in order to place (what he thinks) the true issue before the
> country.

Such energy is magnificent, and the word is more
justified of this than of parallel examples in his past,
because here the matter of his crusade was entirely worthy
of it.

Before the end of July, 1886, the result of the elections
was known. The Conservatives had a majority of
118, and the Liberals had lost over 40 seats. The
dissentient Liberals, among the majority, were almost
exactly the number which had previously abstained.
Scotland and Wales approved the Liberal policy, and
when the total votes were compared, " in contested
constituencies the Liberals of the main body were only
76,000 behind the forces of Tories and seceders combined." Surely there was character no less than compu-
tation in Gladstone's utterance :

> There is nothing in the recent defeat to abate the hopes or to
> modify the anticipations of those who desire to meet the wants
> and wishes of Ireland.

The veteran was unquenchable to the last.

IX

Gladstone resigned immediately, and in August 1886, Lord Salisbury was Prime Minister once more; after but six months in Opposition. At his farewell audience of the Queen, worth remembering for the future ahead, Gladstone came away with the following reflection :

> The conversation of my closing audience on Friday was a singular one, when regarded as the probable last word with the sovereign after fifty-five years of political life, and a good quarter of a century's service rendered to her in office. The Queen was in good spirits; her manners altogether pleasant. She made me sit at once. Asked after my wife as we began, and sent a kind message to her as we ended. About me personally, I think, her single remark was that I should require some rest. . . . The rest of the conversation, not a very long one, was filled up with nothings. It is rather melancholy. But on neither side, given the conditions, could it well be helped.

The Queen was " in good spirits," and remarked that he would " require some rest." Her mood and her remark were not, perhaps, inseparable. Recognition could hardly be smaller after fifty-five years. Yet at this meeting the two Englands that make up the nation confronted each other, and of the two, Property was personified upon the throne. They could never have an understanding sympathy, despite the reverence of Gladstone, and what does property reverence except itself ?

The momentous efforts for the moment were over, and relaxation came in the congenial company of Döllinger and Acton abroad. Döllinger was hale at eighty-seven, and read a pamphlet on Ireland called " The History of an Idea, and the Lesson of the Elections," which Gladstone had found time to write before his Continental holiday began.

A new Land Bill, to abate the judicial rents which a fall in prices made the tenants unable to pay, was quickly introduced by Parnell into the new Parliament, and Gladstone was in his place to make a speech upon it. Then he retired to Hawarden, where he re-read the *Iliad*, wrote on Homer and on the second *Locksley Hall*, taking a more optimistic view of the " sixty years after " than the poet, who was denouncing " the troughs of Zolaism " and all the exposure of industrial society that literature was now bringing into view. Gladstone remembered the improvements, not the new squalor out of which they had come. His eye was for a situation, not an epoch. This and his concern with *Robert Elsmere* need hardly be dwelt upon. Intellectually he never grew. His interest in these works is mentioned only to show that his energies were, even in this interlude, as effusive as ever.

The Land Bill was rejected, and the disturbances which Parnell had prophesied upon this rejection recurred. When the demands of the tenants for a reduction of rents were refused, and evictions were threatened, the Plan of Campaign began. A fair rent was to be offered by the tenant; if it was rejected, the money was to be placed in the bank by a district committee, with whom the landlord would have to deal. If he would not come to terms, the money was to be used to fight him and for the benefit of the evicted tenant. It was not Parnell's plan, and it was devised by others when he was ill. He was not available, besides wishing to give precedence to the political over the agrarian question. With the fall in the price of produce the judicial rents fixed four years before had become rack rents. The landlords were implacable, however; a perpetual Coercion Act was passed; Hicks-Beach retired, to be succeeded by Mr. A. J. Balfour as Irish Secretary. Mr. Balfour, as he then was, applied a policy of rigour, with results that were a hideous repetition of the past.

An attempt to reunite the Liberal party by a round

table conference failed, and of the Plan of Campaign
Gladstone said :

> We all know that such (illegal) devices are the certain result
> of misgovernment. I feel its authors are not one-tenth part
> so blameable as the Government, whose contemptuous
> refusal of what they have now [1887] granted was the parent
> and source of the mischief.

A Commission had reported in the interval that, in
effect, the tenants could not pay, and that this explained
the agitation. "No agrarian movement in Ireland,"
according to Morley, " was ever so unstained by crime."
The Commission reported to the Government the very
facts that they had refused to believe before, and this led
to the passing of an Act affirming the policy previously
repudiated. Despite the opposition of the landlords,
Salisbury gave way because he feared that Ulster would
join the Nationalists if he did not. Those who follow
the contradictions and alternations of the Government
during this year of refusal and capitulation have little
indeed to boast of English statesmanship. It bore out,
alas, every charge that Parnell had brought against us.
Force was the only argument we would admit against
ourselves.

All this brought the Liberals and the Nationalists
closer together, and gave frightful meaning to Gladstone's calm summary of events. Speaking in 1887, he
said :

> I ventured to state in 1886 that we had arrived at the point . .
> where two roads parted; one of them the road that marked
> the endeavour to govern Ireland according to its constitu-
> tionally expressed wishes; the other the road principally marked
> by ultra-constitutional measures, growing more and more
> pronounced in character.

It was now proved that if effective conciliation were
rejected, coercion was the only alternative, and that

meant, as Parliament had learnt, a Perpetual Coercion
Act. Ireland was to be governed by coercion, which
might be momentarily relaxed, and at any moment
revived, at the caprice of the executive. That any man
should build a reputation of statesmanship on this
foundation is not a fact of which Englishmen can be
proud. The bankruptcy of the Government was further
shown by a drastic resort to the closure. The executive
had to make itself irresponsible in England as well.
Gladstone was content to leave the Government entire
responsibility for this, and the majority of Liberals did
not join in the division. Finally, the Liberals retired and
the Irish watched, as spectators, from the galleries. It
seemed as if the pretence of parliamentary government
was at an end.

While Mr. Balfour was defending his policy of repres-
sion with the detachment of a man to whom its rigours
do not apply, steps were taken to enlighten opinion in
England of what was happening. Coercion became
the dividing line between political parties. By thus
entering the consecrated sphere of English strife, coercion
became at last a vivid and appalling reality to the public.
English people even took the unprecedented step of
visiting Ireland, in order to see for themselves how the
island was faring under English rule. It was an undis-
covered country to most of them, and a dark continent
to the audiences which they addressed upon their return.
These were moved to pity and indignation, which spread
the doubt whether such proceedings would be tolerated
for an instant in this country. The one man who was now
free from any taint of approval or co-operation in these
doings was Gladstone. Was it possible that his proposals had been dismissed too lightly after all?

The Irish question was becoming alive in English
feeling, and the wary observer of a former tendency over
the Bulgarian sufferings waited for his chance to fan the

flame of recoil. With his peculiar instinct for the appropriate incident he fixed upon the uproar at Michelstown, a miserable affair in which an old man was shot and two others died from police bullets. On an immediate and unscrutinised report Mr. Balfour promptly decided that the police were in no way to blame, and when the inquest was found to be irregular (it had returned a verdict of wilful murder), a public inquiry was refused. The incredible attitude of the executive must be read in detail to be appreciated, and these details are too perfunctory to need recall. It is enough to say that the effect was to stir indignation in England itself.

It is worth noticing, in passing, that when this state of affairs led the Pope to send an investigator to Ireland, and the conclusion of the Congregation at Rome was embodied in a rescript which condemned the Plan of Campaign and commented upon the circumstances, the Irish refused to let anyone else become the judge of the facts. They took the attitude that the Vatican was being made use of by its enemies and those of Ireland, and repudiated interference in political as distinct from spiritual matters. The bishops had to explain that the Pope was not condemning the Nationalist movement, and his Holiness protested that he had been misunderstood. It is an interesting reminder that Home Rule and Rome rule are not to be confused.

The Nationalists were now commonly heard upon Liberal platforms, and Gladstone's name was becoming popular in Ireland. Parnell alone rigidly preserved his independence. When asked his opinion of Gladstone, he replied : " I think of Mr. Gladstone and the English people what I have always thought of them. They will do what we can make them do."

Gladstone himself was losing no opportunity. In the summer of 1887 he made a wonderful tour of South Wales, where enormous crowds sacrificed their day's

work and wages in order to gain a sight of him. He told
a friend :

> They made this demonstration in order to secure firstly and
> mainly justice to Catholic Ireland. It is not after all a bad
> country in which such things take place.

Of course he was too modest here, and it is a small
example of his manner of sacrificing to a correct attitude
the simpler truth about his personal magnetism. On
that magnetism, however, his public hopes were resting.
He was the cause, which people flocked to see and to hear.
The traditional manifestations greeted him : On June
2nd,

> a tumultuous but interesting journey to Swansea. Half a
> dozen speeches on the way. June 4th. Twelve to four-
> thirty the astonishing procession. Sixty thousand ! Then
> spoke for near an hour. Dinner at eight, near a hundred,
> arrangements perfect. Spoke for nearly another hour.

The next day was Sunday, when he heard two sermons,
the one " notable " and the other " good." On Monday
he received the freedom of the Welsh city. On Tuesday
he was off to London with " processions, hustles and
speeches " at Newport and Cardiff. He summed up the
tour as really a " progress, and an extraordinary one."

He spent the last month of the year quietly at Florence,
after activity both at Birmingham and in the House.
Regarding his speech at Birmingham, Morley says :

> The sight of the vast meeting was appalling, from fifteen to
> seventeen thousand people. He spoke with great vigour
> and freedom ; the fine passages probably heard all over ; many
> other passages certainly not heard, but his gesture so strong
> and varied as to be almost as interesting as the words would
> have been. The speech lasted an hour and fifty minutes ; and
> he was not at all exhausted when he sat down. The scene at
> the close was absolutely indescribable and incomparable,
> overwhelming like the sea.

X

The reception of the Nationalists on English platforms did nothing to lessen the English fear and detestation of Parnell, and a very ugly expression of it soon engaged Mr. Gladstone and the country. *The Times* published a series of articles on "Parnellism and Crime," which sought to make the hated statesman responsible, and concluded with the "facsimile" letter from Parnell, which proved to be a forgery, as we all know. The disgraceful document appeared on April 18, 1887. It purported to be an excuse for having condemned the Phœnix Park murders in public, though the writer thought that one victim met with his deserts. This was the crown upon a mass of innuendo and implied suggestion which the publication of the "facsimile" showed the paper afraid to state but ready to believe.

Parnell described the letter as an audacious and unblushing fabrication, but the House could not believe that *The Times* would stoop to publish a document which it had not verified beyond a doubt. Lord Salisbury was equally credulous, and taunted Gladstone for co-operating with a man "tainted with the strong presumption of conniving at assassination." Parnell decided not to bring his libellers into court. Opinion in London could not be trusted to secure an unprejudiced verdict. The same, in the opposite sense, applied to opinion in Ireland, where a verdict for Parnell would not condemn *The Times* in English eyes. The fatuous notion that respectable institutions are infallible survived Parnell's denial. The series of articles continued. Then another Irish Member sued the paper, which replied that the articles were not directed at him. The jury agreed, but counsel for the paper, the Attorney-General, dragged up again the charges against Parnell, declared that the statements

published were true and the signature genuine, so at last
Parnell was driven to expose the forgery.

He invited the House to appoint a Select Committee
to investigate the authenticity of the letter. This was
refused by the Government, which offered to appoint a
Special Commission of three judges to investigate *every*
charge made. In other words, the specific and definite
charge against one man was to be a minor part of an
investigation into an entire agitation, which, without
discussion, Parnell was invited to accept or to refuse.
Thus the political leaders were to be placed in the dock
with the authors of agrarian crimes, and specific charges
against the former were to be lost in an investigation
affecting countless other people. The constitutional
remedy of a Select Committee was denied and an arbitrary
expedient devised, for a much more extensive purpose, to
replace it. The first reading of the Bill to appoint the
Commission was passed without debate, and its spokesman did " not anticipate being able to make provision
for a debate on the second reading " ! While some
Liberals were anxious not to let the first reading pass
without opposition, Gladstone finally held that a wrong
method of inquiry was better than none. At Parnell's
request the second reading was not opposed, and when
the committee stage was reached and Members began to
be aware of the enormity that they were asked to sanction,
the most drastic closure was invoked in order that no
amendments might be moved. Gladstone called the
proceedings the most extraordinary he had known.

The judges sat on September 17, 1888, and did not
finally rise until fifteen months later. In Morley's
summary, " for the first time in England since the Great
Rebellion, men were practically put upon their trial on a
political charge, without giving them the protection of a
jury. For the first time in that period judges were to
find a verdict upon the facts of a crime." An entire

national revolutionary movement was placed under the review of a tribunal appointed by its political opponents, without reference to its political leaders either in its procedure, powers or scope. The circumstances which occasioned it, and the motives which prompted the agitation, were ruled out, because there was no jury to be affected by them. The crucial issue of the forged letter was relegated to the background, and the court did not arrive at it until February 1889. The manager of the paper said that he accepted the genuineness of the letters—there were three lots in all—apart from their handwriting because they were the kind of letters that he thought Parnell would write. He explained that he had professionally chosen the moment to publish them, or rather the " facsimile," on the morning when the second reading of the Coercion Bill was due. He had paid some £2,500 for them, and had made no investigation into their source.

Thus the reputation of a paper, built on a century of responsibility and experience, can be sacrificed in a moment. There is no doubt that the exposure of this forgery struck a blow to the credit of English journalism from which it has never fully recovered. The unfortunate Pigott, who broke down, confessed, and then committed suicide, was a victim to a weak character and to wretched circumstances, as he pitifully stated himself. With his end were involved what had been a great name in British journalism and a humiliating rebuff to the Government as well. The Liberal opposition were heartened. Gladstone was much encouraged despite his indignation at the atrocious treatment of Parnell.

When the Commission's report came before the House for discussion, Gladstone moved an amendment to the proposal to adopt it. He said that the House should record its reprobation of the false charges, its regret at the wrong suffered, and went on to remind Members

that some of the opinions in the report, from the nature
of the case, could not be judicial findings.   Some of the
events were ten years old; responsible Ministers had
taken different views of some of them, and finally the
judges had rightly declared that not all the essential
evidence could come before them.   The general public
wanted little reminder of that.   They had lately been
instructed upon the circumstances of Ireland.   The
report recoiled upon the heads of those who had manufactured the Commission.   The calumnies ended by
producing sympathy for the victims, and opinion became
readier to consider impartially the Irish case.

In Italy at the end of the year Gladstone took a holiday,
and found difficulty in not engaging himself in the
country's affairs.   He found himself " hardly regarded as
a foreigner."   He wrote an article on the " Triple
Alliance and Italy's Place in it."   He read about the
Old Testament and the Jews, which led him to " the
parallel question " of Homer.   He excuses himself for
having delayed writing to Acton by saying that " every
year brings me, as I reckon, from three to five thousand
new correspondents."   In the same letter he went on :

> Among other things I wish to make some sort of record of
> my life.   You say truly it has been very full.   I add fearfully
> full.   But it has been in a most remarkable degree the reverse
> of self-guided and self-suggested, with reference, I mean, to all
> its best known aims.   Under this surface, and in its daily habit,
> no doubt it has been selfish enough.   Whether anything of
> this kind will ever come off is most doubtful.   Until I am
> released from politics by the solution of the Irish problem I
> cannot even survey the field.

He also planned " something of which a library would
be the nucleus.   I incline to begin with a temporary
building here."

Among the few remarks of Gladstone about himself,
this statement that he is remarkable for the external

T

guidance and suggestion which brought his characteristic
energies into play is one of the most revealing. On the
mountain of his innumerable memoranda, which read so
often like editorial statements composed by someone
else, we find here and there a gleam of true self-knowledge. He was beating perpetually about the bush
because the shy bird that was his soul revealed itself so
seldom. Nothing is so inexhaustible as energy which
is not insight, and of the critical faculty for other than
practical matters he had very little. The fountain rises
higher and higher in its attempt to return to its source.
His vitality was uniquely his own. Its direction was
determined by his surroundings. It is as the embodiment of the public life of his age that he is interesting,
and so we are always losing the man in the stream of
events in which he acted. He brought the same enthusiasm and industry to them all, and it was not until he
found in Ireland a national movement worthy of the
extent of his own sympathies and powers that he and
the right cause for which he was always searching found
a match in one another. National employment was the
object of his life, and for most of it he had perforce to
be content with national business. In his eightieth year
we see him unwilling to be " released from politics "
until a solution for the Irish nation had been found.

In 1889 he celebrated the fiftieth year of his marriage,
which was as fortunate, as characteristic, as appropriate,
as it could well be. Mrs. Gladstone herself was a centre,
almost an institution, of activities, and in her sphere the
same copiousness and abundance displayed itself. Husband and wife were both abounding, and the only thing
that seems to have tried her was her husband's occasional
retirement from political affairs. It is tempting to
imagine her watching the revival of his energies, and
foreseeing, perhaps more quickly than himself, that,
wherever they started, they must return to Downing

Street in the end. The public acclamation in which the latter half of his public life was mainly passed must have become for her the only proper setting for her husband, and the family can hardly have escaped the popular idealism which at length surrounded them. In the odour of general acclamation, the feeling of being a holy family could not well have been escaped, and the assurance that the reputation was deserved must have produced a glow of exalted satisfaction. It was a strange atmosphere in which to exist, and then one shook it off by a quick return to the busy hive of domestic and charitable duties. In this providential order, within and without, as one passed from Westminster to Hawarden, from reclamation to entertaining, it must have been a blessing even to breathe. Everywhere was fullness and abundance; every moment some delightful duty to perform. Mrs. Gladstone's last words were: "I must not be late for church."

The entertaining at Hawarden in 1889 included a visit from Parnell. He spent a night there, and Gladstone found him "certainly one of the very best people to deal with that I have ever known. Took him to the old castle. He seems to notice and appreciate everything." One of the things that he had noticed appeared at dinner. He was sitting next to Miss Gladstone, who happened to ask: "Who is the greatest actor you have ever seen, Mr. Parnell?" Parnell replied: "Your father, undoubtedly," much to her delight. Early in 1890 Gladstone spent a week at All Souls, of which he was an honorary fellow. He found the living very good, and the conversation "that of men with work to do." He gave a "kind of Homeric lecture" to members of the Union, and wrote home that the object of his visit was to make himself as safe as might be in the articles that were subsequently published under the name of *The Impregnable Rock of Holy Scripture*.

XI

After the intense excitement created by the report of the Special Commission, the apology of *The Times*, the confession and suicide of Pigott, there was a brief lull. Parnell had triumphed over his enemies, and in all their encounters his enemies had come off worst. Eyes were now turned upon the Irish leader, and thoughts of the next election were filling men's minds. The visit of Parnell to Hawarden was evidence that the two men without whom Home Rule could not be wrung from England were substantially in accord, and the solution of the Irish question seemed nearer. Even Unionists themselves publicly admitted that their recent system had not only failed but was a discredit to their party, and this was an argument that no one could misunderstand. The Government majority was falling steadily to nearly half what it had been, and in by-elections the Liberals had won eight seats. Of these the last was won, for the first time, from the Conservatives by a Liberal candidate who made the choice between coercion and conciliation expressly his plea.

Those who read the signs of the times could only draw the conclusion that for the undefeated Irish leader only one fence remained, and few doubted that he would take it with Gladstone's aid at the next election. Time, however, had one more surprise in store, which was sprung on December 28, 1889, when Captain O'Shea filed a petition for divorce, with Parnell cited as the co-respondent. Parnell refused to fight the case and, according to his future wife, said to her at the time : " No, Queenie. What's the use ? . . . We have been longing for this freedom all these years, and now you are afraid ! " His attitude was so characteristic that we may quote a few words more from her.

Put away all fear and regret for my public life. I have given, and will give, Ireland what is in me to give. That I have vowed to her, but my private life shall never belong to any country, but to one woman. There will be a howl, but it will be the howling of hypocrites; not altogether, for some of these Irish fools are genuine in their belief that forms and creeds can govern life and men; perhaps they are right so far as they can experience life. But I am not as they, for they are among the world's children. I am a man, and I have told these children what they want, and they clamour for it. If they will let me, I will get it for them. But if they turn from me, my Queen, it matters not at all in the end.

He was a strong man, and a fatalist who, in public or private, neither hoped nor despaired, but decided his course and matched himself against the facts in front of him. As such, his composure remained impenetrable. Compared with Parnell, Gladstone seems an eager child.

Gladstone, of course, was immediately concerned with the effects that the news would produce upon public opinion, for that was the material in which he dealt. " I suppose," he said, " it will end the career of a man in many respects invaluable." On November 15, 1890, after a dull session, the case began, and on the 17th the petitioner was granted a decree nisi. Undefended cases are happily short, and between the two hearings a Sunday had intervened. It was already clear what the issue would be on Sunday morning, when Gladstone wrote to Morley as follows :

It is, after all, a thunder-clap about Parnell. Will he ask for the Chiltern Hundreds ? He cannot continue to lead ? [This question-mark is highly characteristic.] The Pope has now clearly got a commandment under which to pull him up. It surely cannot always have been thus; for he represented his diocese in the Church synod.

Could the contrast between the two men be better seen than in their respective attitudes and expressions ? Shift the subject to politics, and it is manifest that one

type can only govern the other by brute force. In a
week's time Parliament would meet, and while Gladstone
was anxiously waiting to see what the effect would be
upon the leadership of the Nationalist party, Parnell was
as characteristically indifferent. A new difficulty had
come into his path. He would meet it as he had met
others, without acknowledging that it had the smallest
claim to moral respect. The day after the decision of
the court, Gladstone wrote to Morley:

> I think it plain that we have nothing to say and nothing to
> do in the matter. The party is as distinct from us as that of
> Smith or Hartington. I own to some surprise at the apparent
> facility with which the R. C. bishops and clergy appear to take
> the continued leadership for granted, but they may have tried
> the ground and found it would not *bear*. It is the Irish
> Parliamentary party, and that alone, to which we have to
> look.

The tactics of Gladstone at this time have been sometimes questioned; but without prejudice to his conduct
as a matter of political tactics, let us look at the situation
for a moment in a more personal light. We have seen
the young moralist grow, and followed the splendid
fruits of his susceptibility to outside influences. We see
him now, politics first, watching the effect on public
opinion of a certain moral matter. There is no indication
that he gave of personal opinion himself one way or the
other, but his private feeling would be silent before
the attitude adopted by the world. This is perhaps the
most prominent and direct instance of the special quality
of his mind, a pliancy of feeling, and absence of personal
assertion upon the rules of human conduct, compensated
indeed by the fervour of his obedience to external
influence. Once he was told what attitude to take by
the feelings of his fellow-men, he threw the energy of a
Titan into the line that he adopted from them. Of inner
light himself he confessed to having none, and it is this

lack which makes it difficult to accept him as a hero.
The saint and the hero initiate as well as serve. Their
fine conduct is the fruit of exceptionally fine character,
and that character cannot be called exceptionally fine
which owes all its motive force to other people. Gladstone is interesting because his enormous lack was
balanced by an altogether extraordinary degree of the
secondary qualities of genius. If the superabundance of
these secondary gifts could compensate for the want of
its primary virtue, he would be the type of all others to
prove it. But the secondary, even in excess, can never
match with the first, and this is the lesson to be learnt
from the extraordinary personality of Gladstone. In
this matter of Parnell, of course, his long memory could
recall a time when our aristocratic statesmen, as was
mentioned on an earlier page, survived divorce, because
divorce was one of the privileges of their order. Times
had changed, but we cannot expect Gladstone in his
old age to have forgotten the memories of his youth. It
is not necessary to find excuses for his adjustment or to
rebut the charge that he was hypocritical in this matter.
A hypocrite is a man who publicly behaves in a manner
discountenanced by his private conduct or opinions.
But Gladstone had hardly more private opinions than
the nymph Echo, and as conduct is even more imitative
than opinion, and he invariably followed the best-
accredited guides of his class and upbringing, we may
believe that he was, if possible, even more correct in his
behaviour than in his ideas. His personal contribution
was a vitality remarkable in itself and indeed astonishing
in a man who was in most other respects so ordinary.
He would be charitable and compassionate to women
from whom most respectable persons turn anxiously
away, especially when they have the additional excuse
of considering the risks to their public position. The
strain of simplicity in Gladstone's character made him

sometimes exquisitely blind to the reality of these risks, but he was unconventional only in his pursuit of certain virtues. He was really prepared to do what everyone held to be right, and that does look to most of us a terrifying form of originality. The distrust that he always aroused was due partly to his incalculability, for none knew what he would be after next, partly to a constitutional ambiguity of phrase which he was forced to cultivate to safeguard himself against the charge of contradiction, partly to a moral idiom which he dragged in whether the subject required it or not. Incapable of directness, because his intellect was not clear in intellectual things, he used the language of sophistry without being a sophist. Incapable of religious insight, he used a high-sounding style. Because he desired the insight that was not in him, he imitated to the best of his ability the language of those whom he believed to possess what he lacked. Thus, if he had been a hypocrite, he would have spoken as he did, but the style was not the man except in so far as the man, like the style, was an honest attempt at imitation. He took his cue from others, but once started, ran like an express train. Parnell was incomprehensible to him because Parnell was not only the engine but the engine-driver.

For some reason that has never been explained, these islands received a deeper impress than any other part of Europe from the Puritans and the Reformation. The sense of sin is now an English characteristic to an extent that would be incredible to the Englishmen of Shakespeare's time. Reactions there may be which delight the anti-puritans, but the anti-Puritans are often but rebellious Puritans themselves. So matters which raise the question of degrees of sinfulness, and of the appropriate penalty, which is the one delight that the sinful man indulges without any misgiving, excite almost a

superstitious interest in England.* They are given a
false importance which bewilders the rest of Europe,
and this importance is never stronger than when some
public figure is involved. Those who held that a man
who had been living in Parnell's way was not a statesman
who could be relied on, forgot that he had been living
in this way for half of the fifteen years in which he had
had to be reckoned with at all. Three days after the
result of the suit was known a great meeting in Dublin
passed off without a murmur of disparagement, but on
the same day another great meeting was held at Sheffield
by members of the Liberal party. Morley was there,
with the following guidance from Gladstone in his
pocket :

> Your appeal as to your meeting of to-morrow gives matter
> for thought. I feel (1) that the Irish have abstractedly [note
> the adverb] a right to decide the question; (2) that on account
> of Parnell's enormous services—he has done for Home Rule
> something like what Cobden did for free trade, set the argu-
> ment on its legs—they are in a position of immense difficulty;
> (3) that we, the Liberal party as a whole, and especially we its
> leaders, have for the moment nothing to say to it, that we
> must be passive, must wait and watch. But I again and again
> say to myself, I mean in the interior and silent forum, "It'll
> nay dee." I should not be surprised if there were to be rather
> painful manifestations in the House on Tuesday. It is yet
> to be seen what our Nonconformist friends, such as —— or
> such as —— will say. . . . If I recollect aright, Southey's
> Life of Nelson was in my early days published and circulated
> by the Society for Promoting Christian Knowledge. It would
> be curious to look back upon it and see how the biographer
> treats his narrative at the tender points.

If the reader has come with patience thus far, he will
probably agree that nothing that Gladstone ever wrote
is more perfectly in character than this letter. No other

* Gladstone once said : " The sense of sin is the great want in
modern life; it is wanting in our sermons, wanting everywhere " :
quoted by Tollemache.

quite gives to us that exquisite sense of rightness which
we feel when, say, a dialogue of Balzac unfolds itself
upon the page, and every fresh sentence, though beyond
our own imagining, adds another morsel to our taste of
the speaker's character. Morley was clearly briefed to
savour the sense of this meeting, and to do nothing to
commit either himself or his leader or the party till the
precious information had been won. For the moment
Gladstone himself was impatiently expected to denounce
the offender. From the outside this is what simple souls
would naturally fancy he would do, for who was not
the champion of Morality if not the Grand Old Man
himself? It is always amusing to see Gladstone mis-
understanded of the pious, and for a while to watch their
irritation at his plausible explanations. Among other
things they forgot the bare possibility that Parnell himself
might resign, and so for once, as a matter of good taste,
accept the ruling of the English conscience, a local
affair of incalculable reverence to themselves. In this
matter the temptation to quote Gladstone is greater than
usual, for he is so true to himself in every word. Once
more :

> I determined to watch the state of feeling in this country.
> I made no public declaration, but the country made up its
> mind.

We have never waited more eagerly for an echo than
Gladstone was now waiting for the cry that he would
repeat. His daily post was like the vibrations travelling
between the public and his ear. It was a crucial moment
when he was able to write : " All my correspondents are
in unison." At the Sheffield meeting, beside what else
he heard, Morley learned from the Liberal agent that
" three of our candidates had bolted already." Politically
speaking, what more was to be said ? but again Parnell
was still the silent and incalculable. It is to Gladstone's

credit that he steadfastly declined to express any opinion
save upon the political situation as it now stood.   To
carry Home Rule, three factors were necessary in combination : Parnell, Gladstone, and the majority of the
voters.   No two, at this moment, were enough, and
the laboriously coached voter was, at the moment, the
decisive man.   Parnell, impenitent because he was
innocent in his own eyes, disregarded the fellow.   Gladstone did not, and it might have been in vain if he had.
The interesting question was, not what Gladstone would
say, for his " correspondents were in unison," but how
he would say it, and how soon.

Before the Liberal meeting at Sheffield, the Irish,
represented by the National League, as we have seen,
had decided to support Parnell, in spite of the suit, with
acclamation.   Gladstone arrived in London on November
24, 1890, and held a conference with Morley, fresh from
Sheffield, and other Liberal Front Benchers.   The Irish
party did not meet in London till the following afternoon,
the day on which Parliament met.   The upshot of this
conference between the Liberal leaders was that Gladstone
was convinced that his party would lose the General
Election if Parnell continued to lead the Nationalists.
The conviction was embodied in a letter from Gladstone
to Morley, which Morley was to communicate to Parnell.
Mr. Justin McCarthy was similarly informed, with the
same unstated object.   But before the afternoon meeting
of the Irish Nationalists, Parnell, as often happened,
could not be found.   When he entered Committee
Room 15 he was received enthusiastically, and looked,
said an Irishman afterwards, " as if we had committed
adultery with his wife."   He was re-elected chairman
amid cheers, and thanked the party for the latest proof
of their confidence in him.   It was a fine proof, for
they were unanimous.   They did not know of Gladstone's letter.   Did Parnell ?   According to Morley,

McCarthy, who was present, told Parnell of Gladstone's conviction just before the meeting began. Mr. Barry O'Brien, Parnell's biographer, does not tell us, but he quotes some words of McCarthy which imply, if anything, that he did not speak to Parnell about it. We learn that Gladstone talked with McCarthy, who told Mr. O'Brien as follows :

> Gladstone said that the Liberals might lose the General Election if Parnell remained leader of the Irish party. He did not ask that Parnell should resign. He did not show me any letter. He did not at our meeting ask me to convey anything to Parnell, and besides, I should not have done so at his bidding. It was a matter for us to settle without the interference of Mr. Gladstone or any Englishman.

This certainly looks as if Mr. McCarthy kept his conversation to himself. Morley says, however : " the Irish Member who had seen Mr. Gladstone the previous evening, at the last moment was able to deliver the message that had been confided to him. Mr. Parnell replied that he should stand to his guns." Morley's suggestion is that Parnell purposely kept in the background in order that he might be re-elected chairman before the news of Gladstone's attitude was known to his party. When Gladstone arrived at the House, and Morley then told him that Parnell would not budge, and presumably that he had been re-elected, Gladstone " stood at the table, dumb for some instants, looking at me as if he could not believe what I had said. Then he burst out that we must publish at once his letter to me; at once, that very afternoon. I said, ' 'Tis too late now.' ' Oh, no,' said he, ' the *Pall Mall* will bring it out in a special edition.' " Gladstone added that Parnell must be told of this plan, and when Morley had informed him, Parnell remarked : " Yes," amicably, as if it were no particular concern of his. " I think Mr. Gladstone will be quite right to do this; it will put him straight

with his party." There was no flaw in his courage.
The crucial words of Gladstone's famous letter were as
follows :

> " While clinging to the hope of a communication from Mr.
> Parnell," and " viewing the arrangements for the commence-
> ment of the session to-morrow," my conclusion is that " not
> withstanding the splendid services rendered by Mr. Parnell
> to his country, his continuance at the present moment in the
> leadership would be productive of consequences disastrous
> in the highest degree to the cause of Ireland.
>
> " I think I may be warranted in asking you so far to expand
> the conclusion I have given above as to add that the con-
> tinuance I speak of would not only place many hearty and
> effective friends of the Irish cause in a position of great
> embarrassment, but would render my retention of the leader-
> ship of the Liberal party, based as it has mainly been upon
> the presentation of the Irish cause, almost a nullity."

Whatever the last sentence meant about Gladstone, and
it is one of his ingenious ambiguities, it meant that
Parnell must go, and the publication of the letter, in
Morley's words, made it " a humiliating public ultimatum." Still the threat was there; and the intention
to publish it, if necessary, and its publication, were both
Gladstone's. Morley thinks, perhaps truly, that had the
Nationalists known of the letter, they would not have
re-elected Parnell. If so, then the odium would have
rested upon them and not on Gladstone, an arrangement that would have suited Gladstone perfectly. The
Irishmen would have been his agents, but their controller
would have been himself. If Parnell kept them in
ignorance, is it not likely that he was very well aware of
this, and is it not certain that he would never endure it ?
If his men were to desert their leader at Gladstone's
command, the Irish nation at least should know who had
caused them to do so, and Gladstone should not be
allowed to let it be assumed that the Nationalists were
acting of their own freewill. Parnell, if he kept back

the letter, defeated this covert influence, and Gladstone countered by publishing it instantly. Thus Parnell won the first move, and Gladstone the second, in a duel which, ultimately, did neither statesman good. I fancy that the bitter words in Parnell's subsequent and shortly published manifesto reveal, what Morley misses, Parnell's keen resentment at the plan which he spoilt.

News that a letter of Gladstone's about Parnell was being published ran through the House like fire, and its contents were known there before it appeared in print the next morning. It was a crucial moment for the Irishmen. The choice for them was to lie between Parnell and Gladstone, and Gladstone had told them to choose. " I thought," Gladstone recorded, " that it would be best that (Parnell) should be impelled to withdraw, but by an influence conveyed to him, at least, from within the limits of his own party." It seems to me that Gladstone need not have uttered his threat of retiring, for so the phrase about nullity was generally construed, and that had not the clause containing it been added, he had said enough to put himself right with his party and to justify the party to itself. To say that Parnell was for the moment politically impossible would have been enough : to imply that Gladstone would himself retire if Parnell remained was a term of dictation that does not seem to have been essential. One may say this because it is certain that this threat would have " nullified " the rest of the letter for Parnell, to whom it was actually directed. One cannot say that the omission of the clause would have led Parnell to show the letter to his party before they met, but it is arguable. The letter, having failed to make Parnell retire, split the Irish party into two after it was published, and this added a new confusion that Gladstone could not have desired and probably did not foresee. Presumably Gladstone wanted them, if Parnell stood firm, to reject him all but unanimously, and therefore inserted his threat. He miscalculated the force of Parnell, just as Parnell miscalculated, or rather was indifferent to, the panic of public opinion. He thought he could reunite his Irish followers in five years, but he died before the first was over. The original source of the whole trouble lay, of course, with Parnell himself : the prejudice against him may have been absurd, but he knew its force, and public and private crusades against prevailing opinions cannot be carried on with success at the same time. None the less all Gladstone accomplished was to divide the Irish party, and all that Parnell accomplished was a refusal to accept English dictation, and his own death. It is far from certain, however, that even Parnell's retirement would have been more than a flattery to English sentiment, or would really have made a decisive difference at the next elections. If Home Rule was indefinitely to be postponed by the divorce case, then we may sympathise with Parnell in refusing to accept a public verdict, plus English dictation, both of which he had repudiated in private conduct and in political life. After all, in the end Home Rule was only won after civil war, and at any previous time almost anything startling would have been excuse enough to postpone it.

Parnell replied to Gladstone's letter with a manifesto to the Irish people which " will enable you to understand the measure of the loss with which you are threatened unless you consent to throw me to the English wolves now howling for my destruction." He said, in effect, that the substance of Gladstone's proposals, as gathered by himself during his visit to Hawarden, was unsatisfactory ; and that, if he was to be expelled from politics, the Irish at least should see that they were gaining solid value for his loss. When the Nationalists met again to reconsider their position, after the publication of the letter, and the manifesto, Parnell proffered them the same advice. Gladstone, of course, refused to be drawn, and on December 6th Parnell was left with twenty-six followers, while forty-four, who preferred to pin their hopes to obedience to Gladstone, withdrew.

Two elections followed, one in Ireland, the other here. In Ireland the Parnellite was defeated, and in England the Liberal vote declined. Gladstone appeared to be astonished that Parnell had any followers at all, and thought outrageous Morley's suggestion that, in Parnell's opinion, the General Election might be lost by the Liberals whether he retired or not. Morley found the old man looking like the Ancient of Days, but after many busy hours he was found at the theatre, and " as he drove away the crowd cheered him with cries of ' Bravo, don't you mind Parnell ! ' " for political war was now declared between them. We are told that even now Gladstone was unshaken by this disappointment, but he told Acton, " the blow to me is very heavy—the heaviest I ever have received. It is a great and high call to work by faith and not by sight." The defeat of Parnell's candidate at the Kilkenny election was now to make Gladstone say in a letter : " I would rather see Ireland disunited than see it Parnellite." One cannot help wondering if this would have been his opinion if Parnell's candidate had been returned. For the moment he inclined to " some affirmative legislation " to rally the Liberals and encourage the liberal-minded Irish Members. Three elections in Ireland, however, were three defeats for Parnell, and in less than twelve months from the split in his ranks, on October 6, 1891, at the age of forty-five, he was dead.

XII

While the Irish strife was raging and Parnell wearing himself out, there was a lull in England. In the summer Gladstone lost his eldest son in the prime of his life after a lingering illness. The blow was sharp, but " setting this apart, there is nothing lacking to us in consolations human or divine. I can only wish that I may become less unworthy to have been his father." After a visit to Scotland Gladstone attended the annual meeting of the Liberal organisation at Newcastle, the scene of his amazing tour in 1862, and here, as a supplement and change to the eternal Irish preoccupation, was born the set of proposals, nursed by the Fabians, to be known in time as the Newcastle programme. After this Gladstone, now nearly eighty-two, visited Biarritz, where he spent Christmas of 1891, with Morley and Mr. Armitstead.

The General Election, the prospect of which had influenced so many of the preceding events, occurred in 1892. We are told that Gladstone expected a majority of nearly a hundred, and Morley remarks that this mood of confidence was " indispensable to him." On July 13, 1892, the result in his own constituency of Midlothian was known. His majority had shrunk from several thousand to less than seven hundred votes. He felt this keenly, for he had spared no effort in the contest despite his years, and the question was what Irish policy could be devised for at best an evidently narrow majority. His eyesight too had been giving him trouble, and now a cataract had formed. Time would not wait for the benefit of Ireland, and Gladstone attributed to the Irish quarrel the bewilderment in English minds. A month after the death of Parnell, that is to say, in November 1891, Gladstone put the position to Morley as follows :

Herein [the division among the Irish] we see the main cause why our majority is not more than double what it actually

U

numbers, and the difference between these two scales of
majority represents, as I apprehend, the difference between
power to carry the Bill as the Church and Land Bills were
carried into law, and the default of such power. The main
mischief has already been done; but it receives additional
confirmation with the lapse of every week or month.

In August 1892 Gladstone again became Prime
Minister for his fourth and final time. He was in office
for eighteen months with abated powers, not only from
defects in his sight and hearing. In February 1893 the
Home Rule Bill was introduced. On the disputed point
of the retention or otherwise of Irish representatives at
Westminster, it was now decided to retain eighty members with the right to vote only upon any Irish questions
that might arise, but this again had to be modified. In
the conduct of the measure, especially on the committee
stage, Gladstone seemed as vigorous and resourceful at
eighty-four as he had been a generation earlier. It was
the spectacle of his exhaustless energy which lent excitement to a subject that, in spite of the feeling it was bound
to arouse, had begun to grow wearisome. He changed
one concession that looked like defeat into an alteration
which he persuaded his hearers was no less proper than
inevitable. As a parliamentary display his handling of
this awkward moment was thought, even by the oldest
hands, to have been unsurpassed. He was so expansive
that the very wealth of his resources gave new occasions
for discussion, and, because also of obstruction, the
progress of the measure was slow. Despite universal
fatigue the committee stage was prolonged for over
sixty sittings. The Bill passed its second reading, in a
full house, by a majority of forty-three and the third
reading by thirty-four. In the Lords it was thrown out
by an overwhelming majority. A similar fate, though
in the form of crucial amendments, befell the Government's other measures concerning employers' liability

and the setting up of elective councils for certain parochial work.

At the beginning of 1894, soon after his eighty-fourth birthday, the session over, Gladstone went once more to Biarritz. As usual he looked ahead, and thought that the House of Lords, which was standing in the way of a crusade that he had carried to success in the Commons, was now open to legitimate attack. He proposed to dissolve Parliament, and appeal to the country on this issue, but his colleagues were averse and he reluctantly gave way. It is possible that, had he been younger, he might have pressed his point with success. If so, the campaign he would have led can be imagined, and the renewed disapproval of the Queen.

What then should he do next ? His sight and hearing were hardly equal to the demands of the House of Commons. He still seemed an indispensable institution to his party, and, so long as he was not an invalid, to himself. His age and deafness led to the appointment of Sir Algernon West as Gladstone's political attendant. At this date West sadly compared Gladstone to King Lear, and had to observe some almost frenzied exhibitions. The personnel of the Cabinet was not harmonious. At the beginning of 1894, West wrote : " we never had to deal with an old man before." Again, three weeks later : " We went over the old and new stories again and again. How terribly sad it all is ! We must try and get him to go, on the grounds of his failing eyesight, at the end of this session—that is the best solution of a miserable state of affairs." His physical and nervous condition was not fully realised by himself. Thus something more was required before retirement became inevitable. The added argument was found in the naval estimates, which, unlike his colleagues, Gladstone thought excessive for the time. His counter-argument to West is pathetic : " The plan is mad; and who are they who propose it ? Men who

were not born when I had been in public life for years."
The time had come when such an argument had ceased
to be valid. The old passion for economy, whether
objectors thought it effective or not, survived; besides
in his own backward-looking words,

> " I have come to be considered not only an English but a
> European statesman. My name stands in Europe as a symbol
> of the policy of peace, moderation, and non-aggression.
> What would be said of my active participation in a policy
> that will be taken as plunging England into a whirlpool of
> militarism ?"

To the last, what would be said was a vital consideration
to Gladstone, though, when he had occasion to explain
misunderstandings, he was never at a loss to show how
unfounded they were. On economy, for example, he
admitted that at least four times he had to make extraordinary provisions, but he justified them, as everyone
would, by reference to special emergencies.

The one emergency he could not meet was old age.

XIII

From Biarritz the rumour spread that he intended to
resign upon his return, and he contradicted the rumour
with his customary verbal evasiveness. When he was
back in London in February, his colleagues, says Morley,
begged him to remain. To retain or to part with him
became equally embarrassing. A Liberal party without
Gladstone was as inconceivable during his lifetime as the
parallel concept that Victoria's reign would ever end.
On February 27, 1894, Gladstone told Morley that he
would send in his resignation two days after the proroga-
tion speech was made, at or after the council to be held
on the ensuing Saturday. At an audience of the Queen
beforehand he told her what she must expect. He

also wrote a letter to the Prince of Wales in which he said :

> The devotion of an old man is little worth; but if at any time there be the smallest service which by information or suggestion your Royal Highness may believe me capable of rendering, I shall remain as much at your command as if I had continued to be an active servant of the Queen.

His last Cabinet council took place on March 1st, when he received calmly " words undeservedly kind," as he told the Queen, " of acknowledgment and farewell." Before he rose he almost whispered " God bless you all," and went quietly out of the room. On the same afternoon he launched a vigorous attack upon the House of Lords, but no one realised that they were listening to his last speech in the House of Commons. To the last thinking of the morrow of affairs, he declared that the question once raised between the Houses " must go forward to an issue." When the matter was ended he left the chamber which he had been addressing almost without interruption for sixty-one years. It was a characteristic exit, forward-looking like its chief actor, and a better memorial of his activity within the walls of Westminster than any grand farewell.

One hope he nursed still, but that depended upon the watcher at Windsor. He hoped that she would seek his advice as to his successor, and his hope led him to believe that he was right. On the following day he was dining at the Castle, when his last audience would take place. He talked with Ponsonby, the private secretary, who was anxious to hear Gladstone's views. This was not exactly what Gladstone would have chosen, and his old caution and tenacity were aroused. He replied, therefore, with a proviso :

> All my thoughts . . . were absolutely at the command of the Queen. And I should be equally at his command, if he inquired of me from her and in her name; but that other-

wise my lips must be sealed. I knew from him that he was in
search of information to report to the Queen, but this was a
totally different matter.

It was discouraging, but perhaps could be explained,
thus :

> I received various messages as to the time when I was to
> see the Queen, and when it would be most convenient to me.
> I interpret this variety as showing that she was nervous.

The hour was eventually fixed, after the council was
over and before luncheon. " I carried with me a box
containing my resignation, and, the council being over,
handed it to her immediately. . . . She asked whether
she ought then to read it." He replied that this was
not necessary. Then the central moment came. What
would she say, and how would she phrase her acknowledgment of a retiring statesman who had served her for
half a century ? It was awkward for both of them, and
Gladstone's suspense can be felt.

> When I came into the room and came near to take the
> seat she has now for some time courteously commanded, I
> did think that she was going to " break down." If I was not
> mistaken, at any rate she rallied herself as I thought, by a prompt
> effort, and remained collected and at her ease. Then came
> the conversation, which may be called neither here nor there.

" There was not one syllable on the past." There was
even " no touch on the subject of the last Ponsonby
conversation." Moreover, before he left, he " saw no
sign of embarrassment or preoccupation." The Queen
was thinking of herself, and he of her in relation to his
career. To the last the gulf of temperament between the
odd pair was unbridgable, and she had not imagination
enough to understand how much the occasion was meaning
to him. The man who had the appropriate and sonorous
word for every occasion was confronted with a sovereign
who, on this day of days to him, was dumb. That he

had deceived himself about her suppressed emotion at
the beginning of their interview seems probable from
the subsequent letter that Gladstone received. The Queen
deemed that his letter of resignation required, not only
personal acceptance, but an answer.

> She therefore writes these few lines to say that she thinks
> that after so many years of arduous labour and responsibility
> he is right in wishing to be relieved at his age of these arduous
> duties. And she trusts that he will be able to enjoy peace
> and quiet with his excellent and devoted wife in health and
> happiness, and that his eyesight may improve.

The Queen's " perfect manners," to which Gladstone
had often testified, were not accompanied by a vivid
imagination, and the tone of her leave-taking would have
been perfectly appropriate to a man about to take a brief
cruise. Gladstone's painful sense of her inadequacy
appears in a last letter to Ponsonby :

> The first entrance of a man to Windsor Castle in a responsible
> character is a great event in his life; and his last departure
> from it is not less moving. But in and during the process
> which led up to this transaction on Saturday, my action has
> been in the strictest sense sole, and it has required me in
> circumstances partly known to harden my heart into a flint.

He had failed to carry Home Rule, though he had
brought it through the Commons. The Queen had
taken leave of her old Minister without any outward
sign of appreciation or regret. A great occasion in his
life, for his enormous and active career had given to him
no reason for diminishing the seriousness with which he
had regarded himself from the first, had been allowed to
pass as a " mere nothing." It was probably the keenest
disappointment of his career. The defeat of his last
crusade had not been due to any want of effort on his
own part, but in the matter of the royal farewell the
emotional support to which he had inevitably looked

forward, as a man and as a statesman, with the peculiar sense of what was due to every occasion, had not been forthcoming. It left him in the helpless position of a famous actor whose partner spoils his exit from a great scene.

CHAPTER VII

THE ABBEY

FOUR years of life remained to him, and slowly, one by one, time and health loosened his hold upon this world. A year passed before he severed his political connection with Midlothian, and during that year his eyesight grew painfully worse. He spent the leisure, which he had often contemplated but which seemed so unnatural when it came, gathering up the fragments of the past : as if to recollect was to prolong the life that was virtually over. He found in this leisure no cause for petulance, but " excellent opportunities for brief or ejaculatory prayer." One could still write, still compile memoranda of doubtful points possibly yet in need of elucidation. It was the one form of activity that was left, and without activity, whatever he might say, his life was empty and meaningless. He could not bear repose, or to be alone with himself. Surely by this mode of recollection and compilation something might be preserved from the jaws of Time, for the tragedy of a life of action is that it consists of memories which are fleeting. One could follow and check every step, not now of a changing political situation, but of the waning of one's own powers. One could note the falling off in that correspondence, which had been a burden too precious not to be missed. It was a wistful change to listen to a reader, to confine one's attendance at church to the mid-day communion, to be visited by doctors instead of politicians, to have a nurse in place of a private secretary at one's side.

These changes brought a new stage of existence to which he was not "thoroughly accustomed" in a few months. Nevertheless, he protested that he was content with his retirement and "cast no longing, lingering look behind." The protest is in character, but so is the absence of self-knowledge that it masked. Some difficulties could be overcome by rearrangements, and when he was forbidden to rise in time to attend the daily morning service, "two" evening services, one at five and one at seven, "afford me a limited consolation." He was dismayed by having to take drives, but once, even now, succeeded in walking more than two miles "by a little." Luckily, the letters that arrived at Hawarden were still sufficient to seem a weight. He compared himself to a soldier on parade awaiting orders, feeling "no desire to go," but no reluctance. To the very last he was tenacious of his life. Some authorship and editing remained to him, and it is curious to learn that when he was engaged upon his edition of Bishop Butler, his traditional anchor, "organic evolution," now seemed to him "a Butlerish idea." The notion of evolution, he discovered, was "without doubt deeply ingrained in Butler," and the bishop seemed to entertain the possibility of animals elevating to a higher state, and in the conception of evolution itself Gladstone discerned no right "to say that the small increments effected by the divine workman are not as truly special as the large." This was his nearest approach to mental accommodation with a later idea. As Mr. Tollemache puts it, "he caught the evolutionary contagion. He became so far a *philosophe malgré lui* that he more or less levelled up the chief religions as an alternative to levelling them down. . . . He essayed to hear and at last imagined that he really heard, the far-off echo of a revelation in Homer."

The library in his village was successfully established in 1896, and the subject of religious reunion again

occupied him.   There were more *Gleanings* to be collected,
and the past seemed to return when fresh Turkish mis-
deeds occured in Armenia and led him to protest at one
last public meeting more.   Only strength was wanting
to prevent him from starting on another campaign, and the
Queen probably read of this meeting with an uneasy, if
momentary, shiver.

On his eighty-seventh birthday he had lived beyond
his father's age by four months, and he was now the
longest-lived member of a very long-lived family.   Lord
Stratford, he noted, when he was a nonagenarian, had
told him that such a great age was " not a blessing."
He does not give us his own view, but is content to
remark, I do not enter on " interior matters.   It is so
easy to write, but to write honestly nearly impossible."
The long diary ends on the page that contains these
words, and of Gladstone's formal writings it may be said
that it would do him less than justice to examine them
critically.   The verbal style does indeed resemble that
which he used in his public speeches, but there is no
personal revelation to compensate for the want of those
physical virtues of voice, of look, of gesture which the
most observant of his critics agreed were the life and the
soul of Gladstone's oratory.   On paper he is hardly
readable to-day, and every element in his style, its
impersonality, its ambiguity, its qualifications, its exalted
and conventional note, which has necessarily passed with
the age to which it was peculiar, is suggested in those
extracts from speech, letter or diary that, with the aid of
his several biographers, we have been able to give.   As
a man of letters, the style of Gladstone is as dead as the
dust upon his volumes.   His quality is heightened by
the admission, for it lay in the marvellous voice, and that
voice was a magnificent echo.   It needed, and had the
fate to find, the one period and the one chamber in which
it could ring with complete effect, for Gladstone would

not have been the great success he was had he not happened to be alive in the the palmiest day of Parliament. The example of the French Revolution had given a new sanction to the arts of persuasion and debate in the one European country that had escaped the revolutionary movement. These arts, the seemly alternative to bloodshed and disorder, were devoutly pursued by the newly arisen middle classes, a portion of the community always keenly imitative, and outwardly more solemn than the aristocratic politicians whom they were actively replacing. They further brought with them a solemn moral ideal which received a religious tone because at the beginning of the century formal religion was alive among the Evangelicals and nowhere else. All these characteristics were found in the Gladstone family, and he emerged into public life at the moment when the appropriate audience was awaiting him. Economic and political changes completed the transformation of society which made him the most typical public figure of his age. The time, and the place, and the man appeared simultaneously together.

With his splendid physical endowment, his wealth of energy and abundant means, he was, on the shifting surface of our polity, what Victoria was upon the throne, the constitutional voice, as she the settled emblem, of British government. But if his ideas were all inherited and few, he held them earnestly, and his belief in accord was real enough to carry him at times beyond other politicians, so that the settlement of the Alabama claim by arbitration, and the adoption of the Irish cause, on the ground of constitutional justice, made him stride beyond his political peers and represent, justly, to innumerable ordinary men and women, the practical application of principles which others in his position thought chimerical in politics. Living an active life through several generations, he continued to voice successive political aspirations as they arose. He disguised the changes in his attitude by a tone of unction and an art of qualification which seemed hypocritical and sophistical to those who, pursuing different policies, had not the clue.*   The nineteenth century's ideal of political speech and deportment was embodied to an extraordinary degree in one man, and, just in so far as he was extraordinarily true to type and time, he is liable to decline in interest to-day when his age is over.

Such a pilgrimage could have only one culmination, and when he began to be a victim to much pain the end was sensibly near. His old resort to sunshine in the south failed, and he was carried home from Cannes to Bournemouth on what proved to be a stage of his last journey. There, in March 1898, he was told that he could not recover, and he left for Hawarden knowing that he had but a few weeks to live. In May it became a matter of days, and on May 19, 1898, he died.

In both Houses of Parliament an address was presented to the Queen, praying that Gladstone should be buried in the Abbey, and the speeches then made properly remarked the prestige that he had added to the assembly of which he was the most venerable member. All who believed in Parliament were aware of their tremendous debt, for representative institutions could hardly lose their hold upon public respect when conducted after the public manner of Mr. Gladstone. He belonged to the world of contemporary statesmen, and his death was felt in many of the nations. On Wednesday, May 25th, the body was brought from Hawarden to Westminster Hall, where it lay in state for two days before the State funeral on Saturday. Every rank and class of person was represented in the multitude that thronged that Hall.

* Cf. Jowett's remark : " Gladstone is not dishonest; but it is natural that people who do not understand him should think him dishonest."

The famous voice was silent, but the famous audience still attended him. They, at least, were not unmindful of his reputation and his past. He had no doubt himself that he had lived through a great period, and the people had no doubt that he was a great man. His last word, expressing with masterly obliqueness the wish that the Abbey fulfilled, was respected two years later when the body of his wife was laid in the Abbey tomb. It is so perfectly in character that it must not be passed over.

I wish to be buried where my wife may also lie.

His ambition for both of them was realised. The pair of pious pilgrims had reached Westminster Abbey at last. Thus the public figure, who was a prodigy if not a genius, was laid with his wife to rest in the Collegiate Church of St. Peter, where the shades of dead statesmen, soldiers and poets are gathered, in a building which represents to the people who mourn them a parliament of the great spirits of the past. In this shadowy Assembly we leave him, to rest, as he had liked to live, in the countenance and the company of a throng.

THE END

SHORT BIBLIOGRAPHY

The Life of William Ewart Gladstone. By John Morley. 1903.

Catherine Gladstone. By Edwin A. Pratt. 1898.

Catherine Gladstone. By her daughter, Mary Drew. 1919.

Mr. Gladstone. By H. W. Lucy. 1895.

My Memory of Gladstone. By Goldwin Smith. 1904.

Talks with Mr. Gladstone. By Hon. Lionel A. Tollemache. 1898.

A Modern History of the English People : 1880–1898. By R. H. Gretton. 1913.

Mr. Gladstone : a Study. By Louis J. Jennings, M.P. 1887.

Recollections. By Sir Algernon West, K.C.B. 1899.

T. H. Huxley. By Leonard Huxley. 1900.

Alfred, Lord Tennyson : A Memoir by his son. 1897.

London Letters. By George W. Smalley. 1890.

The Life of Parnell. By R. Barry O'Brien. 1910.

Charles Stewart Parnell. By Katherine O'Shea (Mrs. Parnell). 1914.

Life of Gladstone. By Herbert Paul. 1901.

Right Hon. W. E. Gladstone. By G. W. E. Russell. 1891.

Macaulay's Essays.

The Religious Life of Gladstone. By D. C. Lathbury. 1910.

Eminent Victorians, and *Queen Victoria.* By Lytton Strachey. 1918 and 1921.

The books by Mr. Russell and Mr. Paul are political; Lucy's is the best and liveliest of the shorter lives; Tollemache summarises Gladstone's religious view of Homer; Jennings' is a hostile contemporary account.

INDEX